Terrorism Challenges in the Indo-Pacific

This edited volume focuses on contemporary terrorism challenges that remain serious in the Indo-Pacific region long after the seminal terrorist attacks on 11 September 2001.

Since then, the emergence of the new terrorism has been epitomised by rise of radical Islamist terrorist groups such as Al Qaeda and the Islamic State. Through the use of new terrorism techniques and strategies, such movements have been able to transform themselves into worldwide, global jihadist movements. While both Al Qaeda and the Islamic State have suffered greatly from vigorous and sustained global counter-terrorism operations led by the United States, their local affiliates in the Indo-Pacific, as well as other local radical Islamist and non-Islamist groups, have continued to pose serious terrorist challenges in the Indo-Pacific region. While the threat has somewhat abated in recent times in Southeast Asia, the terrorist threat remains very serious in South Asia. The chapters in this book assess the key threats and counter-terrorism responses of South and Southeast Asia to these on-going challenges.

This book will be indispensable to students, scholars and policy makers working on Asian Security, Politics, International Relations and the security dynamics of the Indo-Pacific region. The chapters in this issue were originally published as a special issue of *Journal of Policing, Intelligence and Counter Terrorism*.

Andrew T. H. Tan is Non-Resident Principal Fellow at the Institute for Indo-Pacific Affairs, New Zealand, and was previously Professor of Security Studies at Macquarie University, Sydney, Australia. He specialises in defence studies, terrorism and regional security and is the author, co-author, editor or co-editor of 24 books.

Julian Droogan is Associate Professor and Director of Research and Innovation at the Department of Security Studies and Criminology at Macquarie University, Sydney, Australia. He is also Editor-in-Chief of the *Journal of Policing, Intelligence and Counter Terrorism* (Routledge). His academic research focuses on online extremism, terrorism and disinformation.

Nell Bennett has a PhD from Macquarie University, Sydney, Australia, in terrorism and insurgency. Dr Bennett is Managing Editor of the *Journal of Policing, Intelligence and Counter Terrorism* and is research fellow with the Blue Security Consortium and La Trobe Asia.

Terrorism Challenges in the Indo-Pacific

Edited by
Andrew T. H. Tan, Julian Droogan
and Nell Bennett

LONDON AND NEW YORK

First published 2025
by Routledge
4 Park Square, Milton Park, Abingdon, Oxon, OX14 4RN

and by Routledge
605 Third Avenue, New York, NY 10158

Routledge is an imprint of the Taylor & Francis Group, an informa business

Introduction, Chapters 1, 2 and 4–7 © 2025 Department of Security Studies and Criminology.
Chapter 3 © 2024 Nuri Widiastuti Veronika. Originally published as Open Access.

With the exception of Chapters 3, no part of this book may be reprinted or reproduced or utilised in any form or by any electronic, mechanical, or other means, now known or hereafter invented, including photocopying and recording, or in any information storage or retrieval system, without permission in writing from the publishers. For details on the rights for Chapters 3, please see the chapter's Open Access footnote.

Trademark notice: Product or corporate names may be trademarks or registered trademarks, and are used only for identification and explanation without intent to infringe.

British Library Cataloguing in Publication Data
A catalogue record for this book is available from the British Library

ISBN13: 978-1-032-85554-7 (hbk)
ISBN13: 978-1-032-85555-4 (pbk)
ISBN13: 978-1-003-51865-5 (ebk)

DOI: 10.4324/ 9781003518655

Typeset in Myriad Pro
by codeMantra

Publisher's Note
The publisher accepts responsibility for any inconsistencies that may have arisen during the conversion of this book from journal articles to book chapters, namely the inclusion of journal terminology.

Disclaimer
Every effort has been made to contact copyright holders for their permission to reprint material in this book. The publishers would be grateful to hear from any copyright holder who is not here acknowledged and will undertake to rectify any errors or omissions in future editions of this book.

Contents

Citation Information vi
Notes on Contributors viii

Introduction: contemporary terrorism challenges and responses in the Indo-Pacific 1
Andrew T. H. Tan

1 The Indonesian military and counter terrorism in Poso, 2015–2022 9
   Muhamad Haripin, Chaula Rininta Anindya and Adhi Priamarizki

2 Countering radical terrorist ideology through psywar: lessons from the Malayan Emergency 24
   Andrew T. H. Tan

3 Women, intelligence and Countering Terrorism (CT) in Indonesia: Where are the women? 41
   Nuri Widiastuti Veronika

4 Militant jihadist exploitation of youth and young adult vulnerabilities in the Maldives 61
   Anne Speckhard, Molly Ellenberg and Sheikh Ali

5 Evolving dynamics of China-Pakistan counter-terrorism cooperation 77
   Khuram Iqbal, Muhammad Shoaib and Sardar Bakhsh

6 An Indonesian way of P/CVE and interpreting the whole-of-society approach: lessons from civil society organisations 94
   Chaula Rininta Anindya

7 The false dawns over Marawi: examining the post-Marawi counterterrorism strategy in the Philippines 110
   Tom Smith and Ann Bajo

Index 127

Citation Information

The following chapters in this book were originally published in the *Journal of Policing, Intelligence and Counter Terrorism*, volume 19, issue 3 (2024). When citing this material, please use the original page numbering for each article, as follows:

Introduction
Contemporary terrorism challenges and responses in the Indo-Pacific
Andrew T. H. Tan
Journal of Policing, Intelligence and Counter Terrorism, volume 19, issue 3 (2024), pp. 297–304

Chapter 1
The Indonesian military and counter terrorism in Poso, 2015–2022
Muhamad Haripin, Chaula Rininta Anindya and Adhi Priamarizki
Journal of Policing, Intelligence and Counter Terrorism, volume 19, issue 3 (2024), pp. 305–319

Chapter 2
Countering radical terrorist ideology through psywar: lessons from the Malayan Emergency
Andrew T. H. Tan
Journal of Policing, Intelligence and Counter Terrorism, volume 19, issue 3 (2024), pp. 320–336

Chapter 3
Women, intelligence and countering terrorism (CT) in Indonesia: Where are the women?
Nuri Widiastuti Veronika
Journal of Policing, Intelligence and Counter Terrorism, volume 19, issue 3 (2024), pp. 337–356

Chapter 4
Militant jihadist exploitation of youth and young adult vulnerabilities in the Maldives
Anne Speckhard, Molly Ellenberg and Sheikh Ali
Journal of Policing, Intelligence and Counter Terrorism, volume 19, issue 3 (2024), pp. 357–372

Chapter 5
Evolving dynamics of China-Pakistan counter-terrorism cooperation
Khuram Iqbal, Muhammad Shoaib and Sardar Bakhsh
Journal of Policing, Intelligence and Counter Terrorism, volume 19, issue 3 (2024), pp. 373–389

Chapter 6
An Indonesian way of P/CVE and interpreting the whole-of-society approach: lessons from civil society organisations
Chaula Rininta Anindya
Journal of Policing, Intelligence and Counter Terrorism, volume 19, issue 3 (2024), pp. 390–405

Chapter 7
The false dawns over Marawi: examining the post-Marawi counterterrorism strategy in the Philippines
Tom Smith and Ann Bajo
Journal of Policing, Intelligence and Counter Terrorism, volume 19, issue 3 (2024), pp. 406–422

For any permission-related enquiries please visit:
http://www.tandfonline.com/page/help/permissions

Notes on Contributors

Sheikh Ali, International Center for the Study of Violent Extremism, McLean, USA.

Chaula Rininta Anindya, Ritsumeikan University, Kyoto, Japan.

Ann Bajo, University of Portsmouth, UK; Former Defense Analyst of the Armed Forces of the Philippines.

Sardar Bakhsh, Department of International Relations, National Defence University, Islamabad, Pakistan.

Molly Ellenberg, International Center for the Study of Violent Extremism, McLean, USA.

Muhamad Haripin, National Research and Innovation Agency (BRIN), Jakarta, Indonesia.

Khuram Iqbal, Department of International Relations, National Defence University, Islamabad, Pakistan.

Adhi Priamarizki, Rajaratnam School of International Studies, Nanyang Technological University (RSIS NTU), Singapore.

Muhammad Shoaib, Department of International Relations, National Defence University, Islamabad, Pakistan.

Anne Speckhard, International Center for the Study of Violent Extremism, McLean, USA.

Tom Smith, Associate Professor in International Relations, University of Portsmouth, UK; Academic Director, Royal Air Force College Cranwell, UK.

Andrew T. H. Tan, Non-Resident Principal Fellow, Institute for Indo-Pacific Affairs, Christchurch, New Zealand.

Nuri Widiastuti Veronika, Monash University, Melbourne, Australia.

Introduction: contemporary terrorism challenges and responses in the Indo-Pacific

Andrew T. H. Tan

ABSTRACT
Since the seminal terrorist attacks on 11 September 2001, the emergence of the new terrorism has been epitomised by rise of radical Islamist terrorist groups such as Al Qaeda and the Islamic State. Through the use of new terrorism techniques and strategies, such movements have been able to transform themselves into worldwide, global jihadist movements. While the Islamic State appeared to have gained the upper hand over Al Qaeda in the competition over the radical Islamist cause due to its successes in Iraq and Syria in 2014, analysts believe that in the long-run, Al Qaeda remains the greater danger. While both Al Qaeda and the Islamic State have suffered greatly from vigorous and sustained global counter-terrorism operations led by the United States, their local affiliates in the Indo-Pacific, as well as other local radical Islamist and non-Islamist groups not affiliated to either, have continued to pose serious terrorist challenges in the region. While the threat has somewhat abated in recent times in Southeast Asia, the terrorist threat remains very serious in South Asia.

The new terrorism, Al Qaeda and the Islamic State

The seminal terrorist attacks in the United States on 11 September 2001 (or 9–11), in which the World Trade Towers, the iconic symbols of Western finance and economic domination, were attacked and demolished with just under 3,000 killed, galvanised radical Islamists throughout the world. The attacks were unprecedented in their impacts as well as lethality (Tan, 2008, pp. 1–2). They demonstrated what was possible: that it was in fact possible to strike at the most powerful perceived enemies of the faith, which radical Islamists hold responsible for the many political, economic and social travails in the Muslim world.[1]

It also highlighted the arguably 'new' terrorism that now emerged, one that was different from past terrorisms due to its unique and innovative features. This included its sheer lethality that Bruce Hoffman had argued was without precedent (Hoffman, 2002, p. 31). According to Steve Simon and Daniel Benjamin, the string of terror attacks before 9–11, such as the 1993 World Trade Center bombing, the 1998 East Africa bombings and the Tokyo sarin nerve gas attack in 1995, were all 'unmistakably harbingers of a new and vastly more threatening terrorism, one that aims to produce casualties on a mass scale' (Simon & Benjamin, 2000, p. 59). Kevin O'Brien also drew attention, writing in 2002, to the revolution in computing, telecommunications, and data-transference capacities, or the 'Information Revolution', that has immense implications for global security. This has, for instance, enabled terrorist organisations such as Al Qaeda to coordinate and plan activities around the world. Thus, O'Brien observed the 'ability of terrorists, organised criminal groups or other sub-state malicious actors to use the … information and knowledge resources available in the Information Society to plan and organize, finance and communicate, and ensure command and control (C2) over real-world operations' (O'Brien, 2002, pp. 78–79).

In addition, the increased pace of globalisation, which has led to the 'democratization of finance, technology and information' has in turn resulted in the creation of flexible and diffused organisational structures in terrorist groups. Hoffman therefore argued that Osama bin Laden functioned like a 'terrorist CEO', presiding over a flexible organisational structure and strategy that has enabled it to function at multiple levels, through top-down and bottom-up approaches. While Al Qaeda has planned strategic terrorist attacks such as those on 9–11, it has also taken a venture capitalist approach in supporting local regional initiatives and proposals. Thus, it has utilised a professional cadre, local regional radical groups, like-minded insurgent movements and trained amateurs (Hoffman, 2002, pp. 38–40).

Al Qaeda had therefore arguably pioneered new terrorism techniques and strategies, enabling it to transform itself into a worldwide, global jihadist movement. The Islamic State (IS) that emerged following its spectacular territorial gains in Syria and Iraq in 2014 has followed a similar template, exploiting the transnational opportunities afforded by globalisation, the use of modern communication and information technology, as well as organisational flexibility resulting in networked trans-national operations around the world.

In particular, the IS has proven very adept at using information technology, particularly social media, as well as other forms of mass communication to effectively spread its radical Islamist ideology and message around the world. Daniel Byman thus noted its 'impressive social media efforts and overall appeal', concluding that Al Qaeda has become 'weaker and less dynamic than the Islamic State' (Byman, 2015). The IS also differed from Al Qaeda in that it was able, at least initially, to wage war on the central state in both Syria and Iraq, capturing large swathes of territory, and achieving what Al Qaeda could not, i.e. the proclamation of an actual caliphate, in 2014. In doing so, the IS proved itself to be a worthy successor to Al Qaeda, which had suffered enormous losses since 9–11 in the face of sustained worldwide security operations led by the United States against it.

Since 2014, Al Qaeda and IS have been locked in a global competition for regional affiliates throughout the Muslim world, including in the Middle East, Africa and Asia. However, the IS has had the upper hand in this competition, as 'local groups seem to want to attach themselves to a brand that has caught the attention of jihadists worldwide' (Byman, 2015). Yet, it is noteworthy that this competition between Al Qaeda and IS has not led to an escalation of terrorism. Tore Hamming has argued that this is due to the 'pre-conflict methodological re-orientation within Al Qaeda and in the pacifying role played by influential Al Qaeda-affiliated ideologues' (Hamming, 2020, p. 20). He explained that the absence of competitive escalation or outbidding in the relationship between Al Qaeda and the Islamic State illustrates how Al Qaeda successfully stuck to its analysis of what works in a long-term perspective and did not react to the initial provocation and success of its competitor. (Hamming, 2020, p. 32)

The IS used brutal terror tactics in the territory it has controlled, carrying out mass executions, public beheadings, rape and symbolic crucifixion displays to terrorise the population into submission. Al Qaeda, in contrast, has been critical of such tactics as it feels that this would turn the population against them as well as alienate the broader Muslim community. Instead, Al Qaeda has paid greater attention to proselytisation and persuasion, rather than the use of force, to convince local Muslims of the justness of its cause (Byman, 2015). This suggests, at least to some countries surveyed in a UN Security Council report in July 2021, that while IS is an immediate threat, Al Qaeda remains the greater long-term radical Islamist threat (United Nations Security Council (UNSC), 2021, p. 5). Thus, the UN Security Council assessed in 2021 that 'the international context is favourable to Al Qaeda, which intends to be recognised again as the leader of global jihad', and that 'Al Qaeda propaganda is now better developed to compete with the Islamic State as the key actor in inspiring the international threat environment, and it may ultimately become a greater source of directed threat' (UNSC, 2021, p. 6). This is also due to the territorial defeat suffered by the IS in Syria and Iraq in 2019, when it lost its last major stronghold, Baghouz, to the US-backed Syrian Democratic Forces, proving to radical Islamists worldwide that its strategy has not worked (BBC, 2019). Another recent development that could potentially lead to Al Qaeda's revival has been the return to power in Afghanistan of the Taliban following the US withdrawal and subsequent swift collapse of the Western-backed regime in Kabul in 2021 (CNN, 2021). As a result, Al Qaeda now enjoys greater freedom of movement within Afghanistan, since it has remained close to the Taliban and reportedly plays an advisory role to it (UNSC, 2021, p. 16).

The new terrorism and South Asia

The events of 9–11, the emergence of the new terrorism in the form of Al Qaeda and the subsequent rise of IS from 2014 had immense impacts on the Indo-Pacific region. 9–11 and the caliphate declared by IS galvanised radical Islamists around the world, including in North America, Europe, Africa, the Middle East and Asia. The IS attracted large numbers of volunteer fighters to fight on its behalf to defend its caliphate in Syria and Iraq. Both Al Qaeda and IS also inspired terrorist attacks around the world.

In the Indo-Pacific, the impacts have been felt in South and Southeast Asia, where large numbers of adherents to Islam reside and where several countries continue to face serious governance issues. In South Asia, the radical Islamist threat has steadily become more serious since 9–11. From 2002 to 2020, an estimated 21,753 people in Pakistan and 9,685 in India were killed due to terrorist attacks (Ritchie, Hasell, Mathieu, Appel, & Roser, 2013). The threat from radical Islamist groups remains strong in Pakistan. The Tehrik-e-Taliban Pakistan (TTP), an alliance of militant networks formed in 2007 to unify opposition against the Pakistan government and military, has aimed to expel the central government's influence over the Federally Administered Tribal Areas (FATA), the setting up of an Islamic state in Pakistan, and the expulsion of Western troops from

Afghanistan (Office of the Director of National Intelligence, n.d.). In recent years, the TTP has carried out several deadly terrorist attacks, such as the December 2014 attack on the Army Public School in Peshawar that killed around 150 people in the single deadliest attack in the history of Pakistan. The government's response to this attack was to implement a National Action Plan to combat terrorism and extremist ideology across the country, as well as counterinsurgency operations in the FATA region. An estimated 3,500 militants and 500 military personnel were killed in the subsequent two-year operation (Council for Foreign Relations, 2023).

However, deadly terrorist attacks have continued. In 2016, a series of spectacular attacks took place. In March, a bombing in Lahore was carried out by the Taliban-linked Jamaat-ul-Ahrar (JuA), itself a splinter from the TTP, killing 74 people. In August, a bombing claimed separately by the JuA and the Islamic State's local affiliate, namely, the Islamic State Khorasan Province, of a gathering of lawyers in Quetta killed 70 people. In October, a bomb attack carried out by the Lashkar-e-Jhangvi (LeJ) and IS at a police college in Balochistan killed 60 people (Department of State, 2016). In July 2018, an attack by the IS on an election rally in Mastung in July 2018 claimed the lives of 149 people (BBC, 2018). Another deadly attack, claimed by the JuA, took place in January 2023, when a police mosque in Peshawar was targeted in a suicide bombing that killed 100 people (Aljazeera, 2023).

The string of deadly terrorist attacks demonstrates Pakistan's continuing failure in counterterrorism. This has been attributed to the lack of a coherent counter-terrorism strategy and the lack of a national consensus on how to deal with the militants. As Ahmad Rashid observed, Pakistan uses militants as an appendage to foreign policy, with the army and the civilian government having different agendas towards the militant groups. The result has been the 'failure of the state to adopt a common strategy and a believable narrative', which in turn 'is emboldening the terrorists, weakening the state and making solutions harder to find' (Rashid, 2017). The problem is that the terrorist threat to Pakistan has serious and obvious implications for regional and global security. A destabilised Pakistan will also have serious consequences for international security, given that it is a nuclear-armed state.

The collapse of the Western-supported government in Afghanistan in 2021 and the return to power of the Taliban has now enabled militants from Pakistan to establish safe havens in Afghanistan. From there, they could plan and carry out further attacks against the government, further destabilising the Pakistani state, which has been facing on-going political instability as well as serious economic issues in the wake of the COVID-19 pandemic. In particular, the emergence of the IS in Pakistan, in addition to the long-running terrorist threat from Al Qaeda linked militants with ties to the Taliban in Afghanistan, has also worsened the terrorist challenge in Pakistan. Indeed, the return to power of the Taliban in Afghanistan in 2021 could have serious long-term consequences for regional and global security, given the close links between the Taliban and Al Qaeda. Al Qaeda could pose a renewed global terrorist threat from Al Qaeda if it re-establishes a safe haven in Afghanistan. Vast stocks of US-supplied military equipment (eg ammunition, guns, night-vision equipment and mortars) could also now fall into the hands of terrorists. Afghanistan's instability and weakness also enables militant groups to flourish, in turn destabilising neighbouring countries such as Pakistan and India.

India too has had to deal with terrorist and insurgent challenges. In December 2001, an audacious attack by the Pakistan-based Jaish-e-Mohammad (JeM) and Lashkar-e-Taiba (LeT) on the Indian Parliament took place, killing 14 people, including the 5 terrorists (Josh, 2021). The JeM, founded in 2000, aims to separate Kashmir from India and had joined the Afghan Taliban in attacks against government and Coalition forces in Afghanistan (Parliament of Australia, n.d.). In October 2005, bomb attacks attributed to the LeT took place at a market in Delhi, killing 66 people. In 2006, train bombings in Mumbai were carried out by the LeT and the Student Islamic Movement of India (SIMI), killing 209 people and injuring over 700. In May 2008, terrorist attacks in the city of Jaipur killed 80 people. This was followed by the widely-publicized Mumbai attacks in November, when 10 terrorists killed 166 people at five different locations. In 2016 and 2019, the Pakistan-based JeM also carried out attacks targeting the Indian army, killing a total of 57 soldiers (Josh, 2021).

Thus, the bulk of radical Islamist attacks have largely emanated from Pakistan-based militant groups, which have carried out attacks particularly in Jammu and Kashmir – territories which Pakistan also claims. However, the inroads being made by the Islamic State into India itself has been a concerning recent development. Indians had joined the Islamic State Khorasan Province in Afghanistan, though only very small numbers of Indian Muslims have been receptive to radical Islamist propaganda. Nonetheless, the increasing Hindu-Muslim polarisation in India could yet pave the way towards greater radicalisation, especially given that there remain a large number of fundamentalist Muslim religious schools or madrassas in India from which to recruit, the ease of access to IS propaganda online, and the ongoing Muslim separatist violence in Jammu and Kashmir (Sarker, 2020).

Apart from radical Islamist-inspired and/or separatist terrorist attacks, India has also faced left-wing extremist violence carried out by the Communist Party of India (Maoist), though concerted counterinsurgency operations have resulted in the threat becoming much reduced by around 2017 (Aljazeera, 2017). Elsewhere in South Asia, radical Islamist terrorism has also emerged in countries such as Bangladesh and Sri Lanka. This was epitomised by the Dhaka café attack in 2016 in Bangladesh that killed 22 people, mostly foreigners, and the deadly attacks carried out in Sri Lanka in 2019 that killed around 260 people (Department of State, 2019; Reuters, 2019).

The new terrorism and Southeast Asia

Compared to South Asia, the situation in Southeast Asia has been less serious, with 648 people in Indonesia and 19 in Malaysia killed in terrorist attacks from 2002 to 2020 (Ritchie et al., 2013). The figures for Indonesia are significant, as Indonesia does have the largest Muslim population in the world, estimated at 229.6 million in 2020, indicating that while it does face terrorism challenges, it has somehow been less serious and appears to have been better managed (Statistica.com, 2020). The caveat is the largest single terrorist incident in the region, which took place in 2017 when IS-linked local extremists occupied Marawi in the southern Philippines, raised the IS flag over the city and executed civilians. Philippine security forces took months to finally regain control of the city but by then, much of the city had been destroyed, resembling the conflict zones in Iraq and Syria where Western-backed forces had battled the IS. A total of 1,132 people were killed, including 920 militants, dealing a major blow to the IS (Amnesty International, 2017).

Over the same period from 2002 to 2020, 2,503 people were killed in Thailand and 5,035 were killed in the Philippines in terrorist attacks (Global Terrorism Database, n.d.). However, there have been active Muslim separatist insurgencies in both countries and the bulk of the insurgents have in fact distanced themselves from both Al Qaeda and the IS (Tan, 2013, p. 242). In the case of the Philippines, some attacks have also been attributed to the Maoist New People's Army (Global Terrorism Database, n.d.). This suggests that in evaluating terrorism in the Indo-Pacific, the threat landscape is somewhat more complex than the threat emanating from radical Islamist ideology in the form of Al Qaeda and the IS. There remain non-radical Muslim separatist insurgent groups as well as non-Muslim insurgent movements, such as Maoist communist insurgents in the Philippines. As a side observation, as China is not a Southeast Asian country, 839 people were killed in terrorist attacks in China between 2002 and 2020 (Global Terrorism Database, n.d.). However, the bulk is attributed to attacks by Uighur separatists and the extent of radical Islamist penetration of the separatist movement is unclear (Chung, 2019, pp. 119–132).

What is obvious is that sustained and robust counter-terrorism efforts by Southeast Asian governments against local groups affiliated with IS and the Al Qaeda-linked Jemaah Islamiah resulted in a fall in terrorist incidents and deaths as a result of terrorism. By 2022, member states reported to the UN that the threat from groups affiliated with both IS and Al Qaeda had largely receded in the region, although there could still be lone-actor attacks as well as remaining pockets of activity in the Philippines. Indeed, in the southern Philippines, the IS reportedly had, in 2021, an estimated 200 fighters capable of carrying out small-scale attacks (UNSC, 2021, p. 18). Another caveat concerns the fears raised over the potential future threat to the region from the Al Qaeda-linked Jemaah Islamiah. After it carried out its last terrorist bombing in 2009 in Indonesia, the JI has adapted. It has since refrained from directly confronting the state, focusing instead on *dakwah* activities, such as religious education and proselytising in order to build grassroots support. With an estimated membership in 2021 of between 6,000 and 10,000, there remain relatively large numbers of radical Islamist individuals who could potentially be involved in terrorist activities (Channel News Asia, 2021).

From the short survey above, it is thus clear that terrorism threats remain very serious in South Asia. Whilst somewhat under control in Southeast Asia, terrorism continues to be a security challenge. How states in Asia have responded to contemporary terrorist challenges is the subject of this Special Edition, which consists of articles written by scholars and analysts on the evolving terrorist threats and the state's responses to them. The analyses in these articles will contribute greatly to the sharing of experiences and strategies, helping to improve counter-terrorism in the region and beyond.

Note

1. Radical Islamists refer to the fringe extremist elements who advocate the use of violence to establish a state ruled strictly according to Islamic laws as interpreted by them. It is not a reference to Islam or adherents to the religion. The overwhelming majority of Muslims do not subscribe to radical ideology and indeed, have been the main victims of radical Islamist terrorist violence.

Disclosure statement

No potential conflict of interest was reported by the author(s).

References

Aljazeera. (2017, 27 April). India's Maoist Rebels: An explainer. http://www.aljazeera.com/indepth/features/2017/04/india-maoist-rebels-explainer-170426132812114.html

Aljazeera. (2023, January 31). Death toll from Pakistan Mosque bombing rises to 100. https://www.aljazeera.com/news/2023/1/31/pakistan-rescue-operation-peshawar-mosque-suicide-bombing

Amnesty International. (2017, November 17). Philippines: Battle of Marawi leaves trail of death and destruction. https://www.amnesty.org/en/latest/press-release/2017/11/philippines-battle-of-marawi-leaves-trail-of-death-and-destruction/

British Broadcasting Corporation (BBC). (2018, July 16). Pakistan Mourns 149 dead in Country's second deadliest terror attack. https://www.bbc.com/news/world-asia-44847295

British Broadcasting Corporation (BBC). (2019, March 23). Islamic State Group defeated as final territory lost, US-backed forces Say. https://www.bbc.com/news/world-middle-east-47678157

Byman, D. L. (2015, April 29). Comparing Al qaeda and ISIS: Different goals, different targets. Testimony before the subcommittee on counterterrorism and intelligence of the house committee on homeland security. *Brookings*. https://www.brookings.edu/testimonies/comparing-al-qaeda-and-isis-different-goals-different-targets/

Channel News Asia. (2021, December 13). The big read: Jemaah Islamiyah emerges from the shadows, playing the long game. https://www.channelnewsasia.com/singapore/jemaah-islamiyah-terrorist-group-indonesia-isd-20th-anniversary-al-qaeda-2373556

Channel News Asia (CNN). (2021, August 24). *Who are the Taliban and how did they take control of Afghanistan so swiftly?* https://edition.cnn.com/2021/08/16/middleeast/taliban-control-afghanistan-explained-intl-hnk/index.html

Chung, C. P. (2019). China's uighur problem: Terrorist acts and government responses. In B. Schreer & A. T. H. Tan (Eds.), *Terrorism and insurgency in Asia: A contemporary examination of terrorist and separatist movements* (pp. 119–132). London: Routledge.

Council for Foreign Relations. (2023, February 7). *Instability in Pakistan*. Center for Preventive Action. https://www.cfr.org/global-conflict-tracker/conflict/islamist-militancy-pakistan

Department of State. (2016). *Country reports on terrorism 2016*. Chapter 2: South and Central Asia. https://www.state.gov/reports/country-reports-on-terrorism-2016/

Department of State. (2019). *Country reports on terrorism 2019: Sri Lanka*. https://www.state.gov/reports/country-reports-on-terrorism-2019/sri-lanka/

Global Terrorism Database. (n.d.). https://www.start.umd.edu/gtd/

Hamming, T. R. (2020). The Al qaeda–islamic state rivalry: Competition yes, but no competitive escalation. *Terrorism and Political Violence*, *32*(1), 20–37.

Hoffman, B. (2002). The emergence of the new terrorism. In K. Ramakrishna & A. T. H. Tan (Eds.), *The new terrorism: Anatomy, trends and counter-strategies* (pp. 30–49). Singapore: Eastern Universities Press.

Josh, J. (2021, May 21). Anti-terrorism day 2021: List of 8 major terror attacks that shook India. https://www.jagranjosh.com/general-knowledge/list-of-major-terror-attacks-that-shook-india-1590080570-1

O'Brien, K. (2002). Networks, netwar and information Age terrorism. In K. Ramakrishna & A. T. H. Tan (Eds.), *The New terrorism: Anatomy, trends and counter-strategies* (pp. 73–106). Singapore: Eastern Universities Press.

Office of the Director of National Intelligence. (n.d.). *Counterterrorism Guide: Tehrik-e-Taliban Pakistan (TTP)*. https://www.dni.gov/nctc/groups/ttp.html

Parliament of Australia. (n.d.). *Appendix D – Statement of Reasons– Jaish-E-Mohammad (JeM)*. https://www.aph.gov.au/Parliamentary_Business/Committees/Joint/Completed_Inquiries/pjcis/four%20terrorist/report/Appendix%20D

Rashid, A. (2017, February 24). Militant groups forge ties as Pakistan havens remain. *FT.com*. http://blogs.ft.com/the-exchange/2017/02/24/militant-groups-forge-ties-as-pakistan-fails-to-tackle-their-havens/

Reuters. (2019, November 27). Bangladesh sentences seven to death for 2016 cafe attack. https://www.reuters.com/article/us-bangladesh-attack-verdict-idUSKBN1Y10JD

Ritchie, H., Hasell, J., Mathieu, E., Appel, C., & Roser, M. (2013). Terrorism. *OurWorldInData.org*. https://ourworldindata.org/terrorism

Sarker, S. (2020. March 30). The islamic state's increasing focus on India. *The Diplomat*. https://thediplomat.com/2020/03/the-islamic-states-increasing-focus-on-india/

Simon, S., & Benjamin, D. (2000). America and the new terrorism. *Survival*, *42*(1), 59–75.

Statistica.com. (2020). *Forecasted share of the muslim population in Southeast Asia in 2020, By country*. https://www.statista.com/statistics/1113906/southeast-asia-muslim-population-forecasted-share-by-country/

Tan, A. T. H. (2008). *U.S. Strategy against global terrorism: How it evolved, why it failed and where it is headed*. New York: Macmillan.

Tan, A. T. H. (2013). Terrorism in Southeast Asia after 9–11. In A. T. H. Tan (Ed.), *East and Southeast Asia: International relations and security perspectives* (pp. 236–245). London: Routledge.

United Nations Security Council (UNSC). (2021, July 15). *Thirtieth report of the analytical support and sanctions monitoring team submitted pursuant to resolution 2610 (2021) Concerning ISIL (Da'esh), Al-Qaida and Associated Individuals*. file:///C:/Users/Andry/Desktop/Documents/JPICT%20Special%20Edition/S%202022%20547.pdf

The Indonesian military and counter terrorism in Poso, 2015–2022

Muhamad Haripin [ID], Chaula Rininta Anindya [ID] and Adhi Priamarizki [ID]

ABSTRACT
The Indonesian National Armed Forces (TNI) has been applauded for its contribution in eradicating the East Indonesia Mujahideen (MIT) networks in Poso Regency, Central Sulawesi Province. The military contributed to the operation in various ways, particularly intelligence gathering, and territorial and counter-guerrilla operations. The operation in Poso is a case whereby the threats are beyond the police's capabilities. On the one hand, counter terrorism against MIT requires deep involvement of the military primarily due to the strategic and structural challenges surrounding the conflict area. On the other hand, such profound entanglement can produce detrimental impacts toward democratic security arrangement. We argue that TNI involvement is indeed valuable but should be on a case-by-case basis. This article highlights that the operation has been able to nurture coordination between the police and the military. However, there are also potential risks for the future of counter terrorism efforts in Indonesia. Counter terrorism requires a multidisciplinary approach, yet the involvement of TNI in all sectors would only lead to suboptimal achievements of the military. This article also discusses the militarisation approach in counter terrorism is likely to escalate the use of violence.

Introduction

This article focuses on the use of military force in domestic counter terror operations in Indonesia. TNI, Tentara Nasional Indonesia or the Indonesian National Armed Forces, has taken more active and direct roles in counter terrorism in recent years. Amidst opposition from civil society groups, TNI continues to gain support from President Joko 'Jokowi' Widodo, top government officials, and political elites (Anindya, 2017). Out of the military's wide-ranging involvement, this article examines the direct participation of TNI in counter terror missions against the MIT, Mujahidin Indonesia Timur or the East Indonesia Mujahideen, in Poso Regency, Central Sulawesi Province. The operation was initially launched in 2015 under the banner of 'Operation Camar Maleo', and later renamed as 'Operation Tinombala' and 'Operation Madago Raya' consecutively. The joint operation has been applauded as a success story of the partnership between the TNI and Polri

(Kepolisian Negara Republik Indonesia or the Indonesian National Police) (Singh, 2023). Indonesia's 'war on terrorism' in Poso presents an intriguing case study of military involvement in a domestic counter terror operation, in which the role of the military has been extended to not only intelligence gathering and analysis but also joint operation with the police force.

MIT undoubtedly constitutes a security threat. Nevertheless, the terrorist group hardly presents a grave danger to state sovereignty, a requisite needed to employ the armed forces. The terror group also does not possess highly dangerous and sophisticated weaponries. Despite its small and unorganised structure, MIT's modus operandi of aggressive insurgency and tactic of indiscriminate killing against the local population posed a challenge towards national security as well as the political legitimacy of the Joko Widodo government (2014–present).

The recurring attacks from MIT and other Islamic radical groups put heavy pressure on President Jokowi to demonstrate his leadership amidst the turmoil. In addition, there was a deep concern that MIT could ignite a greater Islam radicalism movement in Indonesia (Mahar, 2022). Particular segments of Indonesian society had openly expressed their allegiance to the Islamic State of Iraq and Syria (ISIS), not to mention the departure of hundreds of Indonesians to the Middle East to join the caliphate. MIT, which also declared its allegiance to ISIS' leader Abu Bakr Al-Baghdadi, used the momentum to recruit new members, collect funds, and propagate radical teachings. The circumstance put tackling MIT's terror as a priority for the Indonesian government.

Meanwhile, the use of military force is often seen and justified as the last resort in responding to imminent terror threats. The failure of law enforcement agencies to contain the threats consequently allows the military to take responsibility for deploying its coercive power to deter and neutralise the terror threats. The military's wide range of instruments and organisational resources made it a suitable choice for conducting counter terror missions (Boyle, 2018). For example, the military's structure that stretches across the nation can help to sustain military operations to every edge of the country.

This general proposition brings us to the question of the extent of the military's use of force in countering the threats of terrorism. Under what condition is the military's use of force in counter terrorism justified? This important question from time to time has attracted thorough attention from the academic community. Terrorism used to be seen as a form of low-intensity security threats, committed by small groups to achieve their radical political aspirations. But as terror organisations have developed sophisticatedly and formed highly vigilant networks, established meticulous recruitment systems, and obtained easy access to modern communication technology, terror attacks consequently have become deadlier and harder to deter. Moreover, the nature of terror networks now has become more transnational, and even globalised. To effectively counter such escalating threats, scholars and policy makers in many countries have been in a position to support the military warfare model of counter terrorism. The military's use of force is considered to be pivotal in not only inflicting a major blow against the active, existing terror organisations' assault capabilities but also to deter the establishment of similar groups in the future. In contrast with the law enforcement personnel, the military personnel is equipped with certain equipment and trained in a specialised skill that is useful to fight against terrorist organisations. The military involvement is also paramount in cases where the terror groups hold access to sophisticated conventional weapon or weapons of mass destruction (Wilkinson, 2011).

In this sense, we can see that there are two different yet related strategic rationales for the mobilisation of armed forces in counter terrorism: it is either as a rapid reaction force to provide immediate results or as a part of the government's middle- and long-term strategy to maintain stability. Based on our examination of the dynamics surrounding TNI involvement in counter terrorism operations in Poso, we argue that military deployment in counter terrorism should be treated using case-by-case basis. On the one hand, the military can supplement the role of the police in counter terrorism and boost the efficacy of counter terrorism governance. On the other hand, there are some potential inherent risks, namely competition between police and military, continued presence of the military in internal security realm, and possible militarisation of counter terrorism governance.

Our article comprises five distinct yet interconnected sections. Following this initial overview, we will delve into the evolution of the TNI's roles in countering terrorism in post-authoritarian Indonesia. The third section will centre on military activities, including joint operations with the police force, in Poso Regency against the MIT group. Consequently, it is crucial to explore the impacts of TNI involvement on the military-police relationships. Finally, the article concludes with a closing and several policy implications.

TNI and counter terrorism in post-Suharto period

Indonesia, the largest nation-state in Southeast Asia and the third biggest democracy in the world, adopts a mixture of 'criminal justice' and 'counter insurgency' models for its counter terrorism regime (Haripin, Anindya, & Priamarizki, 2020). This mixed approach involves a wide array of actors, ranging from national police and its special counter terrorism unit to the intelligence agency and military command. Aside from those defence and security actors, the government also brought in other relevant governmental and non-governmental agencies, such as the ministries of religious affairs, education and research and development, foreign affairs, civil society organisations, and academic community. Indonesia has been developing a whole-of-government and a whole-of-society approach in its counter terrorism efforts. Indonesia's counter terrorism regulation, which was initially promulgated in 2002–2003 and then amended in 2018, provided a broad framework of policy coordination and division of labour. In practice, such a seemingly comprehensive national strategy faces several challenges. One of them, as the main context of our argument, is the shaky relationships between police and military institutions.

Prior to the existing arrangement of police and military separation, these two organisations used to be integrated under the roof of ABRI (Angkatan Bersenjata Republik Indonesia or the Indonesian National Armed Forces). This police-military's unified set up was established in the 1950s during the era of Sukarno, the first president of the Republic of Indonesia, and remained intact throughout the authoritarian regime of President Suharto (1966-1998). Such an arrangement made the police under the subordination of the military's chain of command. The circumstance made the police not only fell behind in terms of policing effectiveness, organisational autonomy, and logistics but also suffered from militaristic culture.

The fall of President Suharto in May 1998 caused a drastic change in police-military relations. An anti-authoritarian people's movement urged the end of military rule and the separation of the police (then named Polri) from the military. The separation proceeded gradually and was completed in 2002, four years after the democratic transition took off, with the formal promulgation of Law No. 2/2002 on the Indonesian National Police and Law No. 3/2002 on the National Defence. The disengagement was formulated to emphasise the police's law-enforcing responsibility and strict the military into defence roles. The new arrangement mandated the military in the post-Suharto period to focus more on taming external threats.

Such strict separation of police and military roles, nevertheless, did not hold up long. Indonesia's turbulent political transition, which was unfortunately followed by inter-religious violent conflicts in several cities, for example Ambon, Poso, and Sambas, generated the urgency to restore the military's domestic deployment. Regardless of past human rights violations and excessive violence against civilians committed by the military, the post-Suharto governments had to mobilise TNI to swiftly de-escalate the tension and reinstate public order in the respective conflict hotspots. The cycle of violence continued through the early years of the democratisation period, including the rise of terrorist group Jemaah Islamiyah (JI)[1] that eventually culminated in the first Bali bombing on 12 October 2002. This instability further bolstered the domestic roles of the TNI.

Law No. 34/2004 on TNI put counter terrorism under military operations other than war (MOOTW). TNI's involvement requires an official presidential order and national parliament's approval to execute counter terrorism. The military's counter terrorism roles consist of hard and soft approaches. The hard approach takes the form of troops deployments, intelligence gatherings and analyses, and the mobilisation of military assets to monitor and intercept targets' communication and movements. Meanwhile, the soft approach encompasses a de-radicalisation programme in the form of public seminars with local religious figures as speakers, reminding the general public of the danger of radical Islamic teachings and the importance of tolerance. These public gatherings usually take place in the army's local territorial command headquarter (komando teritorial) and mosques or other religious facilities.

TNI's further affirmed its position in Indonesia's counter terrorism efforts through the BNPT (Badan Nasional Penanggulangan Terorisme or the National Counter Terrorism Agency). In 2010, President Susilo Bambang Yudhoyono established BNPT which serves as a coordinating body for the counter terrorism efforts in the country. TNI acquires the position of Deputy I on Prevention, Protection, and Deradicalisation. This position remains in the hand of a military man until now (Haripin et al., 2020). In addition, the revised law on terrorism Law No. 5/2018 allows more leeway for TNI due to vague definitions of TNI's roles.[2] Following the ratification of the revised law, TNI established a counter terror unit in July 2019, called 'Koopsus TNI' (Komando Operasi Khusus or TNI Special Operations Command), whose members originated from the selected personnel of each military services' special units. Although the overall security arrangement after the collapse of the New Order regime limits direct involvement of TNI in counter terrorism operations, TNI gradually regains its prominence. The vagueness of legal framework and the escalation of terror attacks allow TNI to infiltrate various aspects of counter terrorism policy.

The hunt of the East Indonesia Mujahideen

Poso emerged as a hot bed of Indonesia's terrorist networks in the early 2000s when a communal conflict between Islam and Christian communities broke out in the regency. The conflict generated a mass mobilisation of the jihadi networks, including JI, to defend and support the Muslim groups. JI saw the conflict as an opportunity to secure a base (qoidah aminah) for their future goals of establishing an Islamic State (ICG, 2004; Karnavian, 2015). The conflict further justified their presence by enhancing their paramilitary skills and training their members while defending fellow Muslims. Santoso alias Abu Wardah, the leader of East Indonesia Mujahideen (MIT), is a Javanese descent who was raised and born in Poso. His family was affected by the interreligious conflict (Diprose & Azca, 2019). His jihadism journey started back when he joined Jamaah Ansharut Tauhid (JAT), a JI's splinter group. Santoso was appointed as the head of JAT's military training (tadrib asykari) whereby he trained aspiring jihadists from Java, Sumatera, Sulawesi, and West Nusa Tenggara (Jones & Solahudin, 2015). However, Santoso always aspired to establish his own organisation (Jones, 2014). In 2012, in an online video, Santoso declared the establishment of MIT as an independent group and claimed himself as the 'Abu Mus'ab Al-Zarqawi al Indunesi' or the Indonesian Al-Zarqawi, an Al-Qaeda leader in Iraq. Santoso was able to recruit aspiring jihadists from various regions in the archipelago thanks to his networks while he was a member of JAT. Santoso gained attention when he circulated an online video urging his followers to attack Polri's special counter terrorism unit, Densus 88 Antiteror (Detasemen Khusus 88 Antiteror or Special Detachment 88 Anti-Terror). In 2012, MIT was responsible for various terror attacks against the police (VoA Indonesia, 2016). In 2014, Santoso pledged his allegiance to the Islamic State (IS) and its leader, Abu Bakr Al-Baghdadi, making MIT one of the first terrorist groups in Indonesia to declare its faithfulness to IS.[3]

Counter terror operations against Santoso dan his MIT lasted for approximately seven years, from early 2015 until the end of 2022. In the span of such a long period, the Indonesian government launched counter terror missions under three different codenames: (1) 'Camar Maleo' [January 2015-December 2016]; (2) 'Tinombala' [January 2017-December 2020]; and (3) 'Madago Raya' [January 2021-December 2022]. This series of security operations in Poso is so far the largest that had been launched by the Indonesian government in modern times.

Santoso and MIT remained at large while continuously attacking the police and threatening the locals. In September 2014, the Indonesian government was further alarmed by the arrest of four Uyghurs who attempted to join MIT in Poso (Tribun News, 2014). The Uyghurs were reported to join the fight of MIT while learning paramilitary skills for their own struggle in China (Soliev, 2017). In January 2015, Polri began Operation Camar Maleo to hunt down Santoso and his members. During a two-month operation, the police arrested fifteen terrorist suspects who allegedly provided logistical support for MIT members (OkeZone, 2017). However, the police failed to arrest Santoso and other MIT members who were listed on its most-wanted list.

In the early stage of the hunt, TNI also conducted their own 'unofficial' operation through the Quick Reaction Strike Force (Pasukan Pemukul Reaksi Cepat or PPRC) combat exercise. TNI initially was reluctant to claim that the exercise was to hunt down the MIT members.[4] Nevertheless, the exercise activities clearly indicated that it was indeed to track down and deter MIT members. TNI's battleships, for instance, launched their rockets and naval gunfire supports (bantuan tembakan kapal or BTK) to Mount Biru where Santoso and his members were hiding (TNI, 2015). At the end of exercise, TNI stated that its personnel discovered the training locations of MIT members. The military also explained that the exercise was able to deter MIT members as they fled to other locations during the exercise (VoA Indonesia, 2015). Following the end of the training, TNI stated their willingness to support the police in the hunt for MIT, but the military had yet to acquire approval from the government and the police had not formally requested for the backup support (Republika, 2015). The whole exercise aimed to show TNI's counter terrorism effectiveness and convince the relevant authorities to include the military in hunting down MIT members. At last, TNI was involved in Operation Camar Maleo III and IV to support Polri in the operation, doing search operations and disrupting logistical support for MIT (Kompas, 2015).

After a series of extensions, Operation Camar Maleo lasted until early 2016. In a span of one year, the operation apprehended 24 MIT members, resulting in seven deaths and seventeen prosecutions. One of the most remarkable achievements during the operation was the death of Daeng Koro alias Sabar who was Santoso's field commander (IPAC, 2015). Although Polri claimed that the operation significantly undermined MIT's activities in Mount Biru, Santoso and the other 21 MIT members remained at large. The addition of TNI in the last two phases of Operation Camar Maleo did not significantly enhance the effectiveness of the operation. The joint operation team claimed the vast and difficult terrain of Poso had undermined the operation (Antara News, 2016). On the other hand, MIT members are more familiar with the terrain thanks to the locals who helped the group evade the counter-terror team's surveillance.

Despite their suboptimal achievements, Polri opined that the operation should once again extended to chase Santoso. The operation was later extended and re-coded as 'Operation Tinombala'. The first phase of Operation Tinombala was launched in January 2016 and engaged 1,543 police and 1,791 military personnel (Haripin, 2020). Unlike the Camar Maleo, the number of TNI personnel deployed for Tinombala significantly increased (see Table 1). This time the joint operation attempted to make the best use of the military's jungle warfare skills by focusing their personnel to search out in the jungle while the police would focus on curbing the flows of MIT members and the logistical support from their sympathisers (IPAC, 2016b).

During Operation Tinombala II in July 2016, the task force shot to death Santoso and his bodyguard, Mukhtar. In a special mission, The Alfa 29 Team of the Army Strategic Reserve Command's 515th Raider Battalion took around eight days to track down Santoso and another four MIT members (Tempo, 2016). TNI was applauded for their success in hunting down the most wanted terrorist. The success further justified their involvement in counter terrorism operations which had been scrutinised due to the fear of human rights violations and the backsliding of military reform. Behind the success of the military, there were rumours that Santoso could have been arrested faster yet the military tended to prolong the operation for the sake of its institutional interests (Diprose & Azca, 2019). A week after the death of Santoso, an incident occurred between the police and military. A police officer shot to death a military officer due to a miscommunication between the two groups. The police and the military were both trying to clarify the information which they received from the locals on the whereabouts of MIT

Table 1. Anti-terror campaigns in Poso, Central Sulawesi, 2015–2016.

Code Name	Time Period	Force	Outcome
Camar Maleo I	26 January – 26 March 2015	563 personnel from Special Detachment Anti-Terror 88 (Densus 88), Mobile Brigade (Brimob Polri), and Central Sulawesi Regional Police (Polda Sulteng)	6 members of Santoso group arrested; 2 guns confiscated
Camar Maleo II	2 April – 7 June 2015	1,000 of Brimob and Polda Sulteng personnel	3 members of Santoso group dead; 3 guns confiscated; 30 IED (improvised explosive device) confiscated.
Camar Maleo III	9 September – 27 October 2015	1,000 of Brimob and Polda Sulteng; 60 TNI Special Force Command (Kopassus) and 40 Army Strategic Reserve Command (combat intelligence platoon of Kostrad)	14 types of evidence confiscated; 10 documents related with Santoso group confiscated
Camar Maleo IV	28 October 2015–9 January 2016	1,000 Brimob and Polda Sulteng; 700 military	Detect the location of Santoso
Tinombala I	10 January – 10 March 2016	1,543 police; 1,791 military (army, marine)	10 members of Santoso group dead; 3 members arrested
Tinombala II	11 March – 11 August 2016	1,543 police; 1,791 military (army, marine)	Santoso and Mukhtar alias Kahar, one of his followers dead; 9 members of Santoso group arrested

Source: (Haripin, 2020).

members. Unfortunately, the search operation led to the deadly incident as they assumed that the other party was MIT (Republika, 2016).

Operation Tinombala was concluded in 2020 and re-coded as 'Operation Madago Raya' in 2021. Operation Tinombala unfortunately ended with a tragic incident in Lembantongoa Village, Sigi. Four Christian residents were brutally killed, and seven houses were burnt down by MIT members. Moreover, the local residents also grew impatient with the protracted security operation, as their daily life has been heavily affected. Despite the large number of police and military personnel, their presence could not guarantee the safety of the locals from MIT's brutal acts (VoA Indonesia, 2021). Civil society organisations also called the government to re-evaluate the operation. It had been five years since the operation started and the government had deployed thousands of military and police personnel, yet MIT continued to survive and threaten the life of locals.

In response to public fatigue over non-stop security operation, the police and military gradually intensified the territorial operation and social campaign. The Madago Raya Task Force commenced different yet related activities to ensure public support. According to the joint task force, both the military and police stationed in Poso had been involved in approximately 11,175 activities; for instance, pre-emptive sub-task force coordinated the social campaigns.

It is unclear whether other sub-task forces participated in the campaign and the degree of their involvement. As shown in Table 2, we can identify three major activities undertaken by the task force, namely door-to-door contact, direct communication, and face-to-face meetings. Through careful reading and observation of the operations, we find difficulties in differentiating these different yet similar social campaigns. There is also little guidance to verify the degree of efficacy of such public outreach. What we can infer, however, is that counter terrorism in Poso also involves persuasive, non-coercive approaches directed towards the local community at large.

Table 2. Pre-emptive activities (territorial operation and social campaign) Operation Madago Raya 2022.

No.	Type of Activities	Phase I	Phase II
1.	Door-to-door contact	3483	702
2.	Direct communication	3480	1014
3.	Face-to-face meeting	1164	92
4.	Religious gathering	677	81
5.	TNI-Polri's sub-task force of Islamic preachers (*da'i*)	189	83
6.	Sub-task force of de-radicalisation	126	84
	Total activities	9119 activities	2056 activities

Source: Indonesian National Armed Forces (TNI).

Madago Raya Task Force consists of six related sub-task groups, i.e. intelligence, pre-emptive, direct-action, law enforcement, public relations, and supporting team (see Figure 1). Each group holds its own distinct roles and functions. Two particularly prominent sub-task forces are intelligence and direct-action. The intelligence group, as its designated name suggests, is responsible for collecting and analysing the information about the strength and manoeuvre of the MIT. This had been a challenging mission for the group due to the fact that MIT hid in the vast mountainous area of Mount Biru, and the terror group was difficult to track down. Meanwhile, the direct-action task force is the 'foot soldier' undertaking counter guerrilla/jungle warfare operations. It consists of the police's mobile brigade (Brimob) and the military's various special forces, including

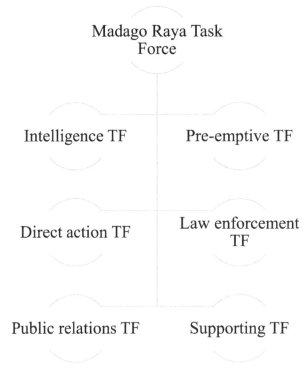

Figure 1. Command structure of Madago Raya Task Force. Source: Indonesian National Armed Forces (TNI).

the Koopsus TNI. These special forces in reality played a bigger role, including to undertake a particular mission called 'insulation' (penyekatan)[5] in which the joint force established a number of checkpoints – or blockade – to prevent as well as intercept logistics supplied by the MIT supporters.

The checkpoints were usually located at the main routes which were used by MIT members to go down from the mountain area to the local villages to pick up logistics. For instance, in a regular patrol in April 2022, the insulation team encountered a suspicious person who was later identified as Suhardin alias Hasan Pranata. He was asked to surrender but he threw a body vest to the team which then forced the team to shoot him (Kompas, 2022).

Operation Madago Raya deployed about 800 TNI-Polri personnel (Merdeka, 2021). In September 2021, the operation gunned down Ali Kalora, the successor of Santoso. This event was one of the turning points of the operation. After the death of Ali Kalora, there were only four remaining MIT members who were on the run as of September 2021. Analyst suggested that MIT had been significantly weakened and they had no potential successors for leaders. They believed that the remaining members would be arrested soon, yet the government should not be complacent. There is a valid reason to believe that Poso will remain a hostile land and the government should formulate suitable programmes to maintain harmony among the locals (BenarNews, 2021).

In May 2022, TNI Commander General Andika Perkasa (2021-2022) stated that the military had withdrawn 167 personnel from the Madago Raya Task Force hence there were only 100 personnel left in the operation zone and all of them were coming from the local military bases (Antara News, 2022). The military announced a change of strategy in Poso whereby they would focus on territorial management instead of combat operation. As the number of personnel had been trimmed down, the compositions of personnel and teams were also adjusted; from forty checkpoints and six chasing teams to twelve military subdistrict command bases (komando rayon militer or koramil) (Perkasa, 2022).

Table 3. The casualties of the East Indonesia Mujahideen, 2015–2022.

Year	Date	Event
2015	April 3	Sabar Subagyo aka Daeng Koro, the field commander of MIT and apparently former member of Indonesian military, was shot dead
2016	July 18	Santoso, the leader of MIT, was shot dead by TNI personnel
	September 14	Basri, the successor of Santoso, surrendered and arrested
2021	March 1	Alvin and Khairul died in Andole, Kampung Maros, Poso Pesisir, Poso Regency. Khairul was Santoso's son
	July 11	Qatar and Ruli, MIT members, were shot dead
	July 17	Abu Alim, a MIT member, was shot dead
	September 18	Ali Kalora, the successor of Basri, and his subordinate, Jaka Ramadhan, were shot dead
2022	January 4	Ahmad Gazali aka Ahmad Panjang aka Basir, a MIT member, died
	April 27	Suhardin aka Hasan Pranata was shot dead
	May 16	Polri's Special Detachment Anti-Terror 88 arrested 24 members of MIT and IS supporters in Central Sulawesi, West Java, and East Kalimantan
	May 18	Nae aka Galuh, a MIT member, was shot dead
	September 29	Askar aka Jaid aka Pak Guru, a last identified active MIT member, was found dead. His death marked the end of MIT activity

Source: compiled from various documents and media reports.

In September 2022, Askar alias Pak Guru was the last remaining MIT member who eventually was shot to death by the task force (see Table 3). No more MIT active members are on the run in the mountainous jungle of Poso. However, the police did not halt the counter terror operation. The police asserted that they would extend Operation Madago Raya in 2023 but the focus would be on the revitalisation of the impacted area and de-radicalisation of MIT sympathisers to prevent the cycle of radicalisation among locals (VoA Indonesia, 2022).

From our discussion above, we see that the TNI has played a crucial role in countering MIT activities. The military's jungle warfare capability was a paramount game changer in the pursuit of Santoso and his accomplices in the dense area of Mount Biru. It took a while, but the military unit assigned to the joint operation successfully tracked and restricted the guerrilla-tactics of the MIT, resulting in the crumbling of MIT leadership and logistics that eventually led to the terror group's downfall in September 2022. The tactics of jungle warfare require the task force to stay in the jungle for a long time which is physically and mentally taxing. TNI has been drilled for jungle warfare and equipped with survival skills for such operations. The impact of TNI's jungle warfare became apparent when there was an increase in the number of military personnel (see Table 1). Inherently related to the jungle warfare capability is the use of military intelligence that assumes crucial positions in the conduct of territorial operations by TNI and Polri. The establishment of Madago Raya Task Force, which aims to fulfil the needs of both coercive and non-coercive measures in dealing with the MIT and the local populace, thus asserts the inalienable roles of the military.

Nevertheless, it took almost seven years for the joint task force between Polri and TNI to hunt down all the MIT members. Thousands of personnel were deployed to locate a handful of terrorists who were hiding inside a jungle in Poso. Many people raised doubts about the real intention behind the operations, and why it took so long for the police and military to crack down on the MIT networks. Although TNI was engaged in the operation to enhance the effectiveness of the operation, the military operation apparently had made the life of the local populace quite complicated. During the height of counter terror operation in 2016–2020, a local community organisation reported that many Poso residents had to evacuate and leave their farms behind. Those who stayed faced difficult living conditions. They complained that the joint operation personnel often accused them of being terrorist accomplices. Moreover, instead of uplifting the social and economic condition of the local community, the territorial operation that was conducted by the military further marginalised the people living in the operation area. The command-in-charge in Poso singlehandedly decided the types of development projects being undertaken.

Implications to TNI and Polri relationships

The involvement of TNI in Operations Camar Maleo and Tinombala, and later Madago Raya, reflected the military's continuing effort to maintain its domestic security roles. The Indonesian military took advantage of both the limited capability of the national police as well as political circumstance. Polri's lack of jungle warfare capability and inability to deliver immediate results provided a compelling reason for the military to take part in hunting down Santoso and the MIT group. On the one hand, the involvement of the Indonesian military in the hunt for terrorist groups in Poso produced some tangible results. On the other hand, such involvement has significantly shaped the TNI-Polri connection. We argue that the joint counter terror operations have resulted in three impacts on their relationship.

First, the experience in Poso has put the police's spearhead position in counter terrorism in a delicate situation. In this context, the security operation in the Poso mountainous area necessitates implementing jungle warfare, for which the military is the only force with the requisite capability. Meanwhile, the diverse scenarios of terrorist attacks require the ability to provide a wide range of solutions. This means that the option for using jungle warfare will never be diminished completely. Given the advantage of its warfare training and equipment, the military has a comparative advantage in tackling terrorist activities (Ganor, 2012). In the context of Indonesia, another example of comparative advantage is TNI's territorial command structure. It provides the military with superior intelligence and surveillance capability vis-á-vis Polri as the command structure covers rural and outer islands area of Indonesia. The territorial command system works as a part of the larger military structure, which enables the military to cover wider ground and employ more organisational resources.

Second, one potential snowball effect of the continued TNI involvement is the overarching presence of the military in the internal security realm. Such involvement in clamping down terrorist activities may result in increasing prioritisation in internal security operations as counter terrorism requires close attention to various domestic affair aspects, such as strengthening surveillance capability and infrastructure development to sustain the operation objective. Nonetheless, such situations can trigger further competition between the Indonesian military and police. For instance, it may hinder them from sharing information with each other in order to gain credit for the success of a special operation.[6] The separation of the police from the military in the early period of democratisation established Polri as the main actor for safeguarding internal security and TNI as the supporting actor. Thus, military presence in internal security has never been completely diminished. In fact, counter terrorism in Indonesia is hardly free from military involvement (Haripin et al., 2020).

Three, the element of militarism in counter terrorism persists. The continued involvement of the military has the likelihood of strengthening militaristic elements in the counter terrorism approach. In the past, Polri's counter terrorism unit, Densus 88 Antiteror (Special Detachment 88 Anti-Terror), was often criticised due to its militaristic approach in apprehending terrorist suspects.[7] The regular inclusion of the military in counter terrorism activities may cause the issue to endure. The military and the police have two different approaches in dealing with the terrorists. The police force primarily employs a law enforcement approach. In a democracy, the main task of the police is the safety and security of citizens, communities, and societies as a whole (Clutterbuck, 2018). The role of the police in reality contradicts the military approach which emphasises the protection of the state at all costs. The use of excessive force will only undermine the law enforcement process. The trial process is important to investigate the activities of the terrorist networks and the roots of their radicalism.

Closing and policy implications

How should we treat the involvement of TNI in Indonesia's counter terrorism governance? We can at least outline three takeaways from the above discussion. *First*, the operational experiences in Poso have helped nurture a mutual institutional trust between the two security apparatuses. Despite the competition between the police and military, not to mention the change of leadership within them, TNI and Polri managed to improve tactical coordination and the cohesion of field task forces operating in Poso throughout 2015–2022. Here we can see that military-police partnership is still probable, though competition between them exists.

Second, the case of Poso showcased the importance of military reinforcements in boosting strategic advantage in counter terror missions. TNI contributed valuable assets and tactical experiences that substantially helped Polri in detecting the movement of MIT members. Nevertheless, it would be potentially counterproductive and undemocratic to suggest that Polri-TNI joint operation should become a default setting of counter terror arrangement. The military deployment must be decided on a case-by-case basis, considering the type and intensity of the terror threats. Otherwise, the use of excessive military force will amplify the grievances of terrorist organisations and justify their cause. Santoso's MIT was an exception rather than a standard practice of radicalism in Indonesia. The terror group was a justifiable military target due to the fact that they were able to exert effective control upon certain territory in Poso Regency – thus it compromised national sovereignty and the government's political legitimacy. Moreover, MIT also committed multiple horrendous crimes against innocent civilians, therefore decisive action was required.

Third, military deployment in counter terrorism must pay attention to the overall TNI's strategic and defence development. Indonesia's all-encompassing counter terrorism style means that TNI participation in this field will be stretched not only on the battlefield, but also in civic duties. This will require the military to optimise its resources into various activities. Nonetheless, optimisation in many fields may result in no optimisation at all. It is important to maintain the position of TNI as a supporting agency within the overall counter terrorism arrangement in Indonesia.

In addition, TNI involvement entails risks of militarisation and, on the other side, police marginalisation. The police may be considered ineffective at handling domestic security issues thus the deployment of the military forces could be a favourable option. It is unlikely that the police will be completely omitted from operations as Indonesia upholds the law enforcement approach. Such conditions, however, will lead to an increasing number of military personnel on the ground. This is the case when we observe security instability and counter insurgency operations in the Papua Province. The Indonesian government has been in a protracted conflict with the Papuan independent movement since the 1960s. Given the violent escalation in recent years, the government conducted a joint operation of military and police to repress the separatist group. It is without coincidence that in 2021 Jakarta designated the Papuan rebels as 'terrorists'. Since then, we have witnessed a steady escalation of violence and hostility in the region. Although the military option is justified when conflict escalates, the government should not ignore the need to address the grievances of the people. Otherwise, public discourses will be dominated by the use of hard approaches instead of providing comprehensive counter terrorism measures.

Notes

1. Jemaah Islamiyah (JI) is a splinter group of Darul Islam (DI), an Islamist rebellion movement which envisioned the establishment of an Islamic state in Indonesia. JI was formally

established in early 1990s by the former DI members, Abdullah Sungkar and Abu Bakar Ba'asyir who decided to split from DI due to ideological differences. JI was responsible for major bombings in Indonesia in early 2000s, including the 2002 Bali Bombing, the 2003 JW Marriott Hotel Bombing, the 2004 Australian Embassy Bombing, and the 2005 Bali Bombing (Solahudin & McRae D, 2013).
2. The Indonesian government is expected to issue a Peraturan Presiden (Perpres) or Presidential Regulation one year after the ratification of revised law on counter terrorism in 2018. The Perpres would draw the boundaries of TNI's engagement in counter terrorism operations. It has been five years since the ratification of the law, but the Perpres is nowhere to be seen. It was only in early 2023 that the House of Representatives or Dewan Perwakilan Rakyat (DPR) brought up the issue of Pepres again. The DPR members urged the government to issue the Perpres due to 'security disturbance' caused by the Criminal Armed Group or Kelompok Kriminal Bersenjata (KKB) in Papua.
3. The Syrian civil war outbreak and the declaration of IS has lured the aspiring jihadist in Indonesia to pledge allegiance to IS. It was reported that Santoso's decision to associate MIT with IS was to attract more Indonesian jihadist to join his forces and to earn financial and material supports from IS. MIT's ability to conquer a small base in Poso also created an illusion among the other jihadists in Indonesia that it was the first step to establishing a larger Islamic state in Indonesia. Hence, MIT was able to garner support and new recruits from other regions (IPAC, 2015; IPAC, 2016a; Mahar, 2022).
4. At that time, TNI required a formal approval from the parliament to be engaged in a counter terrorism operation which had to go through a lengthy process. The form of exercise allowed the government and TNI to bypass such an extended procedure. President Jokowi at that time showed no hesitation towards the overall situation. It should be noted that the president had a rocky relationship with several political parties at that time. The precarious situation made Jokowi turn to the military for its political support.
5. It was reported that the insulation strategy was implemented firstly in January 2016 (Detik, 2016).
6. The competition occurred during the last phase of the hunt for Ali Kalora. The police and the military competed for the credit of capturing Ali Kalora. However, they failed to capture him alive. The hunt ended with a shootout which led to the death of Ali Kalora (IPAC, 2023).
7. Special Detachment 88 Anti-Terror and the police force in general have been heavily criticised by activists and civil society organisations, including Islamic groups, due to their inhumane treatment of terrorist suspects. Furthermore, several reports mentioned that many of these suspects were wrongly apprehended.

Disclosure statement

No potential conflict of interest was reported by the authors.

ORCID

Muhamad Haripin http://orcid.org/0000-0003-3037-4815
Chaula Rininta Anindya http://orcid.org/0000-0001-7898-7245
Adhi Priamarizki http://orcid.org/0000-0001-9078-9903

Bibliography

Anindya, C. R. (2017). *TNI's role in counterterrorism: Impact on military reform*. RSIS Commentary. https://www.rsis.edu.sg/rsis-publication/rsis/co17224-tnis-role-in-counterterrorism-impact-on-military-reform/?doing_wp_cron = 1686222474.8837280273437500000000

Antara News. (2016, January 8). *Operasi Camar Maleo IV Poso Berakhir*. Retrieved from Antara News: https://sulteng.antaranews.com/berita/23187/operasi-camar-maleo-iv-poso-berakhir

Antara News. (2022, May 13). *TNI mulai tarik pasukan Satgas Madago Raya secara bertahap di Poso*. https://manado.antaranews.com/berita/198321/tni-mulai-tarik pasukan-satgas-madago-raya-secara-bertahap-di-poso

BenarNews. (2021, September 20). *Indonesian analysts: MIT leader's killing may bring about militant group's demise*. https://www.benarnews.org/english/news/indonesian/no-scuccessor-09202021150257.html

Boyle, M. J. (2018). The military approach to counterterrorism. In A. Silke (Ed.), *Routledge handbook of terrorism and counterrorism* (pp. 384–394). London: Routledge.

Clutterbuck, L. (2018). Policing in counterterrorism. In A. Silke (Ed.), *Routledge handbook of terrorism and counterterrorism* (pp. 375–383). London: Routledge.

Detik. (2016, April 27). *Kunci Keberhasilan Satgas TNI-Polri Melemahkan Kekuatan Kelompok Santoso*. Retrieved from Detik.com: https://news.detik.com/berita/d-3198124/kunci-keberhasilan-satgas-tni-polri-melemahkan-kekuatan-kelompok-santoso

Diprose, R., & Azca, M. N. (2019). Past communal conflict and contemporary security debates in Indonesia. *Journal of Contemporary Asia, 49*(5), 780–805. DOI: 10.1080/00472336.2019.1619186

Ganor, B. (2012). The use of force to combat terrorism. In R. Jackson & S. J. Sinclair (Eds.), *Contemporary debates on terrorism* (pp. 137–143). London: Routledge.

Haripin, M. (2020). *Civil-military relations in Indonesia: The politics of military operations other than war*. New York: Routledge.

Haripin, M., Anindya, C. R., & Priamarizki, A. (2020). The politics of counter-terrorism in post-authoritarian states: Indonesia's experience, 1998–2018. *Defense & Security Analysis, 36*(3), 275–299.

ICG. (2004). *Indonesia backgrounder: Jihad in central Sulawesi (report No. 43)*. Jakarta/Brussels: International Crisis Group.

IPAC. (2015). *Indonesia's Lamongan network: How East Java, Poso, and Syria are linked (report No. 18)*. Jakarta: Institute for Policy Analysis of Conflict.

IPAC. (2016a). *Disunity among Indonesian ISIS supporters and the risk of more violence (report No. 25)*. Jakarta: Institute for Policy Analysis of Conflict.

IPAC. (2016b). *Update on the Indonesian military's influence (report No. 26)*. Jakarta: Institute for Policy Analysis of Conflict.

IPAC. (2023). *Militant groups in Poso: Down but not out (report No. 86)*. Jakarta: Institute for Policy Anaysis of Conflict.

Jones, S. (2014, October 5). *Lessons learned from Indonesia's conflicts: Aceh, Poso and Papua*. https://www.insideindonesia.org/lessons-learned-from-indonesia-s-conflicts-aceh-poso-and-papua

Jones, S., & Solahudin. (2015). ISIS in Indonesia. In D. Singh (Ed.), *Southeast Asian Affairs* (pp. 154–163). Singapore: ISEAS-Yusof Ishak Institute.

Karnavian, M. T. (2015). *Explaining Islamist insurgencies: The case of al-Jamaah al-Islamiyyah and the radicalisation of the Poso conflict, 2000-2007*. London: Imperial College Press.

Kompas. (2015, September 9). *Terus Buru Jaringan Teroris, Polisi Gelar Operasi Camar Maleo III*. https://regional.kompas.com/read/2015/09/09/16555531/Terus.Buru.Jaringan.Santoso.Polisi.Gelar.Operasi.Camar.Maleo.III

Kompas. (2022, April 28). *Satu DPO Mujahidin Indonesia Timur Tewas Ditembak, Terorisme Diharapkan Segera Selesai*. Retrieved from https://www.kompas.id/baca/nusantara/2022/04/28/satu-dpo-terorisme-poso-tewas-ditembak-mit-diharapkan-segera-selesai

Mahar, I. (2022). *Merekam Jejak Teror ISIS di Indonesia*. Jakarta: Kompas.

Merdeka. (2021, May 31). *80 Gabungan Polisi dan TNI di Luar Satgas Madago Raya Dikerahkan Buru Kelompok MIT*. Retrieved from Merdeka.cm: https://www.merdeka.com/peristiwa/80-gabungan-polisi-dan-tni-di-luar-satgas-madago-raya-dikerahkan-buru-kelompok-mit.html

OkeZone. (2017, March 27). *15 Anak Buah Santoso Diringkus dalam Operasi Camar*. https://nasional.okezone.com/read/2015/03/27/337/1125267/15-anak-buah-santoso-diringkus-dalam-operasi-camar

Perkasa, A. [Andika Perkasa]. (2022, February 16). *Pemaparan Terkait Perubahan Konsep Operasi di Kodam XIII/Merdeka* [Video]. Youtube. https://www.youtube.com/watch?v=canLcDoYksI

Republika. (2015, March 20). *Usai Latihan PPRC, TNI Bakal Gelar Operasi Teritorial di Poso.* https://news.republika.co.id/berita/nlgq7n/usai-latihan-pprc-tni-bakal-gelar-operasi-teritorial-di-poso

Republika. (2016, July 28). *Ini Kronologi Insiden Salah Tembak Satgas Tinombala di Poso.* Retrieved from Republika: https://news.republika.co.id/berita/ob0h8z354/ini-kronologi-insiden-salah-tembak-satgas-tinombala-di-poso

Singh, J. (2023, February 2). *Operation Madago Raya: Indonesia's Joint Military-Police Approach to Counter-Terrorism.* RSIS Commentary. https://www.rsis.edu.sg/wp-content/uploads/2023/02/CO23017.pdf

Solahudin & McRae D. (2013). *The roots of terrorism in Indonesia: From Darul Islam to Jemaah Islamiyah.* Sydney: New South Publishing.

Soliev, N. (2017). *Uyghur militancy in and beyond Southeast Asia: An assesment, 9:1.* Singapore: ICPVTR.

Tempo. (2016, July). The hunt for Santoso. Tempo Magazine English Edition.

TNI. (2015, April 1). *Kapal Perang Koarmatim Gempur Gunung Biru Poso.* Retrieved from TNI: https://tni.mil.id/view-74522-kapal-perang-koarmatim-gempur-gunung-biru-poso.html

Tribun News. (2014, September 15). *Polisi Bingung Terjemahkan Bahasa Uighur 4 WNA yang Ditangkap di Poso.* https://www.tribunnews.com/nasional/2014/09/15/polisi-bingung-terjemahkan-bahasa-uighur-4-wna-yang-ditangkap-di-poso

VoA Indonesia. (2015, April 11). *Latihan PPRC TNI Temukan Jejak Kelompok Teroris di Gunung Biru.* https://www.voaindonesia.com/a/latihan-pprc-tni-temukan-jejak-kelompok-teroris-di-gunung-biru/2715349.html

VoA Indonesia. (2016, March 25). *AS Masukkan Santoso dalam Daftar Teroris Global.* Retrieved from VoA Indonesia: https://www.voaindonesia.com/a/as-masukkan-santoso-dalam-daftar-teroris-global-/3252959.html

VoA Indonesia. (2021, May 9). *Desak Penuntasan Gangguan Keamanan di Poso, Warga Kirim Surat Kepada Jokowi.* https://www.voaindonesia.com/a/desak-penuntasan-terorisme-di-poso-warga-kirim-surat-terbuka-kepada-presiden-joko-widodo/5896441.html

VoA Indonesia. (2022, December 9). *Polda Sulteng: Pemulihan Desa Yang Pernah Terdampak Terorisme Jadi Fokus Operasi Madago Raya di 2023.* https://www.voaindonesia.com/a/polda-sulteng-pemulihan-desa-yang-pernah-terdampak-terorisme-jadi-fokus-operasi-madago-raya-di-2023/6869121.html

Wilkinson, P. (2011). *Terrorism versus democracy: The liberal state response* (3rd ed.). London: Routledge.

Countering radical terrorist ideology through psywar: lessons from the Malayan Emergency

Andrew T. H. Tan

ABSTRACT
Soon after the events of 9–11, it was recognised that the U.S. and the West had to wage effective information warfare if they were to succeed in countering or containing global terrorism as a result of radical Islamism. The West, however, has failed in this endeavour, epitomised by the contemporary onslaught from the Islamic State's ideology resulting in the continuation of the global terrorist threat. Yet, lessons drawn from the case study of British success in the Malayan Emergency experience, with the necessary qualifications, are useful in waging information war today against contemporary radical Islamist terrorism. The key lessons for contemporary counter-terrorism include: the need for psywar operations to be accompanied by legal and security measures in consultation with local Muslim communities to contain the enablers of the adversary's psywar apparatus, establishing better governance over religious schools, enabling local Muslims to lead psywar operations, the use of former terrorists in counter-radicalisation, the promotion of inclusion, addressing underlying causes of alienation and paying careful attention to developments in the Middle East.

Introduction

Soon after the seminal terrorist attacks on the United States took place on 11 September 2001 (or 9–11) and the subsequent U.S. response in attacking Afghanistan where Al Qaeda was based, it was recognised by many, such as Singer, who asserted that 'more important to the success of Operation Enduring Freedom than the fire of any weapons will instead be the use of words, images, and ideas to create an environment amenable to victory.' Indeed, while the actual warfighting is the easy part, the most important task is to 'reshape the information environment and target points of fracture in the opposition' in order to win the battle of hearts and minds which is the crucial centre of gravity in such conflicts (Singer, 2001). In short, the U.S. and the West has to wage effective information warfare if they are to succeed in countering or containing global terrorism as a result of radical Islamism. Radical Islamism here refers to the very small minority who subscribe to extreme interpretations of religion, and who advocate the use of violence in establishing a state that would be ruled strictly according to Islamic laws. The overwhelming majority of the world's Muslim population does not adhere to radical Islamism.

Just as presciently, Taylor observed in 2002 that in the war on terror, 'the challenge for whatever replaces the Office of Strategic Information is daunting, especially since the conflict owes more in character to the Cold War than to any other conflict waged by the United States since 1945, and it may prove to last just as long.' Indeed, he argued that 'the role of strategic information warfare may prove crucial.' Taylor thus called for the waging of information warfare against terrorist networks that uses propaganda as one of its key weapons in its asymmetric struggle against the West. This requires a shift in emphasis in Information War conceptualisations 'away from its early obsession in the 1990s with computer and communication systems at the expense of human factors' (Taylor, 2002, pp. 10–11).

More recently, Droogan and Waldek have observed that 'the impact of social media technology on classic terrorist groups, dissident political groups, and persecuted ethnic and religious minorities in the Asia Pacific has been profound,' with such groups seizing the opportunities that social networking platforms such as Twitter, Facebook, Whatsapp and Telegram have generated, such as the ability to engage with sympathetic audiences globally and create transnational communities for recruitment and funding. Moreover, 'the accessibility and openness of social media has meant that terrorist groups are no longer reliant on traditional mass media for spreading propaganda and fear.' In addition, the migration of terrorist groups online has facilitated structural and operational changes, resulting in a more dispersed, resilient and self-sustaining form of terrorism (Droogan & Waldek, 2019, pp. 31–32).

Taylor observed in 2008 that the West has been losing the propaganda war against radical Islamist terrorism, though the West does not use the term 'propaganda' to describe its information campaign (Taylor, 2008, p. 118). This still holds true today in the face of the onslaught from the Islamic State's ideology resulting in the continuation of the global terrorist threat. It is the contention of this article that lessons, albeit with the necessary qualifications, can be drawn from the experience of the Malayan Emergency in waging information war today against contemporary ideological and misinformation challenges, including from radical Islamist terrorism.

During the Malayan Emergency (1948–1960) and its aftermath, the Maoist, pro-China Malayan Communist Party (MCP) used psychological war operations (or psyops) which also incorporated a 'United Front' strategy of above-ground political and social activities, to complement its violent insurgency, with the objective of subverting the nascent Malayan state and turning it into a Maoist, pro-China communist state. How did the fledging Malayan state, aided by the British colonial power at the time, manage to win the psychological war during the Malayan Emergency and after? What lessons can we learn from how to better manage and even win such wars against contemporary terrorist movements and groups?

Waging psychological war

Psychological operations (or psychological warfare), is part of a broader strategy of Information Operations (or Information War). According to the US Army Field Manual in 2008, Information War is 'the integrated employment of the core capabilities of electronic warfare, computer network operations, psychological operations, military deception, and operations security, in concert with specified supporting and related capabilities, to influence, disrupt, corrupt or usurp adversarial human and automated decision-making while protecting our own' (FM-3-0, 2008, Glossary 7). According to Christopher Simpson however, psychological warfare consists of 'a group of strategies and tactics designed to achieve the ideological, political, or military objectives of the sponsoring organisation ... through exploitation of a target audience's cultural-psychological attributes and its communication system' (Simpson, 1994, p. 11). As psychological warfare played a key role in the overall strategic objective of winning over the hearts and minds of the Chinese population, from which the insurgents drew support during the Malayan Emergency, this article will focus on this aspect of information warfare (Stubbs, 2004).

After the end of the Cold War in 1989, psychological operations became somewhat neglected, as it became subordinated to the military and warfighting, with 'psyops' (or psychological warfare operations; with the term 'psywar' being used interchangeably with psyops) seen as tactics used in a military theatre of operations, with limited objectives in mind (Molander, Riddile, & Wilson, 1996, p. iii). According to Crane, 'the shift would contribute to a lack of understanding among military officers and senior civilians about the broad uses and capabilities of psychological operations' (Crane, 2019). An added challenge today is the rapid evolution of cyberspace, including the widespread use of the internet, the proliferation of social media and the resultant deep influence welded by social media platforms in forming perceptions, beliefs and in forming transnational networks and communities. The result has been the inability of the West to effectively counter psychological operations carried out by Russia and China, which adopt a strategic approach to such operations and integrate them as part of their Information War activities abroad. Just as seriously, it has left the West struggling to counter the propaganda and misinformation spread by radical Islamist terrorist groups and movements.

The Malayan emergency: the challenge of the Malayan Communist Party

On its part, the Chinese Communist Party (CCP) in China has always understood and valued psychological factors. Indeed, by 1945, its propaganda machine had won the battle of hearts and minds for the Chinese people against the then ruling Kuomintang, which eventually lost the Chinese civil war and fled to Taiwan in 1949, where the rump Republic of China continues to exist. The CCP's strategy of waging psychological war has historically been aimed at subverting the state and mobilising the masses towards the destruction of the existing socio-economic-political system to be replaced by a different political order. In this context, its historic United Front strategy of above-ground political and social activities has been an integral part of its quite sophisticated psywar (or propaganda) strategy. The CCP understood from its history that subverting from within is the most economical method of gaining victory. This reflects the long historical Chinese strategic tradition stemming from Sun Tzu's dictum that 'supreme excellence consists in breaking the enemy's resistance without fighting' (Sun Tzu, n.d.).

As Joske observed, the United Front is 'a coalition of groups and individuals working towards the CCP's goals,' under the direction of the United Front Work Department (UFWD), which is today a CCP Central Committee department (Joske, 2020, p. 6). As the current leadership of the UFWD state, 'the united front is a political alliance ... the united front work is political work.' This takes place under the leadership of the Party, for the purpose of enhancing the Party's 'political leadership, ideological leadership, mass organization and social appeal.' Further, to be effective, the objective of the united front is to establish a 'one game of chess' consciousness that will further the goals of the CCP (Yu, 2019). In short, the United Front is very much part of psywar operations designed to change perceptions and win the hearts and minds of the population to support the CCP.

The armed insurgency mounted by the Malayan Communist Party (MCP) in 1948, which was only effectively ended with its disbandment in 1989 at the end of the Cold War, is a useful case study of how psychological war or psywar tactics (and associated above-ground 'United Front' type activities which are a crucial component of psywar) could be successfully countered. The MCP was dominated by ethnic Chinese (many of whom were born in Malaya and had in fact never been to China), looked to China for moral and strategic direction, and took directives from the CCP. Indeed, soon after its founding in 1930, it was instructed in 1933 by the Central Committee of the CCP to infiltrate labour unions and begin establishing 'organisations to oppose imperialism' (Comber, 2019, pp. 77–78).

During World War Two, the MCP established a broad United Front resistance organisation, the Malayan Peoples' Anti-Japanese Army (MPAJA) to resist the Japanese occupation of Malaya. After Japan's surrender in 1945, the MPAJA was disbanded but the MCP kept its arms caches and established a number of other United Front organisations. The extensive use of psywar (otherwise known as 'propaganda') was accompanied by the use of United Front tactics designed to establish the credentials of the MCP as a political force, spread communist propaganda, recruit ethnic Chinese to its cause and raise funding. Both the MCP and its parent organisation, the CCP, understood the crucial importance of winning the propaganda war as it was crucial in recruitment and the building of the popular support needed to subvert and ultimately overthrow the state.

The MCP's use of violence, following the start of the Cold War, led to the declaration of the Malayan Emergency in 1948. While the Emergency officially ended in 1960, the MCP continued its struggle until its ultimate disbandment in 1989. The MCP predictably followed Mao Tse-tung's three-stage revolutionary war model, since this was the template that had led to victory for the CCP in China. The first phase consisted of defensive guerrilla operations and the building of underground organisations within the population. The second consisted of the expansion of underground infrastructure and population control, while the third stage would see the party stage a strategic counter-offensive and seize power (Mao, 1938).

Reasons for the MCP's effectiveness

As Stubbs observed, 'for the many Chinese MCP members who still followed events in their homeland with a keen interest, the success of the Chinese Communist Party in the war against the Kuomintang government was a powerful incentive to adopt a similar strategy' (Stubbs, 2004, pp. 253–254). According to the noted historian Wang Gungwu, prior to the Japanese occupation from 1942 to 1945, there already existed Chinese in Malaya who strongly identified with the nationalist anti-Manchu revolution in China and followed closely developments in the Chinese homeland. According to Wang,

> their keenness to modernize according to China's new needs was infectious and they soon mobilized to try and convert most Chinese to their point of view ... they dominated the two closely related fields of publishing and education, and the strength of the group increased rapidly as literate newcomers were imported to edit the newspapers and magazines and to provide teachers for the increasing numbers of Chinese schools. (Wang, 1970, p. 11)

Ranged against them were a smaller minority of well-assimilated Chinese who were grateful for the law and order provided by the colonial rulers, proud of their superior mastery of English and were critical of nationalistic Chinese for their emotionalism and actions which endangered the community as a whole in the eyes of the British and Malay authorities (Wang, 1970, p. 14).

Japan's aggression towards China and the occupation of Malaya during World War Two sharpened the patriotism of the Malayan Chinese towards China. Building on its United Front work in Malaya in mobilising the Chinese following Japan's attack on China in 1937, the Malayan Communist Party (MCP) dominated the Malayan resistance to Japanese occupation, assisted in no small measure by the brutality of the Japanese occupation especially with regards to the local Chinese. More significantly, the pro-Malay policy of the Japanese created a strong sense of resentment and distrust among Chinese towards the majority Malays (Cheah, 1981, p. 108). Indeed, violent racial clashes broke out between Chinese and Malays in 1945–1946 following the Japanese surrender, sharpening the sense of insecurity amongst the Chinese and also the determination of the Malays to prevent Chinese domination (Cheah, 1981, pp. 108–117).

The MCP's propaganda worked because the ethnic Chinese continued to adopt a China-centric worldview, sustained through Chinese education, language and culture, and their uncertain status as migrants in British colonial territory where the majority Malays were openly hostile to them. There were also economic drivers that made many Chinese susceptible to MCP propaganda. The Great Depression of the 1930s and World War Two had led to the emergence of a large Chinese migrant underclass in Malaya, who now eked out a precarious legal and economic existence as rural farmers on state land that they did not own (Opper, 2020, p. 184).

This set the stage for the MCP to condemn the British colonial government in 1948 for its 'limitless economic exploitation and plunder of Malaya's raw materials in exchange for American dollars, turning Malaya into nothing more than a dollar printing press,' paving the way for a violent Maoist-inspired class-based rebellion against the government (Opper, 2020, p. 176). While the ostensible objective of the MCP's rebellion was independence for Malaya, in practice, the MCP's closeness to the new communist government in China meant that its real aim was to impose Chinese domination of Malaya as well as draw it into the orbit of the People's Republic of China.

The MCP's psychological operations

The above discussion explained the reasons for the effectiveness of the MCP's psywar (or propaganda) apparatus. It is important to note though that the MCP's rebellion consisted of both armed violence waged by its insurgent forces, as well as above-ground United Front political and psywar activities designed to bolster support for the MCP, recruit new activists and insurgents, and undermine the legitimacy of the Malayan government. Both activities were carried out in tandem, complemented each other, and were not mutually exclusive.

One of the main ways that the MCP carried out its psywar operations was through the print media, for instance, the *Min Sheng Pao* (Voice of the People), which was the party organ of the MCP from 1949, the *Vanguard Weekly*, which was the mouthpiece of the communist Pan-Malayan Federation of Trade Unions, and Chinese newspapers, such as the *Malayan Orchid, Nan Chiau Jit Poh, People's Awakening News* and *Modern Daily News* (Comber, 2019, p. 82; Ramakrishna, 2002, p. 56; Yeo, 1973, pp. 225, 227). All these propaganda outlets were eventually banned by the government, or forced to disband. The insurgents and their supporters were also able to listen to broadcasts from Radio Peking, which was broadcast from China. The MCP gained its own radio station much later, in 1969, when the Voice of the Malayan Revolution (VMR) began broadcasts from South China. The propaganda consisted of Maoist writings (often by Chairman Mao Tse-Tung himself) for study, developments in Malaya as interpreted by CCP researchers in China, inspirational propaganda and guidelines for activities (Central Intelligence Agency [CIA], 1973, pp. 11, 118).

The MCP's organisational structures were also set up to implement its United Front strategy of above-ground political and social activities designed to win the hearts and minds of the targeted Chinese population. This strategy was copied from, and indeed was directed by the CCP. According to Stubbs, this could best be understood as a series of concentric circles, with the MCP at the centre, followed by satellite organisations such as the New Democratic Youth League, Ex-Servicemen's Association and the Chinese Women's Association, and then an outer circle of front organisations controlled or influenced, to varying degrees, by the MCP (Stubbs, 2004, p. 47). Such a large collection of front organisations was used for influencing operations, including for recruitment, propaganda, and other purposes.

In 1941, the MCP's front organisations consisted of clan associations, trade unions and student bodies. While the party itself had only around 5000 members at the time, it had some 50,000 members in the Malayan General Labour Union. All these front organisations were organised for patriotic activities in support of a foreign entity, namely, the CCP (Yong, 2019, p. 146). After 1945, the MCP focused on capturing the labour movement in order to mobilise the masses and increase its political power. As recounted by Stubbs, the MCP gained control of the union movement, by infiltrating and then taking over the Pan-Malayan Federation of Trade Unions and the Singapore Federation of Trade Unions (Stubbs, 2004, pp. 47–48). This was achieved 'by placing people in official leadership positions and as well as (through) informal opinion makers,' enabling the MCP to 'steer the policies and actions of the various unions in the desired direction' (Stubbs, 2004, p. 48).

Apart from trade unions, the MCP also attempted to set up legal political fronts. The Malayan Democratic Union was one such attempt, although this was dissolved when the Malayan Emergency was declared in 1948 (History.SG, n.d.). In Singapore, an island at the southern tip of Malaya and a British Crown Colony until self-government in

1959, the MCP infiltrated the trade union movement and attempted to subvert post-war political parties such as the Barisan Socialis and People's Action Party.

Apart from infiltrating trade unions and political parties, the MCP paid particular attention to United Front and propaganda work in Chinese schools in Malaya, as the Chinese valued education. Private Chinese schools had been infused since the 1920s with China-centric nationalistic teaching and thus in the context of rising Chinese nationalist fervour in the years before and after 1945, proved to be a particularly useful base for recruitment. The MCP established branches of the Malayan Communist Youth League to penetrate Chinese-medium schools, coordinate student activism and to recruit from amongst the students (CIA, 1973). As Stubbs noted, teachers and students were targets for recruitment primarily through personal contact. Thus, 'having been persuaded to attend a meeting of a satellite or front organisation, many found themselves swept along by the communist rhetoric,' since MCP speakers (similar to many present-day radical Islamist clerics) were invariably dramatic and persuasive (Stubbs, 2004, p. 49). Chinese high school students were so radicalised that they took part in the assassination of, for instance, their own teachers, as epitomised by the killing of the principal of Chung Ling High School in Penang, David Chen, who was at the time also the President of the Malayan Federation of Chinese Teachers Association (Lee, 2005, p. 106).

Countering the MCP

The response of the British colonial authorities was to conduct counterinsurgency operations against the MCP. At first, counterinsurgency efforts focusing on the kinetic application of military force failed to stem the growing insurgency, which reached a nadir with the assassination of the British High Commissioner, Henry Gurney, in October 1951. However, the Briggs Plan, which was a comprehensive approach involving the police, army and civilian authorities led by General Harold Briggs, the Director of Operations (1950–1951), had already been put in place and required time and adjustments to make it work. The centrepiece of the plan was the resettlement of 500,000 Chinese rural squatters into New Villages, which had the effect of cutting off the MCP's supply lines (Comber, 2019, p. 147).

The new approach focusing on 'hearts and minds' was implemented by the new British High Commissioner and Director of Operations, General Gerald Templer. He oversaw greater emphasis on intelligence and the crucial recruitment of the aboriginal Orang Asli that had been friendly with the MCP to the cause of the government. The successful implementation of the revised Briggs Plan led to the reduction of insurgent attacks from around 6000 in 1950 to 1000 in 1954 (Comber, 2019, p. 189). As Stubbs, observed, it was 'the abandonment of a coercion and enforcement approach in favour of a hearts and minds approach' that led to an end to the fighting (Stubbs, 2004, p. 271).

However, Templer did implement harsh measures, including the forced relocation of Chinese squatters into 'New Villages' (ringed with fences and policed by a vast police force) as envisaged under the original Briggs Plan. However, and more importantly, he also accelerated the psychological campaign to win the people's support, especially the Chinese, as he was aware that no victory would be possible or permanent unless the Chinese were won over (Clutterback, 2003, p. 85). As British strategist Robert Thompson wrote, one of the key lessons of the Malayan Emergency is that 'the government must give priority to defeating the political subversion, not the guerillas' (Thompson, 1966, p. 55).

Propaganda (or psychological operations/war) is a component of what we know today as Information War. In Malaya, it was recognised very early on that this would be crucial in countering communist subversion and propaganda. Thus, General Harold Briggs had brought in Hugh Carleton Greene to establish the Emergency Information Services (EIS) to coordinate psychological operations. Greene was formerly with the BBC's German service and later became Director-General of the BBC after leaving Malaya (Comber, 2019, p. 170). Under him, and building on the Joint Information and Propaganda Committee (JIPC) which first met in 1950, the EIS was transformed when it was amalgamated with the Department of Information in 1952 to become the Department of Information Services, to become a centralised institution responsible for coordinating a vigorous and coherent propaganda effort (Ramakrishna, 2002, pp. 52, 58).

According to Greene in his Report in 1951, the objectives of the EIS were:

1. To raise the morale of the civil population and to encourage confidence in Government and resistance to the Communists with a view to increasing the flow of information reaching the Police;
2. To attack the morale of members of the Malayan Races Liberation Army (i.e. the armed wing of the MCP), the Min Yuen (the MCP's mass organisation) and their supporters and to drive a wedge between the leaders and the rank and file with a view to encouraging defection and undermining the determination of the Communists to continue the struggle; and
3. To create an awareness of the values of the democratic way of life which are threatened by International Communism (Greene, 1951).

This would be achieved through media such as leaflets, word of mouth propaganda, films and radio broadcasts (Greene, 1951). Indeed, Greene introduced a full radio broadcast schedule in the local languages, namely, Malay, Tamil, and four Chinese dialects in 1950 (Stubbs, 2004, p. 181). Greene noted as well that all the State Emergency Information Officers mentioned in his Report, including the British officers, were Chinese-speakers. According to him, 'there would seem to be some mysterious connection between skill in Chinese Affairs and skill in propaganda,' and that 'Malaya now has a nucleus of experienced propagandists,' who might 'be particularly valuable if international developments should ever call for propaganda from Malaya (to be) directed to China' (Greene, 1951).

More significantly, Greene strongly advocated for 'the use of surrendered bandits for propaganda purposes,' arguing that 'wherever the free world has been engaged in any form of psychological warfare against Communism it is the convert and the deviationist who have been recognised in the Communist world as the most dangerous enemies, because these people understand the Communist mentality and methods as no-one else can' (Greene, 1951).

Greene thus recruited local Chinese to help counter the communists, hiring Henry C. C. Too and a surrendered MCP leader, Lam Swee, to join the EIS in 1951. They were entrusted with the responsibility of writing government psychological warfare material. For instance, they edited the *New Path News* which was directed at the rural Chinese (Ramakrishna, 2002, p. 55). Lam Swee's booklet written in Chinese, entitled *My Accusation*, which strongly criticised the MCP leadership, was widely distributed in Malaya (Comber, 2019, p. 159). More broadly, the British also increased the number of Chinese in the security services, such as Special Branch and the Criminal Investigation Department (CID), recruiting 580 new Chinese officers in 1951–1952 alone (Comber, 2019, p. 159).

In particular, the role of C. C. Too, a local Chinese, was crucial in the psychological war against the communists, who were predominantly ethnic Chinese who looked to China's CCP for inspiration and guidance. By 1956, he headed the psychological warfare section, a role he held with distinction until his retirement in 1983. As Clutterback later observed, the obvious lesson here is that 'psy warfare must be directed by a local man,' adding somewhat clumsily that 'it is amazing how many Europeans think they understand the Asian mind' (Clutterback, 2003, p. 106).

C. C. Too, who spoke excellent English and Chinese Mandarin, was a forceful and imaginative person, and was particularly adept at forecasting the MCP's policies and reactions due to his constant contact with current communist thinking. According to Ramakrishna, Too benefitted from a thorough bilingual education before 1945, enabling him to understand communist thinking as well as the British philosophy of psywar that had been developed in the course of World War Two. Indeed, the fundamental principle of the British way of propaganda was to establish credibility with the audience by telling the truth, although the caveat is that this is a strategy and not an iron commitment to telling the truth all the time. However, the point is that if the propagandist is careful to say what is plausible, the audience would eventually trust what the propagandist had to say, thus enabling the propagandist to be able to effectively influence the audience. Thus, Too learnt the basic principle from Greene to be very careful what was said, since any obvious falsehood would eventually be found out (Ramakrishan, 2000, pp. 64–86).

As part of psywar operations, the British also organised civics courses, which began in 1952 with the visit of rural Chinese villagers to government offices for a week for briefings and entertainment. In 1953, 116 of these courses were organised, and included military firing displays as well as entertainment by Commonwealth military units such as the King's African Rifles and sketches by police officers. The courses helped to bridge the psychological gulf between the Chinese and the government, particularly the security services (Ramakrishna, 2002, p. 61).

In the end, psywar operations were successful because concrete measures to address the underlying political and economic issues were also undertaken. One key political issue was the place of the Chinese in the emerging independent Malayan state. In 1952, a new citizenship law enabled all Chinese born in Malaya to automatically became citizens, thus giving stateless Chinese a sense of belonging and forcing them to choose between China and the new Malayan state. The rural Chinese squatters were also granted land titles enabling them to cultivate what had been government lands. Many more Chinese were also recruited into the police and other security agencies, which hitherto had been dominated by Malays (Yadi, 2004, pp. 25–26). These measures addressed the underlying fundamental grievances of the Chinese minority that led to widespread alienation. They also demonstrated to the Chinese that they now had a stake in the new Malaya and that they did not have to look towards a foreign power or entity to protect them.

The British government also addressed the issue of private Chinese schools, which had become hotbeds of communist brainwashing, often carried out by younger teachers infused with communist ideology. The government took measures to control Chinese education by funding it and subjecting Chinese schools to close monitoring (Hong & Huang, 2008, p. 132). Apart from reducing communist infiltration and propaganda amongst students, government funding also won over the Chinese, who highly value education. In turn, this reduced MCP recruitment and the cadre of hard-core communists (Yadi, 2004, p. 27). As the MCP could not penetrate the English and Malay schools which taught a national as opposed to a China-centric curriculum, this meant that its United Front strategy in the education sector failed. After independence in 1957, Malaysia continued to fund Chinese-medium schools, though a small number of private Chinese schools remained in existence to this day (Malay Mail, 2017). In Singapore, the government phased out all Chinese schools in the 1970s, and replaced them with English-medium schools, although a select few Chinese schools were able to continue under government supervision in the teaching of a national curriculum, albeit with an emphasis on bilingualism in both English and Mandarin (Asiaone, 2014, july 14).

Space does not permit a thorough examination of the comprehensive counter-insurgency strategy pursued by the British, but psywar operations clearly played a key role in eventually ending the large-scale insurgency by 1958. However, while the Malayan Emergency officially ended in 1960, the threat from the MCP continued until its disbandment in 1989 at the end of the Cold War. In 1961, China's Deng Xiaoping instructed the MCP to restart its revolutionary war in Malaya (Chin, 2003, pp. 429–430). In 1968, the MCP (now known as the Communist Party of Malaya or CPM) officially announced the resumption of its armed struggle, possibly due to the increased ideological militancy in China as a result of the Cultural Revolution (CIA, 1972, p. 4). The resumption of the armed struggle demonstrated that the CPM continued to take its cue from external sources, i.e. the motherland.

The battle for hearts and minds thus resumed, but this time, it was not the British directing security and psywar operations but the local governments. Malaya had become independent in 1957, and Singapore followed suit when it split from the Federation of Malaysia (which includes the East Malaysian states of Sabah and Sarawak) in 1965. CPM insurgents now operated in the then comparatively lawless Betong salient in southern Thailand, while it continued to attempt to re-build its United Front in Malaysia and Singapore to try to mobilise the masses. Recognising the continuing, long-term threat from the communists, Malaysia passed the Internal Security Act (ISA) in 1960, which provided for the prohibition of quasi-military organisations and the preventive detention of persons deemed a threat to the State or to essential services. More importantly, from the perspective of psywar, the Act also provided for the suppression of subversive publications and the closing of schools that supported subversion (International Labour Organisation [ILO], n.d.). The ISA was very effectively used by Malaysia and Singapore to shut down organisations and publications as well as arrest individuals associated with the CPM.

After Lee Kuan Yew became Prime Minister in 1959 when Singapore became self-governing, the MCP's united front in Singapore gradually crumbled as Lee took decisive measures to end the influence of its United Front organisations and overall psywar capabilities there. This included Operation Cold Store in 1963, under which 107 communist cadres or pro-communist figures were arrested under the ISA. As the MCP leader Chin Peng admitted later, the operation crippled the communist network in Singapore (Chin, 2003, p. 439). Under the Lee government, communist influence on trade unions in Singapore declined rapidly, from 31,000 members in 30 pro-communist unions in 1967, to 6500 members in 13 unions by 1972 (Yong, 2019, p. 70).

China continued to sponsor the CPM, with the establishment of a Malayan National Liberation League in Peking in 1966 headed by Malayan communists (CIA, 1972, p. 12). In 1969, China also began the Voice of the Malayan Revolution (VMR), which broadcast from southern China until it was shut down in 1981. The VMR broadcast propaganda material with the objective of persuading the masses to rise up and overthrow the allegedly illegitimate neo-colonial governments of Malaysia and Singapore, and to replace them with a communist republic (Wang & Ong, 2009). The CPM was handed a propaganda boost in the aftermath of the deadly May 13 race riots in 1969, which epitomised the breakdown in relations between the Chinese and Malay communities. A CIA intelligence assessment in 1972 concluded that while the Chinese in Malaysia were not desperate enough to defect to the communists as a result of this, they also 'saw little reason to cooperate enthusiastically with the government' (CIA, 1972, p. 14).

Thus, despite the Malayan Emergency being declared over in 1960, the MCP/CPM continued to pose a threat, albeit a considerably weakened one, until changes in China's foreign policy led to its demise. Eventually, with the end of the Cold War in 1989, the CPM negotiated the termination of its armed struggle with the government of Malaysia and laid down its arms (Malaysiakini, 2019). The defeat and ultimate demise of the MCP/CPM was also aided by factors such as the rapid economic development of both Malaysia and especially Singapore, as well as China's weakness during much of the Cold War era. In addition, China's policy towards fraternal communist parties in Southeast Asia changed under the pragmatic leadership of Deng Xiao Peng, who launched China's Open Door policy in 1978 and focused on economic development instead of exporting revolutions. This led to China abandoning the region's beleaguered communist parties, including the MCP/CPM, with the VMR radio station shut in 1981. In its pursuit of economic development, the context of serious tensions with the Soviet Union as a result of the Sino-Soviet split and the need to build a regional coalition to oppose Vietnam's invasion of Cambodia in 1978, China's priority from the late 1970s shifted to building friendly relations with the states in Southeast Asia. China's support for the Chinese diaspora has therefore waxed and waned according to the dictates of China's national interests.

As this article has attempted to demonstrate however, the psywar carried out by the British and the subsequent independent governments of Malaysia and Singapore were well-crafted, comprehensive, well-resourced, as well as competently led and decisively implemented, which made the most significant contribution to the relatively swift containment and ultimate victory over the insurgency.

Conclusions: lessons for contemporary counter-terrorism

This article has demonstrated that psychological wars can in fact be managed and even won. In the case of Malaya, the caveat is that it still took end of the Cold War in 1989 to finally defeat the communist insurgents. Nonetheless, the insurgents were very much on the back foot once the British and the subsequent independent governments of Malaysia and Singapore had made significant progress in their psychological war operations relatively early in the Emergency. This demonstrates that in any counter-terrorism and counter-insurgency operation, information war, particularly psychological warfare operations, is a primary means in achieving the objective of winning over the hearts and minds of the insurgent population. Once the psychological war is won, the terrorism or insurgency would eventually collapse as its legitimacy has been eroded and it no longer is capable of recruiting sufficient numbers of foot-soldiers and supporters.

The question then is what a careful examination of the key lessons from Malaya's previous experience might yield in meeting the challenges of the present-day radical Islamist terrorism. The caveat is that there are obvious differences between the Malayan Emergency and the current challenge of global terrorism, particularly the significant advances in communications that has spawned the internet and social media, enabling terrorist groups and movements to now have hitherto undreamed of tools to recruit, propagandise and win support, raise funds and to coordinate operations across borders. Another caveat is that the type of authoritarian measures adopted in Malaya would be difficult in the context of liberal Western democracies in the present-day.

Nonetheless, caveats aside, there are still enduring lessons from the Malayan Emergency that could be useful. One key reason why the British and the subsequent independent governments of Malaysia and Singapore defeated the communist insurgency was that they found ways to dismantle the above-ground United Front organisations that had been a crucial component of the adversary's psywar operations. In Malaya, the authorities enacted legal mechanisms, under which individuals who were communist agents and sympathisers were neutralised (i.e. arrested and forced to undergo rehabilitation), thus rendering United Front organisations ineffective. Crucially, the authorities removed foreign-directed control of the mass media, as the Chinese communist press was shut down, and Chinese media subjected to the close scrutiny of the government and the security services. This removed an important source of subversive propaganda. Indeed, the MCP's psychological (or propaganda) campaign including its United Front strategy was ultimately defeated by the British and the newly-independent governments of Malaysia and Singapore through a combination of internal security measures that led to the banning of communist media such as its newspapers, the arrests of communist operatives, the taking over of control over Chinese education, as well as effective and proactive psywar operations on the part of the authorities.

Thus, it is important to recognise that psywar operations must be accompanied by legal and security measures to contain the enablers and other associated instruments of the adversary's psywar apparatus as well as neutralise radicalised individuals through rehabilitation. A comprehensive approach is needed to stem all the sources of the adversary's psywar capabilities. In the contemporary context, the authoritarian measures undertaken by the British in Malaya would not work in liberal Western democracies.

However, appropriate legal means and security measures can prevent above-ground radical Islamist organisations from controlling newspapers, publishing books and journals, running religious schools and maintaining websites that propagate radical Islamist ideology advocating the use of violence. Furthermore, measures must be taken to prevent the infiltration by radical Islamists in religious places of worship, schools and prisons. This requires better cooperation and consultation between the government and local Muslim communities. The ability to operate in a similar fashion to the United Front must be severely constrained or denied if recruitment, spread of propaganda and the raising of terrorist financing is to be prevented, since it is not sufficient to attempt to merely counter the propaganda of the adversary. Extensive and effective measures are also required to extinguish as many channels of communication for extremist ideology as possible.

In Malaya, aware of the crucial role of Chinese education in spreading communist propaganda and recruitment, the authorities ensured they controlled it by either phasing Chinese schools out or absorbing them into the national education system. Today, traditional Islamic schools exist in countries such as Pakistan, Indonesia and Malaysia, where some have been susceptible to infiltration by radical Islamist elements. This means that the central government has to enact measures to better govern this space, including incorporating such schools into the national education system, or else impose better governance systems in consultation and with the cooperation of local Muslim communities. This is necessary to ensure that the recruitment of teachers and that the teaching curriculum are better regulated, with improved accountability, with the aim of preventing the infiltration by radical Islamists.

More significantly, the authorities in Malaya were also very effective in developing and using expertise on Chinese culture, language and knowledge of China. While this included Chinese-speaking British officers, the British authorities in the 1950s recognised early on the value of using ethnic Chinese. Thus, the authorities succeeded because they knew the adversary well, since those in charge of security and psywar operations spoke and understood the political language of the adversary (Comber, 2019, p. 289). Indeed, the authorities paid careful attention to carrying out centralised, well-resourced and strategically directed psywar operations to counter the propaganda of the adversary and to publicise and promote the government's perspectives. Crucially, this was led by Chinese speakers (often, but not necessarily, ethnic Chinese), who understood the social and cultural contexts and were able to communicate effectively to the local Chinese population.

In the contemporary context, this means that governments, especially those in the West, must be bold enough to trust their own moderate Muslim populations and to recruit extensively from within them to carry out a vigorous counter-propaganda war in print as well as in the online and social media spaces, in both English as well as in the local languages of the Muslim populations. In addition, Western governments must rely on and strongly support moderate Muslim community and religious leaders in their leadership roles within their communities in order to counter radical Islamists and their violent ideology. After all, the radical Islamist challenge emanates from differences and conflicts within the Muslim world, which means that the fight must be carried out within that context, with Muslims themselves taking a prominent role.

This is a lesson that the Singapore government has learnt, as its present-day counter-radicalisation program is led by local Muslims, many of whom are qualified religious clerics, including graduates of Al-Azhar University in Egypt, the most prominent centre for Islamic theology in the Muslim world. This counter-radicalisation program, which is in essence the waging of psychological war, is extensive, and includes countering the claims of radical Islamists in the online space, education in schools, leadership in religious places of worship and Muslim organisations, and strong engagement with the Muslim community (Personal communication, 2018).

Governments in the Malay Archipelago, which has the world's largest population of Muslims, have also learnt to emulate a tactic that stems from the Malayan Emergency, i.e. the use of former terrorists, in waging the psywar against terrorism. Thus, former Al Qaeda-linked terrorists, such as Nasir Abbas, who was a former terrorist trainer, and Ali Imron, one of the Bali bombers (responsible for the deadly Bali terrorist attack in 2002 that killed 202 people), have become prominent in the counter-ideological war being waged by the Indonesian government against radical Islamist ideology (Ilyas & Athwal, 2021). The presence of qualified Muslim religious clerics as well as ex-terrorists in the counter-radicalisation efforts provides a significant boost to the legitimacy and credibility of what amounts to, even if the governments do not wish to frame it that way, a government-led psychological war operation.

Another key lesson from Malaya is the building of a national identity that promotes inclusion. Having unwittingly created a minority Chinese problem by importing large numbers of Chinese who then became disaffected as a result of their economic, social and political marginalisation, the authorities in Malaya realised that they needed to take concrete measures to address the underlying fundamental grievances that had contributed to alienation and the resort to terrorism as a form of redress. Thus, the hitherto stateless Chinese were given citizenship, land and rights in the new Malaysian state, although race relations between Chinese and Malay remain fraught to this day, and the nation-building in Malaysia remains somewhat problematic. In Singapore, where the ethnic Chinese are in a majority, nation-building has been more successful as a result of concerted efforts since independence from the Federation of Malaysia in 1965 to build a Singapore national identity, until the recent challenges posed by the contemporary migration of large numbers of mainland Chinese to Singapore (New York Times, 2015). In other words, psywar operations cannot merely consist of propaganda by the government. In order for it to be credible and to ultimately achieve results, it has to be accompanied by concrete measures to address the underlying grievances that have led to some turning to armed violence as a form of redress.

In countering the present-day radical Islamist challenge, it is important to therefore undertake measures to ensure the inclusion of Muslim populations as well as their identification with the nation-state in which they reside. This is particularly if they are a potentially vulnerable minority. Having welcomed Muslims to enter as well as take up citizenship in their countries, Western governments now do have the responsibility of ensuring their inclusion and their identification with the nation-state of residence, something which might not happen unless proactive legal, political, economic and social measures are taken to ensure their political, economic and social inclusion into Western societies. In this regard, Britain's counter-terrorism strategy, namely, CONTEST, should be lauded for its incorporation of the lessons learnt from 200 years of imperial policing, including the lessons from British Malayan experience with the Emergency. While there have been criticisms of this strategy, the Prevent component of the strategy does consider issues of equity and social participation among members of the Muslim community, and places strong emphasis on the important and vital role played by the leaders and members of the Muslim community in countering extremism (Home Office, 2018, pp. 25–82). Britain's relatively more successful approach can be contrasted to the obvious failures in other parts of Europe, notably in France, where the Muslim community remains strongly alienated, as serious civil disorder in mid-2023 following the police shooting of a Muslim youth demonstrated (New York Times, 2023).

Finally, it is important to recognise that external developments continue to have serious implications for terrorism. The MCP ultimately collapsed when China's national interests changed after 1979. In similar fashion, developments in, for instance in Syria, Iraq, Yemen and Afghanistan will resonate deeply in the broader worldwide Muslim community or *umma*, which has emerged as a result of globalisation and the communications revolution. This means that the rest of the world, including the West, must continue, despite fatigue and ultimate failure in counter-insurgency in Afghanistan, to pay careful attention to what is happening in various *jihadi* theatres around the world, particularly developments in the Middle East, since they will affect local Muslim populations everywhere and could lead to local individuals or groups to take up those causes.

In sum, countering radical Islamist ideology requires the waging of psychological war (or, to use an outdated term, counter-propaganda war). This requires a deep understanding of how psywar operations can be effectively designed, coordinated and competently implemented, albeit adapted to the contemporary era of the internet and social media, and, particularly for the West, the context of liberal Western democracy. The caveat is that this has to be accompanied by appropriate legal and security measures, carefully and sensitively enacted in consultation with local Muslim communities, to deny the adversary the means of spreading propaganda, as well as recognition of and measures to address fundamental grievances that have led to the political, social and economic marginalisation of some Muslim communities.

As Taylor had warned in 2008, and which still holds true today in the face of the onslaught from the Islamic State's ideology resulting in the continuation of the global terrorist threat, the West has failed to win the information war (Taylor, 2008, p. 118). It is the contention of this article that careful lessons drawn from the Malaya experience, with the necessary qualifications, are useful in waging information war today against contemporary radical Islamist terrorism.

Disclosure statement

No potential conflict of interest was reported by the author(s).

References

Asiaone. (2014, July 14). *Chinese schools' role remembered*. https://www.asiaone.com/singapore/chinese-schools-role-remembered

Central Intelligence Agency [CIA]. (1972, February 22). *Communist insurgency in Malaysia: Intelligence memorandum*. https://www.cia.gov/library/readingroom/docs/CIA-RDP85T00875R001100130038-1.pdf

Central Intelligence Agency [CIA]. (1973, April). *Intelligence report: Peking's support of insurgencies in Southeast Asia*. https://www.cia.gov/library/readingroom/docs/polo-37.pdf

Cheah, B. K. (1981, March). Sino-Malay conflicts in Malaya, 1945-1946: Communist Vendetta and Islamic resistance. *Journal of Southeast Asian Studies*, *12*(1), 108–117. doi:10.1017/S0022463400005014

Chin, P. (2003). *My side of history*. Ipoh, Malaysia: Media Masters.

Clutterback, R. (2003). *The long War: The emergency in Malaya, 1948-1960*. Singapore: Cultured Lotus.

Comber, L. (2019). *Dalley and the Malayan security service 1945-48: MI5 Vs. MSS*. Singapore: Institute of Southeast Asian Studies.

Crane, C. (2019, June 14). The United States needs an information warfare command: A historical examination. *War on the Rocks.* https://warontherocks.com/2019/06/the-united-states-needs-an-information-warfare-command-a-historical-examination/

Droogan, J., & Waldek, L. (2019). Social media and terrorism in the Asia pacific. In B. Schreer, & A. T. H. Tan (Eds.), *Terrorism and insurgency in Asia* (pp. 31–44). London: Routledge.

FM 3-0. (2008, February). Operations, Headquarters, Department of the Army. *Glossary-7.* https://people.uwplatt.edu/~hood/FM3-0.pdf

Greene, H. C. (1951, September 14). *Report on emergency information services, September 1950–1951.* https://www.psywar.org/content/greene

History.SG. (n.d.). *The Malayan democratic union is formed: 21 December 1945.* http://eresources.nlb.gov.sg/history/events/90e4ea74-e949-4269-a522-d0cca976b432

Home Office. (2018, June). *CONTEST: The United Kingdom's strategy for countering terrorism.* https://assets.publishing.service.gov.uk/government/uploads/system/uploads/attachment_data/file/716907/140618_CCS207_CCS0218929798-1_CONTEST_3.0_WEB.pdf

Hong, L., & Huang, J. L. (2008). *The scripting of A national history: Singapore and its past.* Singapore: National University of Singapore Press.

Ilyas, M., & Athwal, R. (2021). De-Radicalisation and humanitarianism in Indonesia. *Social Sciences, 10* (87), 1–17. doi:10.3390/socsci10030087. https://www.mdpi.com/2076-0760/10/3/87

International Labour Organisation [ILO]. (n.d.). *Malaysia: Internal Security Act, 1960.* http://www.ilo.org/dyn/natlex/natlex4.detail?p_lang = en&p_isn = 48007&p_country = MYS

Joske, A. (2020). *The party speaks For You: Foreign interference and The Chinese communist party's united front system.* Policy brief report 32. Canberra: Australian Strategic Policy Institute.

Lee, K. C. (2005). *Pioneers of modern China: Understanding the inscrutable Chinese.* Singapore: World Scientific.

Malay Mail. (2017, July 3). *What you should know about Chinese Schools in Malaysia.* https://www.malaymail.com/news/malaysia/2017/07/03/what-you-should-know-about-chinese-schools-in-malaysia/1412233

Malaysiakini. (2019, December 1). *Commemorating Hat Yai Peace accord 30 years later.* https://www.malaysiakini.com/news/501967

Mao, T.-t. (1938). *On protracted war.* https://www.marxists.org/reference/archive/mao/selected-works/volume-2/mswv2_09.htm

Molander, R. C., Riddile, A. S., & Wilson, P. A. (1996). *Strategic information warfare: A new face of war.* Santa Monica: RAND.

New York Times. (2015, February 13). *Being Chinese in Singapore.* https://www.nytimes.com/2015/02/13/opinion/tash-aw-being-chinese-in-singapore.html

New York Times. (2023, July 17). *Riots in France highlight a vicious cycle between police and minorities.* https://www.nytimes.com/2023/07/17/world/europe/france-riots-police-poor.html

Opper, M. (2020). *People's wars in China, Malaya, and Vietnam.* Ann Arbor: University of Michigan Press.

Personal communication. (2018, January 19). Author's observations and conversations with Muslim leaders involved in deradicalization, Singapore.

Ramakrishan, K. (2000). The making of a Malayan propagandist: The communists, The British and C.C. Too. *Journal of the Malaysian Branch of the Royal Asiatic Society, 73*(1), 67–90.

Ramakrishna, K. (2002). Telling the simple people the truth: The role of strategic propaganda in the Malayan emergency. *Journal of the Malaysian Branch of the Royal Asiatic Society, 75*(1), 49–68.

Simpson, C. (1994). *Science of coercion: Communication research and psychological warfare, 1945-1960.* New York: Oxford University Press.

Singer, P. W. (2001, October 23). Winning the war of words: Information warfare in Afghanistan. *Brookings.* https://www.brookings.edu/research/winning-the-war-of-words-information-warfare-in-afghanistan/

Stubbs, R. (2004). *Hearts and minds in Guerilla Warfare: The Malayan emergency 1948-60.* Singapore: Eastern Universities Press.

Taylor, P. M. (2002). Perception management and the 'war' against terrorism. *Journal of Information Warfare, 1*(3), 10–11.

Taylor, P. M. (2008). Can the information war on terror be won? A polemical essay. *Media, War and Conflict*, *1*(1), 118–124. doi:10.1177/1750635207087632

Thompson, R. (1966). *Defeating communist insurgency: Experiences in Malaya and Vietnam*. London: Chatto and Windus.

Tzu, S. (n.d.). *The art of war* (translated by Lionel Giles). http://classics.mit.edu/Tzu/artwar.html

Wang, G. W. (1970). Chinese politics in Malaya. *China Quarterly*, *43*, 1–30. doi:10.1017/S0305741000032392

Wang, G. W., & Ong, W. C. (2009). *Voice of the Malayan revolution: The CPM radio War against Singapore and Malaysia, 1969-1981*. Singapore: S. Rajaratnam School of International Studies.

Yadi, M. Z. (2004, December). *Malaysian emergencies - Anthropological factors in the success of Malaysia's counterinsurgency* [Master Degree Thesis, Naval Postgraduate School, Monterey, California]. https://core.ac.uk/download/pdf/36695031.pdf

Yeo, K. W. (1973). *Political development in Singapore, 1945-1955*. Singapore: Singapore University Press.

Yong, C. F. (2019). Chinese leadership and its political transformation. In C. G. Kwa, & B. L. Kua (Eds.), *A general history of the Chinese in Singapore* (pp. 135–152). Singapore: World Scientific.

Yu, Q. (2019, November 26). Adhering to the work pattern of the Great United Front. *People's Daily*. http://theory.people.com.cn/n1/2019/1126/c40531-31474052.html

OPEN ACCESS

Women, intelligence and Countering Terrorism (CT) in Indonesia: Where are the women?

Nuri Widiastuti Veronika

ABSTRACT
This article explores women's roles in Indonesian intelligence services in response to the rising trend of women's involvement in terrorism in Indonesia. It seeks to understand the extent to which gender dynamics influence women's roles in CT efforts, including detection, surveillance, analysis, and intelligence gathering. Employing Feminist Security Studies and gendered organisational lens frameworks, the paper analyses women's experiences in masculinist intelligence institutions. The Convention on the Elimination of All Forms of Discrimination against Women (CEDAW) adopted in 1979 and The United Nations Security Council Resolution (UNSCR) 2242 adopted in 2015 highlight the importance of gender in promoting women's participation in security sectors, including within the intelligence agencies. Focusing on Indonesia as a case study, this paper conducts a gender analysis to examine how gender and the framing of female bodies construct and affect women's roles within the Indonesian intelligence agencies as institutions of hegemonic masculinity. Drawing from data obtained through interviews with intelligence agents and experts from 2021 to 2023 in Indonesia, this paper argues that despite women's crucial roles in CT efforts, they still encounter gender bias, discrimination, stigmatisation, societal gender norms and systemic neglect of their specific needs.

Introduction

In 2018, a series of suicide bombings committed by three different families struck Indonesian society, raising not only the attention of the national public but also the international community.[1] However, these bombings, albeit shocking, did not emerge in isolation of one another, nor were they without warning. Before these incidents, Dian Yulia Novi and Ika Puspita Sari had both volunteered to commit suicide bombings in Jakarta and Bali respectively in late 2016 (The Institute for Policy Analysis of Conflict (IPAC), 2017b). Yet, the 2018 Surabaya bombing marked two crucial points in the history of terrorist acts in Indonesia: the success of women in becoming suicide bombers and the first family suicide terror attack ever conducted in Indonesia (Dass, 2021).

Indonesian women's engagement in political violence is not new. During the colonisation era in 1908–1945, women were a part of the struggle for independence by fighting side by side with men as well as performing supportive roles (Rohmaniyah, 2020). During the Indonesian struggle for independence, women joined the volunteer troops known as *laskar putri* (literally translated to 'female paramilitary soldiers') and performed battle duties, assisted with supporting roles such as public kitchens, attended to the wounded soldiers and conducted intelligence gathering (Salebaran & Amini, 2022, pp. 2–3).

After independence, post-colonial Indonesia was challenged by the emergence of Darul Islam/Negara Islam Indonesia (DI/NII), an Islamist extremist organisation that aimed to establish an Islamic Caliphate in Indonesia (Solahudin, 2013; The Institute for Policy Analysis of Conflict (IPAC), 2023c). From 1946 until the 1960s, DI/NII fought against the Indonesian government in West Java, Aceh, and South Sulawesi (Robinson, 2021; Solahudin, 2013). Today, all contemporary jihadist organisations in Indonesia are descendants of DI/NII and have played influential roles in the emergence of groups such as Jemaah Islamiyah (Blackburn, 2008; Jones, 2011) and, later, ISIS-affiliated networks in the country in the mid-2010s (Tan, 2019). While these networks and groups are unique, women remain involved in these three organisations and play pivotal roles in supporting these groups' activism.

DI/NII have played influential roles in the emergence of groups such as Jemaah Islamiyah in the early 1990s and later, ISIS-affiliated networks. The emergence of ISIS in 2013 attracted over 2000 Indonesian nationals to travel to Syria and Iraq (The Institute for Policy Analysis of Conflict (IPAC), 2017a) and it has presented a touchstone for the growing support of violent extremist ideology in Indonesia (The Institute for Policy Analysis of Conflict (IPAC), 2015, 2018, 2019, 2023a). The legacy of radical movements, which has strong roots within jihadist groups in Indonesia, has played a significant role in how ISIS has been successful in attracting female followers (Jadoon, Lodoen, Willis, & Jahanbani, 2020; Resnyansky et al., 2022).

Hwang and Schulze (2018) posit that individuals can join terrorist groups through four main pathways: study sessions, local conflict, kinship (which includes marriage), and schools. Extremist groups, including DI/NII, HTI, Jemaah Islamiyah (JI), and ISIS-affiliated groups, predominantly use these pathways to recruit women (Hwang & Schulze, 2018). From here, women affiliated with radical ideologies may be interested in or supported to take their actions further. For the past decade, Indonesian women have been playing active roles in jihadist activism, such as becoming the wives of jihadists, nurturing the next generation of jihadists, conducting terrorist attacks, terrorist financing, facilitating jihadist training camps, recruitment and migrating to ISIS territory (The Institute for Policy Analysis of Conflict (IPAC), 2017c, 2023b). Since 2002, 68 Indonesian women have been involved in terrorist acts, with five of them killed while committing suicide bombings.[2]

Despite the increasing involvement of women in jihadist activism in Indonesia, the government's response still lacks a gender-focused approach. While acknowledging women's roles in terrorism, the government's attention remains disproportionately minimal compared to efforts addressing male terrorism. This leads to the lack of gender consideration in counterterrorism (CT) policies and strategies, notably on how women play significant roles in CT efforts within the security sector. In its efforts to enhance its CT strategies, the Indonesian government established Law 5/2018 on Counterterrorism (the revision of the 2003 counterterrorism law) in the aftermath of the 2018 East Java bombings (Haripin, Anindya, & Priamarizki, 2020). Following this, the Indonesian government adopted the National Action Plan (NAP) on Preventing Violent Extremism in 2021. A few months later, Indonesia adopted its second National Action Plan (NAP) on Women, Peace and Security (WPS) that addresses women's involvement in radicalism. Prior to these frameworks, the Indonesian government ratified the CEDAW in 1984, forming the basis for Presidential Instructions No.9/2000 on Gender Mainstreaming within the Indonesian bureaucracies (Minister of Law and Human Rights, 2000). These policies showcase an impetus for the government's commitment to advancing gender equality and enhancing women's roles within the security sectors responsible for the implementation of CT policies.

Nevertheless, this commitment was challenged by the persistent masculinist culture within the security sectors in Indonesia, particularly in CT sectors. Before the democratisation period in 1998, the Indonesian armed forces controlled most security-related bureaucracies, including the military, police, ministry of defence, intelligence agency, ministry of justice, ministry of home affairs and attorney general (Sukma & Prasetyono, 2003). Despite the ongoing Security Sector Reform (SSR) since the early 2000s, the Indonesian Intelligence Community (IC) responsible for countering terrorist threats still retains its military-oriented characteristics (Sadadi, 2019; Wahyudi & Syauqillah, 2022). The IC comprises agencies such as the Indonesian National Intelligence Body (BIN), National Counter Terrorism Body (BNPT), the Armed Forces' Strategic Intelligence Body (BAIS), Indonesian National Police's Detachment 88 (Densus/ 88/INP) and the Coordinating Ministry for Political Legal and Security Affairs (Kemenko Polhukam). Consequently, since militaristic institutions, and the characteristics associated with them, promote the ideological structures of patriarchy, masculinity and militarism (Enloe, 2000; Kennedy-Pipe, 2000), women's[3] roles in Indonesian intelligence sectors remain subordinate.

Women have historically played vital roles in intelligence and espionage. Perhaps the most famous female spy is Mata Hari, depicted as a seductive and beautiful operative capable of gathering secret information from the high-ranking clientele of the Allied forces in France and passing it to the German forces during the First World War (Taylor, 1998). Additionally, throughout World War I and World War II, women adeptly gathered essential secrets by blending into common spaces, listening, observing and becoming parts of surveillance networks (Proctor, 2003; Taylor, 1998). Meanwhile, in the contemporary Global War on Terror, women continue to hold pivotal positions in intelligence gathering as state agents in CT, navigating culturally and religiously sensitive environments (Nwangwu, Onuoha, Ezirim, & Iwuamadi, 2021). In this sense, intelligence gathering refers to the process of collecting, analysing, producing, and utilising information related to potentially hostile states, groups (such as extremist groups), individuals, or activities to enhance national security (Nwangwu et al., 2021). Despite their pivotal contributions, the portrayal of women in intelligence remains constrained by a gendered view, oscillating between sexualised perversions or demonised objects (Proctor, 2003, p. 3). In other words, women in intelligence are frequently subjected to sexualisation and stereotyping, depicted either as enchanted and controlled or as cunning and seductive (Gasztold, 2022).

This article aims to address the roles of women in Indonesian intelligence services' efforts in CT, focusing on the inequalities, discrimination and structural exclusion that women experience within these security institutions. Employing a gender analysis, this article explores how gender dynamics within a patriarchal society and masculinist institutions shape individuals' behaviours and perceptions within the intelligence sectors, resulting in a lack of willingness to move towards gender equality. Drawing from the framework of Feminist Security Studies, a gender analysis is conducted, focusing on how gender and the reframing of female bodies influence women's roles within Indonesian intelligence agencies as institutions of hegemonic masculinity. Notably, women's roles in the intelligence sector have received limited attention, evident by the dearth of knowledge and absence of literature on their contributions to CT efforts in Indonesia. Therefore, this article seeks to bridge this gap in the existing literature.

The data used in this analysis were obtained through an extensive desk review of relevant literature, complemented by information collected during my doctoral fieldwork conducted from 2021 to 2023 in Indonesia. Primary data was gathered through interviews with informants currently employed as intelligence agents in security sectors with intelligence departments focused on CT. These sectors include the Ministry of Defence (Participant 1), the National Counter Terrorism Agency or BNPT (Participant 4), Detachment 88 of the Indonesian National Police (Participant 2 and Participant 3), and the National Intelligence Body or BIN (Participant 5 and Participant 6). Additionally, an interview was conducted with an intelligence expert affiliated with the Indonesia National Research Agency or BRIN (Participant 7). All intelligence agents who participated in this research consented to be identified solely through their positions and affiliations. It is important to note, however, that this paper focuses on the experiences of women working in security sectors within the intelligence community. In such community, the pervasive hegemonic masculinist culture often reinforces gender inequality, hampering women's meaningful roles within CT-related security sectors.

Following this introduction, this paper presents the theoretical and conceptual frameworks on which the analysis is anchored. The subsequent section discusses the contextualisation of intelligence gathering within the gender mainstreaming framework in CT. The next part presents the analysis of the paper by examining the themes related to how gender operates within the hegemonic masculinity institutions, the framing of female bodies, and socio-institutional challenges of women working in intelligence agencies. The last part is the concluding section that summarises the main findings of this paper.

Women's roles in security sectors: the feminist security studies (FSS) approach

This paper employs a Feminist Security Studies (FSS) approach which aims to look at women's roles in security fields and reformulate the masculinist views traditionally applied to women in conflict situations. Specifically, FSS emerges as a field that seeks to focus on how gender identity and gender politics shape experiences of security and insecurity (Lee-Koo, 2020). This is because gender is not only a tool for the maintenance of power, but also intersects with other identities that enable structural violence – for example, class, religion and race (Gentry & Sjoberg, 2015). Gender lens can describe patterns of sexual violence during war, make sense of women committing violence and explore the reproduction of gender in post-war peacebuilding efforts (Prügl, 2011). In addition, gender is the crucial factors underlying specific international phenomena such as women's engagement as political violence (Sjoberg & Tickner, 2011), women's roles within the military and armed conflicts (Enloe, 2000), and the use of sexual violence as war strategy (Pankhurst, 2014). In the context of this paper, employing a gender lens in examining the radicalisation of men and women to terrorism is crucial as gender plays a significant role in constructing pathways to extremist activism and violence, revealing how radical identities are formed within power structures (Pearson, 2023, p. 165).

Importantly, gender is a non-fixed category constructed through repeated performances and shaped by social, cultural, and historical contexts (Butler, 2002). These performances are shaped by power relations, highlighting the performativity of gender as something that individuals do rather than something they inherent. The concept of gender performativity has implications for power and agency. Therefore, gender significantly impacts human agency, social relations, global politics, and power dynamics, leading to inequalities between women and men (Shepherd, 2014). These inequalities manifest in the assignment of responsibilities, the activities undertaken, access to and control over resources, and opportunities for decision-making (Myrttinen, 2019).

In addition, gender defines norms and relations between men and women within a particular context. In Indonesian Muslim societies, gender norms and gender relations are shaped by Islamic moral code and customary practices, underlining permissible interactions between men and women (Blackwood, 2007). Within a conservative society, gender relations are regulated through the notion of *mahram* or sexual purity. According to this notion, devout Muslim women should only interact with male *mahram* such as their husband or male relatives like father or brothers (Khelghat-Doost, 2017). In Indonesian society, *mahram* dictates social norms and behaviours, especially in public spaces.

Therefore, the application of a gender lens in analysing global security issues and how women play significant roles within the security sectors such as intelligence agencies, is helpful in revealing the gender politics at work and bringing into focus gendered identities, politics and relationships (Lee-Koo, 2020). Additionally, analysing the impacts of gender performativity within intelligence agencies is essential in uncovering gendered practices within a particular context and organisational setting. These practices often lead to the marginalisation of women's roles within highly militaristic institutions such as CT sectors in Muslim-majority Indonesia.

'Disruptive' female bodies: gendered organisation and hegemonic masculinity

In gendered organisations like intelligence sectors, men possess political, economic, and social power, thus favouring masculine traits over femininity. Within such male-dominated workplaces, women's bodies are perceived as deviating from universally accepted (male) bodies, resulting in gender stereotypes and bias. Hence, this article employs both the concepts of gendered organisations and gendered habitus to investigate how societal gender norms regarding women's and men responsibilities shape their perspectives and their career trajectories in intelligence sectors. The integration of both concepts is pertinent because gender norms not only shape how organisations operate and privilege certain gender norms, but also how organisations mould men and women's behaviours under specific gendered constructions of male and female bodies.

The body itself becomes a site where politics unfolds, and inequalities are often the consequences of female bodies being perceived as deviating from the masculine standard (Shepherd, 2014). Social constructions of masculine and feminine bodies produce gendered habitus which is reinforced by social structures, practices, and discourses found in contexts such as the family, education, and the workplace which is referred to as gendered habitus (Lo & Lim, 2023; Bourdieu, 2001 as cited from Steidl & Brookshire, 2019, p. 1273). As a result, gendered habitus significantly shape gender relations and identity in everyday life, as they become embedded and embodied within individual and institutional norms.

The concept of gendered organisation can explain how the individual and institutional gendered habitus marginalised women in workspaces. Joan Acker's (1990) theory of gendered organisations asserts that organisations are structured in a way that reinforces gender distinctions, where advantage, exploitation, control, emotion, meaning, and identity are patterned based on male and female, masculine and feminine (Acker, 1990). She identifies five processes through which organisations are gendered: practices/structures, culture, interactions, identity, and organisational logic (Acker, 1990). The organisational logic, which may appear gender-neutral, perpetuates the assumption of a disembodied and universal worker (Kronsell, 2005). Acker (1990) further asserts that organisations and jobs are inherently gendered masculine, promoting the interests of men.

This is exemplified in the concept of the disembodied and universal worker, which aligns with the notion of hegemonic masculinity – the most honoured way of being a man (Connell & Messerschmidt, 2005). Hegemonic masculinity, associated with authority and power, represents a hierarchy of masculinities (Connell & Messerschmidt, 2005; Duriesmith & Ismail, 2019). Furthermore, Connell and Messerschmidt (2005) emphasise that the characteristics linked to hegemonic masculinity are not fixed but vary across historical periods and locations. Although various changes have been introduced, such as recruitment of women and the gender mainstreaming policies adopted within some of its institutions, the Indonesian intelligence community continues to uphold its hegemonic masculinity and militaristic traits, which further normalise gendered organisational practices towards its female members.

Intelligence gathering and gender mainstreaming in CT

There is no agreed definition of intelligence and there have been attempts to define what is meant by intelligence (Glees, 2015; Lowenthal, 1999; May, 1995). For this paper's purpose, intelligence is defined as the processed information required by an entity to effectively address and mitigate potential threats or unfavourable circumstances that could jeopardise the interests of such entities as individuals, groups, communities, corporations, organisations, or states (Nwangwu et al., 2021, p. 4). The intelligence gathering process entails collecting, analysing, producing, and utilising information that relates to potentially hostile states, groups, individuals, or activities with the objective of bolstering national security (Nwangwu et al., 2021). Although technological advancements and environmental changes have influenced the techniques of intelligence gathering, human sources, including both men and women, have consistently served as an enduring and invaluable resource of information (Nwangwu et al., 2021). In the context of CT, women play crucial roles in intelligence gathering and their involvement contributes to a comprehensive understanding of potential threats and aids in identifying individuals, groups, or activities that pose risks to national security.

Similarly, the global recognition of the gendered impacts of conflicts and the imperative for gender equality and women's participation in peacebuilding was solidified with the adoption of United Nations Security Council Resolution (UNSCR) 1325 on the Women, Peace, and Security (WPS) Agenda in 2000. This acknowledgment has extended to incorporate the need to address the gendered dimensions of terrorism, violent extremism, and their prevention, highlighted by the UNSCR 2242 in 2015 and the UN Secretary-General's Plan of Action to Prevent Violent Extremism in 2016. As a result, there is an increasing emphasis on improving gender equality, implementing gender mainstreaming, and prioritising women's empowerment in CT efforts (Brown, 2021; Gasztold, 2020; Gordon & True, 2019; Pearson, Winterbotham, & Brown, 2020; Rothermel & Shepherd, 2022; White, 2022). In this paper, gender mainstreaming is 'a strategy to include women in the security process and achieve gender equality' (White, 2020, p. 2).

Consequently, the integration of gender mainstreaming, the WPS agenda and preventing violence extremism (PVE) is imperative as it serves two primary purposes. Firstly, the agenda emphasises the importance of including women in security services, recognising the valuable contributions they can make in these roles (Fink & Davidian, 2017). Secondly, the agenda mandates the use of gender analysis to better understand conflict drivers, impacts, and potential resolution options (Asante & Shepherd, 2020). UNSCR 2242 also underscores the significance of integrating a gender perspective into CT, particularly within intelligence agencies. Member states are encouraged to conduct gender-sensitive research and collect data on the specific drivers of radicalisation for women, as well as the impacts of counterterrorism strategies on women's human rights (Asante & Shepherd, 2020). This comprehensive approach aims to address the gender-specific aspects of violent extremism and ensure that policies and strategies are effectively designed to counter such threats while also promoting gender equality and women's empowerment (Asante, Chilmeran, Shepherd, & Tiller, 2021; Mesok, 2022; Shepherd, 2020).

In the Indonesian context, the incorporation of gender mainstreaming policies into the country's state bureaucracies was initiated with the ratification of CEDAW on 13 September 1984. Article 5 of CEDAW obligates states to abolish the prejudices arising from the notion of inferiority/superiority based on sex or gender stereotypes regarding men and women's roles. Intelligence agencies should align with CEDAW by implementing policies that oppose gender discrimination, creating mechanisms to address institutional gender biases, and removing barriers to women's training and advancement, thus ensuring their full participation in the agency (Hutton, 2019).

Additionally, the Indonesian government has adopted the two National Action Plans (NAPs) on WPS agenda in recognising the distinct impacts of armed conflicts and insecurities to women and thus sought to promote women's full and equal participation in the security sector, and in decision making on peace and security matters (Coordinating Ministry for Human Development and Culture of The Republic of Indonesia, 2014, 2021). While the first NAP (2014–2019) has yet to include security threats arising from violent extremism as stipulated within the UNSCR 2242 in 2015, the Second NAP on WPS

(2020–2025) enacted in July 2021, implicitly addresses women's involvement in violent extremism and its prevention (Chuzaiyah & Kholifah, 2021).

Nevertheless, there are only three Indonesian security-related ministries involved in CT which have incorporated gender mainstreaming policies into their planning, budgeting, and policy implementation based on gender analysis. These ministries include the Coordinating Ministry for Political, Legal and Security Affairs through the Coordinating Minister for Political, Legal, and Security Affairs Regulation No 2/2022 (Coordinating Ministry for Political Legal and Security Affairs of the Republic of Indonesia, 2022), the Ministry of Defence through the Minister of Defence Regulation No 9/2020 (Indonesian Ministry of Defence, 2020), and the Indonesian National Police through the Head of Indonesian National Police Regulation No 1/2022 (Indonesian National Police, 2022). This demonstrates the scarce efforts made to establish and implement gender mainstreaming policies in the Indonesian security sectors responsible for CT and reflects the fundamentally militaristic practices permeating the state's security agencies.

In light of these international frameworks on gender mainstreaming, responses to terrorism can be broadly categorised into two strategies: the so-called hard approach, which covers efforts to *counter* terrorist acts, and the so-called soft approach to *prevent* violent extremism. The hard approach involves the use of intelligence, law, policing, and military powers, and this approach prioritises militarised responses and strict legal frameworks to counter violent attacks as they occur or in the immediate aftermath (Agastia et al., 2020; Brown, 2017; Nwangwu & Ezeibe, 2019). They do so through militarised actions and the strict implementation of legal frameworks. Women are key players in this approach such as by performing roles in military and paramilitary forces (Nwangwu & Ezeibe, 2019, p. 169), being soldiers in the global 'War on Terror' (Sylvester & Parashar, 2009), law enforcement, intelligence officers and prison officers (The Institute for Policy Analysis of Conflict (IPAC), 2020) and psychologists for counselling services and risk assessment mechanisms (Sukabdi, 2015). In this context, this article focuses on the intelligence sector as an inseparable part of CT strategies or the hard approach in Indonesia and how women contribute to CT strategies through their roles as part of the Intelligence Community (IC).

Women's roles in the Indonesian IC for CT: evidence from the field

Indonesian women have played significant roles in the struggle for independence, and the postcolonial Indonesian state has continued to employ women in contemporary security sectors. Women serve in the Indonesian Armed Forces branches, including the Army, Air Force, and Navy and policewomen and work as civil servants in civilian security agencies such as the Ministry of Defence, BNPT, the National Intelligence Body and the Coordinating Ministry of Political, Legal, and Security Affairs. Each of these agencies has its own intelligence and counterterrorism division, tasked with conducting intelligence operations for counterterrorism purposes.

All participants in this research concur on the significant roles that women play in intelligence gathering for CT. A prominent role identified is their involvement in accessing women-only communities associated with specific Islamist religious ideologies, characterised by strict gender-segregated norms (Nwangwu et al., 2021). Within these communities, the presence of female agents allows for the establishment of trust and loyalty, as the broader Indonesian society generally associates intelligence agents with males. Consequently, female agents may encounter less suspicion (Participant 7, BRIN, interview, May 31, 2023). This, in turn, facilitates more accessible intelligence data collection, as women are perceived as approachable and adept at engaging with individuals within these communities.

The significance of female agents in accessing female-only groups and forums, though initially appearing to instrumentalise women's roles, is more nuanced and contextually dependent, particularly within fundamentalist Islamist communities. In Indonesia, gender norms, influenced by the Islamic moral code and customary practices, reconstitute ideas about sexuality, shaping what is considered proper gender relations in public (Blackwood, 2007, p. 297). Failure to meet these gender relation patterns is perceived as unacceptable in a religious sense and as jeopardising family honour and community order. While men have more freedom to express their sexuality publicly, women's sexuality undergoes stringent scrutiny and control, adhering to the strict gender relations imposed on them. Within extremist circles, women face strict prohibitions on interacting with men, especially those outside their groups. Amid these cultural and religious sensitivities, female agents play essential role in addressing the barriers of gender relations, sexuality regulations and the notion of *mahram* in conducting intelligence operations for counterterrorism purposes.

In addition, female agents also play important roles in intelligence analysis, bringing in a more gender-aware view within the analysis. This study reveals that female intelligence analysts provide valuable insights and alternative viewpoints regarding women's engagement with terrorism. One participant from BIN emphasises that women possess a unique way of thinking, paying attention to intricate details, and contributing to empathy-based strategies like exploring familial connections to effectively neutralise threats (Participant 5, BIN, interview, May 30, 2023). Additionally, an agent from BNPT contends that women's perspectives in intelligence analysis counter the tendency to view women involved in violent extremism solely as 'more sinister and militant than men', leading to a more comprehensive understanding of underlying factors influencing their involvement (Participant 4, BNPT, interview, July 13, 2021). Furthermore, female agents conduct gender analysis in understanding women's engagement in terrorism by incorporating concepts like power relations and gender inequality as drivers for violent extremism (Participant 6, BIN, June 1, 2023).

Another distinctive role within CT efforts, undertaken by BIN, involves agent handling for intelligence gathering and deradicalisation purposes. A participant from BIN emphasises that her primary responsibilities revolve around supporting deradicalisation programs, which, for an intelligence agency, can be challenging due to the need for subtlety (Participant 6, BIN, interview, June 1, 2023). This can be done through a 'front organisation' and by relying on individuals within these organisations to carry out deradicalisation activities. Within the intelligence field, a front organisation refers to an entity or organisation that is controlled by an intelligence agency in order to conceal its activities ('Front Organisations', Collins English Dictonary, n.d.). These front organisations or proprietaries which can include corporations, business, charities or educational organisations, serve as covert entities representing the interests of intelligence agencies ('Front Organisations', The Central Intelligence Agency, 2016). This research finds that BIN employs these front organisations, such as charities and non-profit foundations to conduct covert CT activities, including deradicalisation programs (Participant 6, BIN, interview, June 1, 2023). In this case, female agents in BIN play essential roles in managing, gathering and analysing reports from these front organisations.

Concurrently, Participant 6 also plays the role as an agent-handler by managing operations conducted by field agents in the front organisations, overseeing the development of appropriate deradicalisation activities, such as engaging with terrorism inmates. Her work also involves training field agents to comprehend the distinct characteristics, leadership styles, and ideologies of each terrorist group. The various tasks performed by this female agent exemplify her significant role in disrupting extremist networks by conducting the deradicalisation programs.

In addition to their involvement in intelligence gathering, intelligence analysis, agent handling, and deradicalisation efforts, female agents also play a critical role in the arrest and repatriation process. Despite the targets being male, situations may arise where the presence of women becomes necessary, especially when dealing with both male and female extremists. Within extremist Islamist organisations, the concept of *mahram* holds significant importance, hence arresting female terrorist suspects may lead to extreme danger without considering this gender-specific aspect. One notable case illustrating this issue is the arrest of Dian Yulia Novi, identified as the first female suicide bomber aspirant in 2016 (Nuraniyah, 2018). An agent from Densus 88/INP recounted the dilemma faced by the team during the operation in arresting Dian Yulia Novi who was in a boarding house with confirmed indications of a 'rice cooker' bomb in the vicinity (Participant 3, Densus 88/INP, interview, May 22, 2021). The team was aware of the potential risk of the bomb being detonated at any moment. However, due to the absence of female personnel, the team confronted difficulties in negotiating with the suspect effectively. Recognising the importance of a gender-sensitive approach, the team deliberated as to whether to proceed with the arrest under such circumstances.

The incident highlights the important roles of women in intelligence as a part of CT strategies, particularly in situations involving female suspects. Additionally, female agents play significant roles in managing the return and deportation of individuals from ISIS territory in 2017 (The Institute for Policy Analysis of Conflict (IPAC), 2019). This is because most returnees are women who prefer to interact with female authorities due to *mahram*. Involving female agents in these situations becomes crucial to address these cultural sensitivities and ensure the safety and effectiveness of the arrest and repatriation procedures.

The gendered dynamics of women's roles in IC: beyond stereotypical 'women's jobs'

Being women in an institution of hegemonic masculinity presents challenges, even when they are meaningfully contributing to CT efforts. A female agent from Densus 88/INP emphasises her crucial role in providing accurate intelligence analysis used for legal proceedings, investigations, and for upholding human rights principles. In addition to completing this complicated task, she also needs to provide recommendations for Densus 88/INP task force members working at the provincial level, responsible for arresting terrorist suspects. However, despite fulfilling these important responsibilities and believing it is her duty as a member of law enforcement forces, she still feels underappreciated due to her gender. She confides that:

> The main challenge I feel as an agent is the 'gender' problem. I feel that as a woman, I am still considered unimportant, for example by them mentioning the phrase 'You are a woman'. Even though we (women) have more workloads, we (women) will not be considered as working as heavily as men. Sometimes I think 'ah I understand this problem better than him', but I am often feel not included because I am a woman. (Participant 2, Densus 88/INP, interview, August 6, 2021)

The statement highlights a significant challenge faced by a female agent in the intelligence community: the persistent issue of gender bias. Feeling undervalued and less important due to being a woman, the informant perceived that her contributions were not considered as substantial as those of her male counterparts. Despite having better expertise and knowledge in certain issues, she experienced gender-based exclusion. This gendered view reinforces biases that lead to women being perceived as less capable or less influential than their male counterparts.

Nevertheless, women in intelligence agencies often find themselves facing contradictory situations. In these agencies, women are frequently confined to tasks labelled as 'women's jobs' or secretarial duties. While some participants in this study challenge this perception and assert their expertise in handling specific important duties (Participant 1, Ministry of Defence, interview, October 30, 2021), others choose to conform and prefer to perform these assigned tasks. One female agent from BIN acknowledged the prevailing tendency in masculine and patriarchal societies to underestimate women's capabilities and suitability for certain tasks based solely on their gender (Participant 5, BIN, interview, May 30, 2023). Despite this awareness, she intentionally chose to work in a 'women's job' as a liaison officer, which entails fewer analytical, substantial, and field-related duties. This decision allows her to prioritise her family's needs and allocate more time to them.

Being a married woman in a patriarchal society means having to fulfil both private and public roles simultaneously, bearing the burdens of responsibilities within households and workplaces. In this context, while acknowledging the significance of women's roles in the intelligence agency, female agents may consciously opt against assuming challenging tasks such as operational and surveillance duties. Caregiving responsibilities and multiple burdens that women face in their personal and professional lives may be the underlying reason for women's marginalisation in assuming critical roles in security sectors. This may lead them to conform to these gendered roles and condone the gendered practices of instrumentalising women as feminine subjects, with pure, maternal, emotional, innocent, and peace-loving traits (Gentry & Sjoberg, 2015), especially within masculine fields like intelligence for CT efforts.

Similarly, a male agent from Densus 88/INP recounted the experience of his female colleague who, upon getting married, decided to shift towards more administrative roles despite previously carrying out operational duties on par with her male counterparts (Participant 3, Densus 88/INP, interview, May 22, 2021). He highlighted his view that:

> When women have married, with dynamic tasks like ours, it would be difficult (for them) to execute the tasks … the tasks would likely to be delayed, sometimes due to issues related to family obligations. It would be hard to evaluate them. (Participant 3, Densus 88/INP, interview, May 22, 2021)

This illustrates that within CT sectors, gender norms impact how men and women perceive their roles and how their roles shift once women are married. It underscores the specific construction of women's nurturing roles as normalised, likely inhibiting their capabilities as security agents or field officers. Hence, the shift to administrative duties becomes a way for women to negotiate between their private and public roles. Meanwhile, men are assumed not to be burdened by familial roles, making them more likely to successfully execute orders. This reveals that CT mechanisms rely on two gendered assumptions: that women are nurturing and, therefore, unsuitable for masculine tasks, which are deemed 'too dangerous' for women with caregiving responsibilities (Brown, 2017).

The issue of women being limited to administrative, secretarial and human resource roles while men dominate decision making, operational and managerial positions is not unique to Indonesia but is prevalent in intelligence services worldwide (Hutton, 2019, p. 11). This highlights how the burden of care placed on women working in security sectors may compel them to choose administrative, secretarial and human resources roles to alleviate their responsibilities while maintaining their employment within the agencies.

While these women exercise agency in their choices, societal expectations imposed on married women and mothers play a role in shaping their decision-making capacities. Engaging in more analytical work, surveillance and intelligence operations is perceived as impeding women's ability to perform their family obligations, as the traditional gendered division of labour places the primary responsibility for caregiving on women. This decision highlights the individual's gendered habitus, wherein societal gender norms regarding women's caregiving responsibilities shape their perspectives. Meanwhile, men are typically afforded the freedom to work without the same considerations for caregiving responsibilities at home. Consequently, women will be less likely to achieve higher rank managerial positions to be able to achieve women's equality within the security sectors reform and create meaningful gender-responsive policies.

Meanwhile, the institutional gendered habitus becomes evident in how the institution perceives married women as incapable of handling the same workloads as men, leading to a diminished importance of their role in intelligence operations. When women are unable to accomplish these employment and societal expectations, they are often stigmatised as disruptive and labelled as having low productivity. Due to the general assumption in Indonesia that married women 'are tied' to their family institutions, organisations tend to hold a certain stereotype regarding the lack of productivity of married female employees (Participant 3, Densus 88/INP, interview, May 22, 2021).

These findings suggest that the issue lies within the organisational gendered views, which idealise universal (male) bodies that are not burdened with caring responsibilities. In addition, married women are confronted with the stereotype that their family obligations bind them, despite men not facing the same expectations. As the burden of care primarily falls on women, they are perceived as less capable than men, and women's absence due to caring responsibilities, for instance, is seen as an inability to handle the same workload as men or as they did before marriage. This highlights the prevailing masculinist perspective that universalises male experiences as the norm within the intelligence sector.

The framing of female bodies

Sexualised objects and intelligence gathering for CT

Being a woman in an intelligence organisation presents challenges related to how agencies may exploit female bodies in CT efforts. In intelligence agencies, women's presence often sparks fascination, depicted through the lens of the male gaze. Women are stereotyped as either enchanted and controlled by secret agents or cunning and seductive agents themselves (Gasztold, 2022). These stereotypes are often strategically utilised in intelligence operations, leveraging societal perceptions of femininity, masculinity, and sexual preferences.

In the Indonesian context, these perceived views of sexualised female agents are exploited when intelligence operations are dealing with funding issues. When funding is short, female field agents are encouraged to establish romantic relationships with male targets. A source from BRIN confirmed the existence of this practice:

> In Indonesia, it is widely known that if there is a shortage of funds for an operation, but the agents still need to gather data, they use a strategy to get romantically involved with the targets … I get this info from the intelligence officers who confided in me, and I can confirm that it is really happening. Women have the advantage because if male agents were to have a relationship with their targets, people would be more suspicious due to the prevailing view that women are not intelligence officers. Thus, it gives women more leverage to use the relationship as cover to do their jobs. (Participant 7, BRIN, interview, May 31, 2023)

This statement highlights how this strategy for gaining operational funding undermines women's authority over their bodies, forcing them to use their bodies as trade-offs for information. It demonstrates how organisations often exploit women's sexuality for the organisation's interests.

Additionally, these dynamics of gender relations and the persistence of gender stereotypes within intelligence agencies reflect broader societal dynamics, blurring the line between the public and private spheres. For instance, participants in this study underlined the existence of gender relations, where intelligence institutions maintain certain stereotypes of female agents as 'the sexier the better' (Participant 7) and as embodiments of 'male standards of attractiveness', (Participant 6) where female agents should conform to notions of sexiness, make-up, and long hair, all of which benefit the institutions.

Additionally, there are risks associated with female bodies when conducting surveillance in Islamist extremist networks. Muslim single women are prohibited from interacting with their non-*mahram* within the extremist groups, due to the strict gender norms within jihadist communities. This means that female agents, to be accepted within these communities, must be tied to men to be seen as pure and not sexually disruptive to the extremist communities. Female agents then face the risk of being married off by these male extremists. An agent from BIN mentioned this challenge:

> I have heard stories of women in the field being asked to marry terrorist targets. If they approach a male terrorist and he sees that the woman is not married, the man will offer to marry her or offer his friends to marry her. This is not only unsettling but also worrying. There is also still a view that if female agents are married, they will be easily indoctrinated. BIN thus immediately withdrew women from their assignments. (Participant 6, BIN, interview, June 1, 2023)

The statement above underscores the risks associated with female agents' abilities to execute their duties in the field due to the stereotypical view that women are easily indoctrinated. This view is based on specific gender binary perceiving women as feminine beings who are relying more on emotions than logic, in contrast to men. However, this assumption does not hold true, as data shows that the majority of terrorists are men, both globally and in the Indonesian context (Dier & Baldwin, 2022). Meanwhile, male agents do not deal with risks associated with gender norms, as they can marry their targets unofficially and then leave without being perceived as weak or disruptive to the assignments. When female agents are at risk of being married by jihadists, the assignments must be ceased due to concern of potential indoctrination, which can disrupt the organisation's operations. This implies that the organisation perceives women as having less capability to resist indoctrination using reason and logic, rather than it being a concern for women's safety.

The myth of gender-responsive supports for women's productivity

In intelligence sectors, women need both intangible support and targeted provisions to contribute to intelligence gathering, intelligence analysis, agent handling and deradicalisation in implementing CT strategies. However, institutional gendered practices, which predominantly cater to male bodies, often neglect the specific needs of women, hindering their productivity. Despite an increase in the recruitment of women in recent years, significant gaps still exist in addressing their fundamental needs. The majority of female participants in this research emphasised several critical issues that need to be addressed to enhance women's meaningful participation within the intelligence community.

The first issue is the lack of adequate restroom facilities for women, such as that of BIN. The two research participants from BIN highlight the lack of regards to women's specific needs for restrooms. Despite starting to recruit female agents in 2016, the women's restroom was only available in 2018. While there is now a women's restroom on every floor, the number is significantly fewer compared to the male restrooms, with only one provided. This inequality in restroom facilities reflects a disregard for the equal treatment of women in the workplace.

Another important concern raised by female agents in BIN and Densus 88/INP is the absence of a proper lactation room. It took a significant event, such as the leadership meeting, for the need for a lactation room to be acknowledged and addressed. Additionally, female agents in both BIN and Densus 88/INP highlight the absence of day-care facilities. As women may face difficulties in finding suitable childcare options, the lack of support for day-care facilities creates challenges when trying to balance work and family responsibilities. This highlights the lack of consideration and support for working mothers in intelligence agencies.

The absence of a day-care facility and lactation rooms further marginalised women, making it even more challenging for female agents to manage their caring responsibilities while fulfilling their professional duties. This is despite the fact that in 2015, the Ministry of Women Empowerment and Children Protection (MOWECP) issued Regulation No. 5/2015 on the Provision of Gender Responsive and Child Care Facilities in the Workplace (Ministry of Women Empowerment and Child Protection, 2015). This regulation mandates that government and private institutions furnish essential facilities, including lactation rooms, day-care centres, health services, and other supportive amenities, aiming to enhance women's work productivity and safeguard their rights in the workplace. However, since this regulation is not legally binding other institutions, there is no guarantee that state and non-state institutions will abide by this rule.

However, entrenched gender bias, pervasive stereotypes about female employees, and a preference for male norms within patriarchal institutions in the Indonesian Intelligence Community have resulted in significant adverse effects on the women involved in this study. Primarily, the perception of women as less reliable due to their marital and maternal status denies them equal opportunities with men for professional development training, crucial for enhancing leadership, managerial, analytical, and operational skills. Consequently, in the long-term, it significantly impacts women's career trajectories for managerial positions. This is because certain bureaucratic roles in Indonesia demand specific training and educational paths upon promotion to higher positions (Asian Development Bank, 2021, pp. 34–35).

Additionally, in terms of analytical and operational expertise, the lack of opportunities to gain specialised professional development training for capacity building hamper women's upskilling and limit their productivity within the dynamic field of intelligence and CT. However, the multitude of burdens that female agents must cope with in their private and public lives often leads women to be complicit in reproducing the gendered roles that consolidate hierarchical relations between men and women (Braat, 2022). Participant 5 from BIN, for instance, expressed contentment despite not being selected for certain assignments or trainings. Due to her marital and familial responsibilities, she believed that conducting specific training and field operations would be challenging for her in balancing between her traditional responsibilities and her roles within the agency.

Overall, these findings suggest the systemic neglect of women's needs within intelligence agencies. This neglect includes limited attention given to restroom facilities, the delayed provision of a lactation room, the absence of a day-care facility and unequal opportunities for professional developments for better career trajectories. Therefore, there is evidence of a lack of commitment to implement gender-responsive policies within the intelligence community, leading to the failure to acknowledge the unique challenges faced by women in the workplace, particularly in highly patriarchal intelligence sectors. Given the vital roles women play in intelligence agencies, it is imperative to provide the necessary facilities and mechanisms that ensure their equitable participation in the security sector, empowering them to contribute significantly on peace and security matters.

Conclusion

Indonesia has adopted various international norms on gender mainstreaming to incorporate women's roles within state security sectors, particularly within the intelligence sector. As a result, there are now more women employed by the intelligence sectors for CT purposes. Yet, there is evidence that women still deal with various challenges that impede their meaningful contribution in security sectors. In Indonesian intelligence agencies, women are dealing with gender bias, discrimination, stigmatisation, systemic neglect of their specific needs, and unequal opportunities for professional development. Women are also pressured to comply with gender norms and societal expectations that continue to perpetuate gender discrimination and inequality within the family, broader society, and state bureaucracy. Nevertheless, the view that women's bodies are disrupting the masculine norm and the way that women's bodies are sexualised for the benefit of organisations demonstrate the individual and institutional gendered habitus that are pervasive within the intelligence agencies presented in this analysis.

A commitment to gender mainstreaming within intelligence agencies requires efforts in addressing the specific societal construction of femininity and masculinity, which continues to marginalise women. In turn, this construction continues to threaten their meaningful roles within the Indonesian IC in performing CT strategies. Failure in acknowledging these societal gender norms and institutional gender biases will lead to the marginalisation of women in contributing to the intelligence community for CT beyond stereotypical 'women's jobs'.

Notes

1. On 13 May 2018, a family of six carried out attacks on three churches in Surabaya, East Java, resulting in the death of 12 worshipers. Concurrently, three individuals from another household, planning a similar attack, died in Sidoarjo when their bomb prematurely exploded. The following day, 14 May 2018, another family on two motorcycles detonated a bomb at the Surabaya police headquarters, injuring 10 people. These incidents were part of the 2018 East Java bombings that evidently prompted the revision of the Indonesian Anti-Terrorism Law in 2018 (Jacob, 2018).
2. This number has been generated based on the author's professional duties as the member of security-related institution in Indonesia. However, for public data on the number of Indonesian extremists behind bars is accessible from an IPAC Report published on 2 February 2023 which mentions that 57 women have been arrested on terrorism charges between 2004 and 2022 (IPAC, 2023b, p. 1).
3. While acknowledging this paper's primary focus on women's roles in intelligence, it also explores the significant role that gender norms play within particular societies, organisations, groups, and cultures. Gender norms refer to a set of expectations regarding how people of each gender should behave, and these standards of behaviour exert significant pressures, particularly on women, to conform (Saferworld & Uganda Land Alliance, 2016). Female agents grapple with gender norms, such as societal expectations for women to perform traditional roles like nurturing and caring for households, while working as female agents. These burdens arising from the gender norms and sets of expectations associated with being born women limit women's meaningful roles in intelligence sectors. Therefore, the use of gender analysis in this context remains relevant to this article.

Disclosure statement

No potential conflict of interest was reported by the author(s).

Funding

This work was supported by the Lembaga Pengelola Dana Pendidikan (LPDP) Scholarship.

ORCID

Nuri Widiastuti Veronika http://orcid.org/0000-0003-1890-1416

References

Acker, J. (1990). Hierarchies, jobs, bodies: A theory of gendered organizations author(s). *Gender and Society*, *4*(2), 139–158.

Agastia, I. G. B. D., Perwita, A. A. B., & Subedi, D. B. (2020). Countering violent extremism through state-society partnerships: a case study of de-radicalisation programmes in Indonesia. *Intelligence and Counter Terrorism*, *15*(1), 23–43. doi:10.1080/18335330.2020.1722317

Asante, D., Chilmeran, Y., Shepherd, L. J., & Tiller, Z. (2021). The impact of UN Security Council Resolution 2242 in Australia, the UK and Sweden. *Australian Journal of International Affairs*, *75*(4), 388–409. doi:10.1080/10357718.2021.1926422

Asante, D., & Shepherd, L. J. (2020). Gender and countering violent extremism in women, peace and security national action plans. *European Journal of Politics and Gender*, *3*(3), 311–330. doi:10.1332/251510820X15854973578842

Asian Development Bank. (2021). A diagnostic study of the civil service in Indonesia. *ADB Publication*, *57*(2), 257–259. doi:10.1080/00074918.2021.1956406

Blackburn, S. (2008). Indonesian women and political Islam. *Journal of Southeast Asian Studies*, *39*(1), 83–105. doi:10.1017/S0022463408000040

Blackwood, E. (2007). Regulation of sexuality in Indonesian discourse: Normative gender, criminal law and shifting strategies of control. *Culture, Health and Sexuality*, *9*(3), 293–307. doi:10.1080/13691050601120589

Braat, E. (2022). The construction of secret intelligence as a masculine profession. *International Journal of Intelligence and CounterIntelligence*, *35*(4), 694–712. doi:10.1080/08850607.2022.2055429

Brown, K. E. (2017). Gender and terrorist movements. In R. Woodward & C. Duncanson (Eds.), *The Palgrave international handbook of gender and the military* (pp. 419–435). London: Palgrave. doi:10.1057/978-1-137-51677-0.

Brown, K. E. (2021). Feminist responses to violent extremism. In T. Väyrynen, S. Parashar, É. Féron, & C. C. Confortini (Eds.), *Routledge handbook of feminist peace research* (1st ed., pp. 136–147). London: Routledge. doi:10.4324/9780429024160-15

Butler, J. (2002). *Gender trouble: Tenth anniversary edition*. New York: Routledge. https://ebookcentral-proquest-com.ezproxy.lib.ryerson.ca

Chuzaiyah, Y., & Kholifah, R. (2021). *Laporan Final Konsultasi Digital Nasional Review RAN P3AKS 2014–2019*.

Connell, R. W., & Messerschmidt, J. W. (2005). Hegemonic masculinity rethinking the concept. *Gender and Society*, *19*(6), 829–859. doi:10.1177/0891243205278639

Coordinating Ministry for Human Development and Culture of the Republic of Indonesia. (2014). *Peraturan Menteri Koordinator Bidang Kesejahteraan Rakyat Republik Indonesia Nomor 8 Tahun 2014 Tentang Rencana Aksi Nasional Perlindungan Dan Pemberdayaan Perempuan Dan Anak Dalam Konflik Sosial Tahun 2014–2019*. Jakarta: The Government of the Republic of Indonesia.

Coordinating Ministry for Human Development and Culture of the Republic of Indonesia. (2021). *Peraturan Menteri Koordinator Bidang Pembangunan Manusia Dan Kebudayaan Republik Indonesia Nomor 5 Tahun 2021 Tentang Rencana Aksi Nasional Perlindungan Dan Pemberdayaan Perempuan Dan Anak Dalam Konflik Sosial Tahun 2020–2025*. Jakarta: The Government of the Republic of Indonesia.

Coordinating Ministry for Political Legal and Security Affairs of the Republic of Indonesia. (2022). *Peraturan Menteri Koordinator Bidang Politik, Hukum, Dan Keamanan Nomor 2 Tahun 2022 Tentang Pedoman Pengarusutamaan Gender Di Lingkungan Kementerian Koordinator Bidang Politik, Hukum, Dan Keamanan* (Issue 1113, pp. 1–7).

Dass, R. A. S. (2021). The use of family networks in suicide terrorism: A case study of the 2018 Surabaya attacks. *Journal of Policing, Intelligence and Counter Terrorism*, *16*(2), 173–191. doi:10.1080/18335330.2021.1906932

Dier, A., & Baldwin, G. (2022). *Masculinities and violent extremism*. https://www.ipinst.org/wp-content/uploads/2022/06/Masculinities-and-VE-Web.pdf

Duriesmith, D., & Ismail, N. H. (2019). Militarized masculinities beyond methodological nationalism: Charting the multiple masculinities of an Indonesian jihadi. *International Theory*, *11*(2), 139–159. doi:10.1017/S1752971919000034

Enloe, C. (2000). *Maneuvers: The international politics of militarizing women's lives book*. Berkeley: University of California Press. https://www.jstor.org/stable/10.1525j.ctt14qrzb1.10%0AJSTOR

Fink, N. C., & Davidian, A. (2017). Complementarity and convergence? Women, peace and security and counterterrorism. In F. N. Aoláin, N. Cahn, D. F. Haynes, & N. Valji (Eds.), *The Oxford handbook of gender and conflict* (pp. 157–170). New York: Oxford University Press. doi:10.1093/oxfordhb/9780199300983.013.13

Front Organisations. (2016). *The Central Intelligence Agency: An encyclopedia of covert ops, intelligence gathering, and spies* (pp. 151–152). Bloomsbury Publishing USA.

Front Organisations. (n.d.). *Collins English dictionary*. HarperCollins Publishers.

Gasztold, A. (2020). *Feminist perspectives on terrorism: Critical approaches to security studies*. Cham: Springer. doi:10.1007/978-3-030-37234-7

Gasztold, A. (2022). Beyond or in the midst of the masculinized intelligence community in Poland. *International Journal of Intelligence and CounterIntelligence*, 35(4), 654–673. doi:10.1080/08850607.2022.2052535

Gentry, C. E., & Sjoberg, L. (2015). Introduction: A woman did that?. In C. E. Gentry & L. Sjoberg (Eds.), *Beyond mothers, monsters, whores: Thinking about women's violence in global politics* (pp. 1–26). London: Zed Books. doi:10.5040/9781350218628.ch-001

Glees, A. (2015). Intelligence studies, universities and security. *British Journal of Educational Studies*, 63(3), 281–310. doi:10.1080/00071005.2015.1076567

Gordon, E., & True, J. (2019). Gender stereotyped or gender responsive? Hidden threats and missed opportunities to prevent and counter violent extremism in Indonesia and Bangladesh. *RUSI Journal*, 164(4), 74–91. doi:10.1080/03071847.2019.1666512

Haripin, M., Anindya, C. R., & Priamarizki, A. (2020). The politics of counter-terrorism in post-authoritarian states: Indonesia's experience, 1998–2018. *Defense and Security Analysis*, 36(3), 275–299. doi:10.1080/14751798.2020.1790807

Hutton, L. (2019). Intelligence and gender. In *Gender and security toolkit*. https://www.osce.org/files/f/documents/f/2/447061.pdf

Hwang, J. C., & Schulze, K. E. (2018). Why they join: Pathways into Indonesian jihadist organizations. *Terrorism and Political Violence*, 30(6), 911–932. doi:10.1080/09546553.2018.1481309

Indonesian Ministry of Defence. (2020). *Peraturan Menteri Pertahanan Republik Indonesia Nomor 9 Tahun 2020 Tentang Perubahan Atas Peraturan Menteri Pertahanan Nomor 42 Tahun 2012 Tentang Pedoman Pelaksanaan Pengarusutamaan Gender Kementerian Pertahanan*.

Indonesian National Police. (2022). *Peraturan Kepala Kepolisian Negara Republik Indonesia Nomor 1 Tahun 2022 Tentang Pengarusutamaan Gender Di Lingkungan Kepolisian Negara Republik Indonesia* (Issue 8.5.2017).

Jacob, J. (2018, May 31). The May attacks: Is Indonesia facing a new form of terrorism? *Indonesia at Melbourne (Blog)*.

Jadoon, A., Lodoen, J. M., Willis, C. N., & Jahanbani, N. P. (2020). Breaking the glass ceiling? Female participation in militant organizations in Islamic state affiliates in Southeast Asia. *Terrorism and Political Violence*, 34(8), 1774–1796. doi:10.1080/09546553.2020.1838904

Jones, S. (2011). The ongoing extremist threat in Indonesia. *Southeast Asian Affairs, SEAA*, 11(1), 97–106. doi:10.1355/aa11-1g

Kennedy-Pipe, C. (2000). Women and the military. *Journal of Strategic Studies*, 23(4), 32–50. doi:10.1080/01402390008437811

Khelghat-Doost, H. (2017). Women of the Caliphate: The mechanism for women's incorporation into the Islamic State (IS). *Perspectives on Terrorism*, 11(1), 17–25.

Kronsell, A. (2005). Gendered practices in institutions of hegemonic masculinity: Reflections from feminist standpoint theory. *International Feminist Journal of Politics*, 7(2), 280–298. doi:10.1080/14616740500065170

Lee-Koo, K. (2020). Feminist interventions in security studies. In M. Sawer, F. Jenkins, & K. Downing (Eds.), *How gender can transform the social sciences: Innovation and impact* (pp. 1–197). Cham: Springer International Publishing. doi:10.1007/978-3-030-43236-2

Lo, J., & Lim, A. (2023). Sexism without sexists: Gender-blind frames in police work. *Gender, Work and Organization*, 30(6), 1885–1902. doi:10.1111/gwao.13020

Lowenthal, M. (1999). Teaching intelligence: the intellectual challenges. In R. Swenson (Ed.), *A flourishing craft: Teaching intelligence studies, Occasional Paper No. 5*. Washington, DC: Joint Military Intelligence College.

May, E. R. (1995). Studying and teaching intelligence. *Studies in Intelligence, 38*(5), 1–5.

Mesok, E. (2022). Beyond instrumentalisation: Gender and agency in the prevention of extreme violence in Kenya. *Critical Studies on Terrorism, 15*(3), 610–631. doi:10.1080/17539153.2022.2036422

Minister of Law and Human Rights. (2000). *Instruksi Presiden Republik Indonesia Nomor 9 Tahun 2000 Tentang Pengarusutamaan Gender Dalam Pembangunan Nasional* (Vol. 2000, Issue 1, pp. 1–14). Government of Republic of Indonesia.

Ministry of Women Empowerment and Child Protection. (2015). *Peraturan Menteri Pemberdayaan Perempuan Dan Perlindungan Anak Republik Indonesia Nomor 5 Tahun 2015 Tentang Penyediaan Sarana Kerja Yang Responsif Gender Dan Peduli Anak Di Tempat Kerja: Vol.* Nomor 6588.

Myrttinen, H. (2019). Security sector, governance, security sector reform and gender. In *Gender and security sector reform toolkit* (Issue January). http://www.usaid.gov/our_work/democracy_and_governance/publications/pdfs/Maritime-Security-Sector-Reform.pdf

Nuraniyah, N. (2018). Not just brainwashed: Understanding the radicalization of Indonesian female supporters of the Islamic state. *Terrorism and Political Violence, 30*(6), 890–910. doi:10.1080/09546553.2018.1481269

Nwangwu, C., & Ezeibe, C. (2019). Femininity is not inferiority: Women-led civil society organizations and 'countering violent extremism' in Nigeria. *International Feminist Journal of Politics, 21*(2), 168–193. doi:10.1080/14616742.2018.1554410

Nwangwu, C., Onuoha, F. C., Ezirim, G. E., & Iwuamadi, K. C. (2021). Women, intelligence gathering and countering violent extremism in Nigeria: A postcolonial feminist discourse. *Democracy and Security, 17*(3), 278–295. doi:10.1080/17419166.2021.1920929

Pankhurst, D. (2014). Sexual violence in war. In L. J. Shepherd (Ed.), *Gender matters in global politics: A feminist introduction to international relation* (3rd ed., pp. 159–170). London: Routledge.

Pearson, E. (2023). Gender perspectives on radicalisation. In J. Busher, L. Malkki, & S. Marsden (Eds.), *The Routledge handbook on radicalisation and countering radicalisation* (pp. 164–179). London: Routledge. doi:10.4324/9781003035848-13

Pearson, E., Winterbotham, E., & Brown, K. E. (2020). *Violent extremism making gender matter*. Cham: Palgrave Macmillan.

Proctor, T. M. (2003). *Female intelligence: Women and espionage in the First World War*. New York: New York University Press. doi:10.18574/nyu/9780814771457.001.0001

Prügl, E. (2011). Feminist international relations. *Politics and Gender, 7*(1), 111–116. doi:10.1017/S1743923X10000619

Resnyansky, L., Smith, C., Taylor, C., Sulistiyanto, P., Merryman, G., & Mujahiduddin. (2022). Reasons behind reasons: A communitarian reading of women's radicalization and family bombings in Southeast Asia. *Studies in Conflict and Terrorism*, 1–26. doi:10.1080/1057610X.2022.2034229

Robinson, K. (2021, September 24). Invoking memories of Darul Islam. *New Mandala.Org*. https://www.newmandala.org/invoking-memories-of-darul-islam/

Rohmaniyah, I. (2020). Perpetuation of radical ideology: Depersonalization and agency of women after the banning of Hizbut Tahrir Indonesia. *Al-A'raf: Jurnal Pemikiran Islam Dan Filsafat, 17*(1), 45–66. doi:10.22515/ajpif.v17i1.2361

Rothermel, A., & Shepherd, L. J. (2022). Critical studies on terrorism introduction: Gender and the governance of terrorism and violent extremism. *Critical Studies on Terrorism, 15*(3), 523–532. doi:10.1080/17539153.2022.2101535

Sadadi, P. (2019). *Intelligence reform in Indonesia: Transparency and effectiveness against terrorist threats* (Issue September). Leicester: University of Leicester.

Saferworld & Uganda Land Alliance. (2016). *Toolkit gender analysis of conflict*. http://www.saferworld.org.uk/resources/view-resource/1076-gender-analysis-of-conflict.

Salebaran, S., & Amini, M. (2022). Women, military, and state: Indonesian women's military representation during the early independence period. *International Journal of Military History and Historiography, 33*(2), 1–27. doi:10.1163/24683302-bja10032

Shepherd, L. J. (2014). Sex or gender? Bodies in global politics and why gender matters. In L. J. Shepherd (Ed.), *Gender matters in global politics: A feminist introduction to international relations* (2nd ed., Issue 2014, pp. 24–35). London: Routledge.

Shepherd, L. J. (2020). The paradox of prevention in the women, peace and security agenda. *European Journal of International Security*, 5(3), 315–331. doi:10.1017/eis.2020.15

Sjoberg, L., & Tickner, J. A. (2011). Introduction: International relations through feminist lenses. In J. A. Tickner & L. Sjoberg (Eds.), *Feminism and international relations: Conversations about the past, present and future* (pp. 1–21). Florence: Taylor & Francis Group.

Solahudin (2013). *The roots of terrorism in Indonesia: From Darul Islam to Jemaah Islamiyah*. Ithaca, NY: Cornell University Press.

Steidl, C. R., & Brookshire, A. R. (2019). Just one of the guys until shower time: How symbolic embodiment threatens women's inclusion in the US military. *Gender, Work and Organization*, 26(9), 1271–1288. doi:10.1111/gwao.12320

Sukabdi, Z. A. (2015). Terrorism in Indonesia: A review on rehabilitation and deradicalization. *Journal of Terrorism Research*, 6(2), 36–56.

Sukma, R., & Prasetyono, E. (2003). *Security sector reform in Indonesia: The military and the police Rizal*. Working Paper Series: Vol. Working Pa (Issue 12). doi:10.1287/mnsc.22.12.1396

Sylvester, C., & Parashar, S. (2009). The contemporary 'Mahabharata' and the many 'Draupadis': Bringing gender to critical terrorism studies. In R. Jackson, M. B. Smyth, & J. Gunning (Eds.), *Critical terrorism studies: A new research agenda* (pp. 178–193). London: Taylor & Francis Group. doi:10.4324/9780203880227

Tan, A. T. H. (2019). Terrorism in Southeast Asia: A clear and present danger. In C. Ungerer, D. M. Jones, M. L. R. Smith, & P. Schulte (Eds.), *Handbook of terrorism and counter terrorism post 9/11* (pp. 327–339). United Kingdom: Edward Elgar Publishing. doi:10.4337/9781786438027.00036

Taylor, S. C. (1998). Long-haired women, short-haired spies: Gender, espionage, and America's War in Vietnam. *Intelligence and National Security*, 13(2), 61–70. doi:10.1080/02684529808432476

The Institute for Policy Analysis of Conflict. (2015). *Support for 'Islamic state' in Indonesian prisons* (Issue 15).

The Institute for Policy Analysis of Conflict. (2017a). *Mothers to bombers: The evolution of Indonesian women extremists* (Issue 35). http://www.jstor.com/stable/resrep07796.1%0A JSTOR

The Institute for Policy Analysis of Conflict. (2017b). *The radicalisation of Indonesian women workers in Hong Kong*.

The Institute for Policy Analysis of Conflict. (2017c). *The radicalisation of Indonesian women workers in Hong Kong* (Issue 39).

The Institute for Policy Analysis of Conflict. (2018). *The Surabaya bombings and the future of ISIS in Indonesia* (Issue 51).

The Institute for Policy Analysis of Conflict. (2019). *Indonesia: Urgent need for a policy on repatriation of pro-ISIS nationals from Syria* (Issue 59).

The Institute for Policy Analysis of Conflict. (2020). *Extremist women behind bars in Indonesia* (Issue 68).

The Institute for Policy Analysis of Conflict. (2023a). *Indonesia's villa mutiara network: Challenges posed by one extremist family* (Issue 84).

The Institute for Policy Analysis of Conflict. (2023b). *The consequences of renouncing extremism for Indonesian women prisoners*. IPAC Report (Issue 83). https://understandingconflict.sgp1.digitaloceanspaces.com/dashboard/e309e305470abdfea89ebbd1b863c9b3.pdf

The Institute for Policy Analysis of Conflict. (2023c). *The search for an Islamic state in Indonesia: The many guises of DI/NII* (Issue 82).

Wahyudi, R., & Syauqillah, M. (2022). Strengthening cooperation among intelligence agencies in the enforcement of law on terrorism: The case of Indonesia. *JISPO Jurnal Ilmu Sosial Dan Ilmu Politik*, 12(1), 23–38. doi:10.15575/jispo.v12i1.14370

White, J. (2020). Gender in countering violent extremism program design, implementation and evaluation: Beyond instrumentalism. *Studies in Conflict and Terrorism*, 46(7), 1192–1215. doi:10.1080/1057610X.2020.1818435

White, J. (2022). *Gender mainstreaming in counter-terrorism policy: Building transformative strategies to counter violent extremism*. Milton: Taylor & Francis Group. doi:10.4324/9781003195023-1

Militant jihadist exploitation of youth and young adult vulnerabilities in the Maldives

Anne Speckhard, Molly Ellenberg and Sheikh Ali

ABSTRACT
There is little research on militant jihadist radicalisation, particularly the psychosocial factors underlying radicalisation, in the Maldives, which is often overshadowed by its larger neighbours. As militant jihadist terrorism continues in the Indo-Pacific region and as tourism returns to its pre-COVID levels, the threat of militant jihadist attacks in the Maldives must be addressed. The present article uses qualitative interviews from incarcerated men and women in Maafushi Prison to explore the ways that militant jihadist cells in the Maldives radicalise and recruit youth to join them. We identified three primary vulnerabilities that are exploited by Maldivian militant jihadists to radicalise and recruit youth and young adults: Lack of education and employment opportunities, lack of nuanced Islamic education, and substance abuse. Amplifying these vulnerabilities are responses to feeling insignificant and hopelessness, leading to susceptibility to promises of opportunity, redemption, and rehabilitation from militant jihadists.

The Maldives, known to many Westerners for its pristine beaches and expensive resorts, has garnered increased focus in recent years for an apparent rise in militant jihadist[1] violent extremism in the islands. According to some measures, the Maldives was the nation with the highest per capita number of foreign terrorist fighters [FTF] joining ISIS and al Qaeda (U.S. Department of State, 2022). The threat of foreign fighters leaving the islands has been complemented by domestic attacks; the past two decades have seen several high-impact attacks by militant jihadists, including the Sultan Park bombing in 2007 and the 2021 attempted bombing assassination of former President and current Speaker of Parliament Mohamed Nasheed, alongside ISIS-claimed attacks on tourists (Makan, 2007; Mashal, 2021; Sayed & Hamming, 2023; Zahir, 2020). Maldivian nationals have also been known to be involved in attacks elsewhere, such as the 2009 suicide attack on the headquarters of the Pakistani Directorate of Inter-Services Intelligence (Shahid, 2014). Alas, there is little research on the phenomenon of militant jihadist radicalisation, particularly with regard to the psychosocial factors underlying radicalisation, in the Maldives, which is often overshadowed by its larger neighbours, such as Pakistan and Indonesia. As militant jihadist terrorism continues in the Indo-Pacific region and as tourism returns to its pre-COVID levels, the threat of militant jihadist attacks on Maldivians and foreigners alike must be addressed.

Background on psychosocial factors of radicalization

Before considering the specific Maldivian context, it is useful to understand the psychosocial mechanisms which underly radicalisation to militant jihadism or any other type of violent extremism. According to the 'lethal cocktail' theory posited by Speckhard (2016), radicalisation requires a group, an ideology, social support, and individual vulnerabilities and motivations that are dependent on context and whether an individual is residing in a conflict or non-conflict zone. The group may exist in-person or online, and an individual may feel connected to it even without extensive communication. The group also provides an ideology, which often includes religious themes or is based in fundamentalist and violent interpretations of religious texts which most mainline and reputable religious scholars dispute, which provides a worldview that names culprits responsible for one's grievances, and most importantly in the terrorist context, justifies violence in pursuit of the group's social or political goals (Kruglanski et al., 2013). The group also provides social support to those who adhere to its ideology and commit violence on its behalf, thus rewarding those who are willing to sacrifice themselves for the group and its goals with acceptance, dignity, and respect. Finally, the individual vulnerabilities and motivations are those psychosocial characteristics which lead a person to desire the social support of such a group and to believe in its ideology. These vulnerabilities and motivations may include the effects of trauma, a desire for revenge, anger at geopolitics, grief, lack of upward social mobility, and many others (Speckhard, 2016). Common to nearly all of these vulnerabilities and motivations is their relationship to a feeling of insignificance, that one does not matter and is not respected (Kruglanski et al., 2022). This theory is consistent with others surrounding the psychology of terrorism, including the '3N model of radicalisation', which names needs (i.e. individual vulnerabilities and motivations, namely the need for significance and mattering), narrative (i.e. ideology), and network (i.e. the group and the social support it provides) as the necessary components of radicalization (Kruglanski, Bélanger, & Gunaratna, 2019). Other models of radicalisation similarly feature the role of the group and the violence-justifying narrative which allows one to feel as though their deviant or illegal behaviour is morally right or even divinely ordained (e.g. Doosje et al., 2016; Horgan, 2008; McCauley & Moskalenko, 2017).

Radicalisation and militant jihadist violent extremism in the Maldives

Although the psychosocial processes of radicalisation can be applied across groups and ideologies, each component of the process is informed by the cultural context in which it is occurring (Kruglanski et al., 2014). One cannot assume, therefore, that understanding radicalisation in general, radicalisation to militant jihadism, or even radicalisation in Muslim or Muslim-majority countries is sufficient to understanding radicalisation to militant jihadism in the Maldives.

The militant jihadist groups which operate in the Maldives are linked to a number of different global terrorist organisations, including al Qaeda and ISIS, as well as to regional groups such as Lashkar-e-Taiba [LeT] (Dharmawardhane, 2015) and ISIS's Khorasan Province [ISKP] (Sayed & Hamming, 2023). As a result, Maldivian militant jihadists have travelled to Pakistan for training as well as to Iraq and Syria to fight with ISIS and Jabhat al Nusra. Those travelling to join ISIS in the mid-2010s also brought their wives and children to live under the so-called Caliphate (Dharmawardhane, 2015). The groups operating in the Maldives are continuously evolving in response to security activities, but consistently adhere to a general militant jihadist ideology, including a strict, fundamentalist interpretation of *shariah*; a belief in the obligation to migrate to lands ruled in accordance with such an interpretation (*hijrah*) and a belief that those who do not agree with their interpretation of *shariah* are apostates who can be killed (*takfir*); and an acceptance of suicide attacks as a form of Islamic martyrdom. However, these groups also have goals that are specific to the Maldives, namely that *shariah* should be enforced in the Maldives using their interpretation of the punishments (*hokum*) prescribed by the Quran, and that the democratic governments of the Maldives (past and current) are illegitimate for failing to adhere to their interpretation of *shariah* (Bonofer, 2010). As a result of these goals, militant jihadist groups in the Maldives have primarily targeted their attacks at political figures and tourists, as they view the former as catering to the latter by permitting un-Islamic behaviour such as alcohol consumption at resorts (Niyaz, 2010).

Radicalisation in the Maldives occurs in face-to-face interactions as well as online; while some propaganda content is translated into Dhivehi, other Maldivian militant jihadists have been found to consume English-language ISIS online content and the lectures of the deceased Yemeni American al Qaeda ideologue Anwar al-Awlaki (personal communication, National Counter Terrorism Center, 2021). During the height of ISIS's reign, Maldivian militant jihadists were also known to be in contact with members of ISIS and Jabhat al Nusra over Telegram (personal communication, National Counter Terrorism Center, 2021). As in other countries, militant jihadists in the Maldives have also been known to recruit petty criminals and gang members both on the streets and in the prisons (Dharmawardhane, 2015). Face-to-face recruitment and training have largely occurred on the island of Himandhoo, which, although frequently targeted by security forces, continues to be a hub for militant jihadism on the islands (Shama, 2018). According to officials from the National Counter Terrorism Center (personal communication, 2021), the core group of militant jihadists outside of the prisons in the Maldives includes about 36 people, some of whom had previously fought in Syria.

With regard to the vulnerabilities and motivations contributing to radicalisation in the Maldives, Shama (2018) identified 'unemployment, housing crisis, drug problem, gang culture, and [...] ongoing periods of political unrest' as grievances that may mobilise Maldivians, and particularly Maldivian youth and young adults, to radicalisation (p. 207). Indeed, the United Nations Development Programme, in a report by Templer (2019), found that Maldivian FTFs travelling to Syria tended to have histories of substance abuse and petty crime. Many of these issues show no signs of abating, with some likely to worsen with the effects of climate change (Shahid, 2014; Thoha, 2020). Other research has highlighted, however, that official education and religious materials used in the Maldives may also promote extremist views that, although not inherently violent, can be easily manipulated by militant jihadists to serve their purposes, including those materials and ideologies exported from Saudi Arabia to the Maldives (Maldives Democracy Network, 2016; Shahid, 2014). There have also been reports of political figures and organisations aligning themselves with both gangs and violent extremist groups for the sake of increasing their power (Shahid, 2014). In contrast, some efforts by the Maldivian government to curb radicalisation, including issuing a 2015 fatwa decrying extremists' claims that fighting in foreign wars is a religious obligation, have been met with backlash against 'state-sanctioned Islam' and a perception that government-trained imams are illegitimate or surveillance agents (Bureau of Counterterrorism and Countering Violent Extremism, 2015). Despite the awareness of these potential vulnerabilities, however, there has not yet been academic scholarship exploring the psychological mechanisms by which Maldivian militant jihadists radicalise and recruit youth and young adults by exploiting these very vulnerabilities.

The present study

Given this gap in the literature on the psychosocial aspects of radicalisation and recruitment to militant jihadism in the Maldives, as well as the concern over grievances and other vulnerabilities which impact youth and young adults in particular, the present study aimed to explore the ways that Maldivian militant jihadist groups exploit youth and young adults to their advantage. The study utilises grounded theory (Charmaz, 2014) to identify the themes most commonly mentioned in 17 incarcerated men and three incarcerated women in Maafushi Prison, all of whom were identified by prison officials as potentially being radicalised to militant jihadism or associated with militant jihadists operating in the prison. Notably, in the Maldives, 'youth' are defined as people aged 18–34 (Maldives Bureau of Statistics, 2006), and all of these individuals were older than 18 at the time that they were interviewed. The interviewees, including those older than 35, reflect retrospectively on their experiences in childhood and adolescence, as well as in young adulthood. Thus, the study aims to explore not only which vulnerabilities contribute to youth and young adults' susceptibility to militant jihadists' radicalisation and recruitment efforts, but why these efforts are successful among vulnerable youth and young adults.

Method[2]

The present study utilises the data from a larger project on prison-based radicalisation in the Maldives. The study's results are based on interviews conducted by the lead author, along with a trained Islamic scholar (the third author), with 20 incarcerated individuals (17 male and three female). The results are corroborated by stakeholders from Maldives Correctional Services including officials from Asseyri Prison; Male' and Hulhumale Prisons and Maafushi Prison; Department of Juvenile Justice; National Counter Terrorism Center; National Drug Agency; Drug Rehabilitation Center (K. Himmafushi); Ministry of Education; Ministry of Islamic Affairs; Ministry of Gender, Family, and Social Services; President's Office; Human Rights Commission of the Maldives; Juvenile Court; Inspectorate of Prisons; United Nations Development Programme in the Maldives; Journey; and Advocating for the Rights of Children. Results were also corroborated by one man who was formerly incarcerated in Maafushi Prison. Such corroboration came in the form of informational interviews conducted virtually and in-person prior to the prison interviews, during which representatives from these stakeholder organisations provided insights into the militant jihadist landscape in the Maldives, Maldivian prisons, and Maldivian juvenile detention centers. After the prison interviews were conducted, subsequent meetings were held with several stakeholder organisations, during which information provided by the interviewees was probed further, albeit without providing any identifying details about which interviewees provided which pieces of information.

The research was organised by the non-governmental granting organisation, Transparency Maldives. The 20 incarcerated individuals were interviewed at Maafushi Prison, and the one formerly incarcerated man was interviewed at the Drug Rehabilitation Center in K. Himmafushi. The interviews were conducted in both English and Dhivehi, with the help of two translators provided by Transparency Maldives.

Each interview began with an informed consent process. Because incarcerated people are a vulnerable population, extra care was taken to ensure that the interviewees were not coerced to participate and did not fear that their answers would be used against them; for instance, to justify segregating them from the rest of the prison population. Careful explanation of the study was given orally and in written form and consent was given orally on video and in writing. The videos and consent forms are securely stored and accessible only to the research team. The interviewees were told that the purpose of the project was to learn about how and why radicalisation occurs in prisons and what can be done to prevent and counter it. They were told that they would be asked about their childhood, family, life experiences, and experiences in prison, but that they should not incriminate themselves. The interviews lasted approximately one and a half to two hours. Risks included emotional distress in recalling painful experiences, which was mitigated by the researcher, a trained psychologist, proceeding slowly and helping the interviewee deal with any emotions that arose and an Islamic scholar who could elaborate on any Islamic discussions that occurred, particularly surrounding guilt and Islamic forgiveness for serious crimes. Additionally, interviewees were told that although the researcher would anonymize and observe confidentiality with the data, there is always a risk in prisons that a conversation is being monitored. There was also a risk that other incarcerated people might retaliate against interviewees for speaking with a researcher, although there is no evidence that this has occurred with regard to this project. It was clear, however, that some militant jihadist cell members were warned and questioned before the interview or debriefed afterward by other members of the cell. Benefits to the participants included the opportunity to talk to and reflect with an experienced psychologist about their lives, experiences, and feelings in a confidential setting. Indirect benefits included improving people's understanding of the radicalisation process in prison and helping officials gaining a better understanding of people's experiences in prison in the Maldives. Participants were ensured that no information from the interviewees would be shared with the authorities without the interviewee's explicit permission, unless they indicate future harm to themselves or others. They were also told that their name or video would not be used in any future research article or report unless they explicitly gave permission to do so; later all data was anonymized regardless of permission, given the interconnectedness of the Maldives and potential risks to interviewees. Finally, participants were told that they could refuse to participate, stop participating at any time, or refuse to answer any questions without penalty from the prison authorities, and that they could ask questions of the research team as well.

Participants and procedure

The present sample includes 20 incarcerated individuals currently held in Maafushi high-security prison, 17 men and three women. The interviews started with a life and family history, leading to experiences in adolescence and any experiences of drug abuse, criminality, and extremism. Beliefs and relationships throughout the lifespan were probed as well as plans, hopes, and expectations for after release. Participants were asked about the prison units in which they had experiences and were currently housed, education, counselling, Islamic guidance, experiences and relationships with staff and other incarcerated people, desires and concerns, and their experiences upon arrest, in remand, and under interrogation during their time in investigation and prison. They were also asked about their view of the Maldivian government as well as their views on various topics espoused by militant jihadists (i.e. ideologies put forward by groups such as al Qaeda, ISIS, and others that promote the concepts of suicide terrorism, violent jihad, overthrow of governments, and establishment of *shariah* states via violence). The interviews were run by the lead author, who uses a nonjudgmental, open approach to psychological interviewing. Questions posed and discussion that arose regarding Islamic topics during the interviews included the Islamic scholar, who was able to deepen the discussion with the interviewees.

Demographic information for the interviewees, disaggregated by gender, is provided in Table 1. Reporting on the participants' statements throughout this report refers to them by pseudonyms. Notably, 'age at first arrest' refers to the first time the individual was arrested in the Maldives, and not necessarily the age at which they were arrested for the crime for which they were currently incarcerated.

Using the verbatim notes from the interviews, the second author coded each of the interviews in SPSS Version 26 using a coding scheme designed *a priori* based on previous research interviews with militant jihadists (Speckhard & Ellenberg, 2020). Each of the 20

Table 1. Demographic information.

Variable	Minimum	Maximum	Mean	Standard deviation
Age at first arrest				
Men	16	36	21.56	5.40
Women	13	31	20.00	9.64
Age at interview				
Men	19	46	33.12	5.96
Women	32	37	34.00	2.65
Education (in years)				
Men	6	10	8.20	1.21
Women	8	13	10.50	3.536
Prison time prior to current sentence (in months)				
Men	0	144	69.70	58.87
Women	9	156	75.00	74.64
Socioeconomic status				
Men	64.7% lower/working class; 29.4% middle class; 5.9% upper class			
Women	33.3% lower/working class; 66.7% upper class			
Marital status				
Men	41.2% single, never married; 11.8% married; 47.1% divorced			
Women	66.7% single, never married; 33.3% divorced			
Legal status				
Men	64.7% serving time-limited sentence; 35.3% serving life sentence			
Women	100% serving time-limited sentence			

interviews was coded on 329 variables covering demographic details, life histories and vulnerabilities, criminal and prison histories, influences and motivations for radicalisation, roles and experiences within the militant jihadist cell, sources of disillusionment with the group (if any), and present psychological state and level of radicalisation.

Results

All but three of the male participants and one of the female participants referenced adherence to militant jihadist views such as those described previously. These statements were usually made upon probing and only once rapport had been established. It was also clear from their carefully worded speech that the interviewees did not reveal all of their violent beliefs. For example, one man stated that he admired Anwar al-Awlaki (an al Qaeda and ISIS ideologue), but then backtracked, saying, 'I like him because he's a Muslim and a human. I love Awlaki like I love all humans'. One participant who did not appear currently radicalised implied that he had previously associated with the militant jihadist cell in the prison but disengaged, and he spoke about his previous beliefs. The other three participants who did not appear radicalised spoke openly about what they had witnessed from radicalised fellow incarcerated people. Three primary vulnerabilities stood out following the coding of the interviews as contributing to radicalisation and recruitment of youth and young adults by militant jihadists in the Maldives. These vulnerabilities were lack of education and employment opportunities, lack of nuanced Islamic education, and substance abuse. Each of these vulnerabilities, and the ways that they are exploited by militant jihadists in the Maldives, are discussed in turn in the forthcoming sections. The number of interviewees who made comments reflecting these three issues are displayed in Table 2.

Lack of education and employment opportunities

The first was lack of education and employment opportunities. None of the men and only one of the women reported having completed secondary school, but their lack of opportunity was rarely by choice. Reasons for leaving school prior to completing secondary education included issues related to deviant or illegal behaviour such as being expelled from school ($n = 3$), using drugs ($n = 1$), and being arrested ($n = 1$), but other individuals who did not complete their schooling did so for financial reasons. They either wanted to work ($n = 1$), left school unwillingly because their families needed them to work ($n = 2$), could not afford to purchase books necessary for school ($n = 1$), or could not afford to move from their home island to the capital city, Malé, for more schooling ($n = 1$). Only three men and one woman left school due to lack of interest. This vulnerability has also been highlighted by UNICEF as a risk factor for a slew of poor outcomes for youth in the Maldives, noting that although schooling through twelfth grade is free in the

Table 2. Vulnerabilities.

Vulnerability	Number reporting (percentage of total)
Lack of Education/Lack of Employment Opportunities	16 (80%)
Lack of Nuanced Islamic Education	16 (80%)
Substance Abuse	18 (90%)

Maldives, only 59 of 212 schools in the Maldives offer education beyond tenth grade, meaning that, in reality, a complete secondary education is accessible only to those who can afford to move to an island where such education is available. Additionally, those who travel to Male' for secondary education are exposed to increased risk that arises from living on their own or with adults other than their parents (UNICEF, 2015, 2018).

In general, by the time the interviewees were old enough to work legally, they had typically already found that their best option for earning money was to work for criminal gangs, usually selling drugs. Of the 20 interviewees, 10 of the men and all three of the women reported a history of non-violent, non-ideological crime prior to the offense for which they were incarcerated. Eleven of the men and one of the women stated that they had experienced poverty in their lives, making them desperate to find any opportunity to support themselves and their families. Rafiq, for example, grew up poor in a thatch house after his father left the family. At age 14, he joined his father in Male'. His father told him he would put him in school, but instead forced him to work without pay in his business and prevented him from contacting his mother. He recalls, 'There was no happiness once I came [to Male']. Father kept promising when this project is finished, I will enlist you in school. I never lived with my father. [I] lived in the workers' housing unit. My father lived at home with his wife'.

Lack of opportunity is exploited in multiple ways by militant jihadists in the Maldives, both inside and out of the prisons. In this particular sample, one individual stated that he joined the militant jihadists in prison expressly for the employment opportunities he believed would come out of such connections once he was released from prison. More broadly, criminal gangs in the Maldives are known to work closely with militant jihadist cells (Ramakrishna, 2021; U.S. Department of State, 2022), leading to cross-pollination wherein a member of a gang is exposed to the militant jihadist ideology and also learns that increased connection with the militant jihadists will result in more opportunities for earning money. Finally, the general lack of education and opportunity resulted in feelings of insignificance and low self-worth. The interviewees felt that they would never be able to achieve even a medium-level social status within the mainstream society, especially after being released from prison. Joining the militant jihadists provided an alternate means to the same goals of significance, dignity, and purpose.

Lack of nuanced Islamic education

Related to this first vulnerability is the second vulnerability, lack of Islamic education. Although few of the participants had received a secondary education, all of them were literate and they generally had a rudimentary understanding of the basic tenets of Islam. They did not, however, have an extensive or nuanced Islamic education, which was something they desired. Like their lack of general education, the interviewees' lack of a nuanced Islamic education was not due to a lack of interest, but rather a lack of opportunity. Given the presence of Islamic education provided in upper secondary school in the Maldives (Di Biase & Maniku, 2021), it is possible that this second vulnerability, lack of nuanced Islamic education, can be partially explained by the general lack of education highlighted as the first vulnerability. However, given that many Islamic scholars in the Maldives preach a *Wahhabi* interpretation of Islam which validates many of the extreme, albeit not necessarily violent, ideological positions of militant jihadist groups (Ranjan, 2023) and support texts which legitimize overthrowing what is defined as an apostate government,[3] even those who completed upper secondary school did not receive the type of nuanced education required to refute the arguments of militant jihadist ideologues. Indeed, past research has found that Islamic education in Maldivian schools 'focused more on the history of Islam instead of the practical aspects of Islam' (Shiuna & Sodiq, 2013, p. 30).

The interviewees were thus eager to absorb any Islamic knowledge that was presented to them, which, whether by virtue of being in prison or in a gang, tended to come from militant jihadists. Given their elementary understanding of Islam, the participants were essentially able to understand what a recruiter or propagandist or ideologue meant when he said that he was quoting directly from the Quran and/or Sunnah, but they were unable to identify when these people were misquoting or misinterpreting these scriptures. And, although imams associated with the Maldivian government did visit the prisons and provided rehabilitation programming, many of these imams were dismissed by the militant jihadists in the prison as non-credible representatives of 'state-sanctioned Islam' (Bureau of Counterterrorism and Countering Violent Extremism, 2015). Other participants claimed that their militant jihadist beliefs were taught to them in the prison rehabilitation programs, perhaps in an effort to protect the militant jihadist leaders in the prison or to legitimize their beliefs as non-extreme. As noted, the government rehabilitation scholars do teach from some of the same texts upon which the militant jihadists base some of their violent claims.

The motivation to learn more about Islam is exemplified by Jabbar, who recounted, 'Before I came to prison, I literally didn't know anything about religion. My mom told me to pray, so I did [...] I learned here the principles and tenets'. The third author, a trained Islamic scholar, gently pressed Jabbar to expand upon those principles and tenets. About becoming a *shaheed* (martyr), Jabbar said, 'All I know is that in Islam one of the highest positions you can attain is to die a martyr in the way of jihad. Everyone wishes for this'. Asked about suicide bombers, he admitted, 'I don't know if they would become a *shaheed* or not'. Another man, Mansur, said that he was the imam of his prison-based cell, but claimed that he had learned his extremist views from the prison-run religious education program, though this was not corroborated by prison officials or representatives from the Ministry of Islamic Affairs. Mansur recalled, 'In the [prison] rehabilitation program in phase one, I was taught if a person gives up the prayer, then all of the religious scholars of the *ummah* agree that this person should be beheaded'.

Perhaps what was most appealing about the militant jihadist recruiters and ideologues, in and out of prison, was their willingness to answer questions. Some stakeholders expressed that parents and teachers are hesitant to answer difficult questions from young people about Islam and its followers' obligations. When adolescents are exposed to confusing messages online, particularly regarding whether their government is legitimate and whether they are obliged to wage militant jihad either in their own countries or in foreign countries, it is imperative that they feel comfortable asking trusted and knowledgeable adults about the veracity of those claims. If not, they will turn to self-professed scholars, whether online or in-person, who will answer their questions and often guide them toward violent extremism. During his interview, one research participant, Khalid, took the opportunity to ask the third author one such question, demonstrating his desire to learn: 'What I am confused about it, who are the true people who are fighting in wars? ISIS, Hezbollah, al Qaeda. Among these groups, who are the people who are on the true path?' Without the opportunity to ask a learned scholar, the interviewees turned to the leaders of the militant jihadist cell in the prison. For instance, Abbas recounted the lessons he learned from another interviewee, Daoud, which simultaneously improved his self-concept and turned him against the Maldivian government:

> He taught me tawheed [the oneness of God]. He's a teacher. If someone wants to become good and start praying, they become a source of information and mentor him [...] I was taught [that] taghut [is those] who makes a non-Islamic constitution and tries to get people to obey it. These institutions are taghut. Prison officials are part of this [...] He taught me that the sentence I got was not Islamic. In Islam, if you commit a murder, if the inheritors forgive you, then you are forgiven, but you are still here in jail. You are serving an unjust Islamic sentence.

Daoud was identified by another interviewee, Faisal, as the 'emir', though it was not clear whether Daoud was the emir for the entire militant jihadist group operating in the Maldives or whether he simply led the cell within Maafushi Prison. Faisal, who did not espouse militant jihadist beliefs, claimed that Daoud had 'declared [Faisal] a kafir and [said] I had to be executed'. Faisal's quarrel with the militant jihadists stemmed from his more extensive knowledge of Islam than the other interviewees, which led him to doubt what Daoud and his followers were saying:

> One group told me that if you are a drug user, you have to be executed. I said show me evidence from the Quran. They wouldn't show it but said this is the law of God, this is the Islamic religion. I responded that this is not the religion I know. I have heard the story of the Prophet where during battle they had someone cornered and because he was cornered he said the shahada, but they killed him even. When they returned and told the Prophet, he said what you did was wrong, multiple times.

Thus, it is clear that Faisal's more nuanced Islamic education served as a buffer against the radicalisation efforts of the militant jihadists in Maafushi Prison.

Substance abuse

The third vulnerability identified in the data was substance abuse, alongside long prison sentences for the same. As adolescents and young adults, all but two interviewees struggled with substance abuse, with most reporting using hard, addictive drugs like a form of heroin they called 'brown sugar'. One interviewee, Ehan, was arrested on drug charges for the first time when he was a teenager in 2001. He reported being tortured and humiliated by the guards and said that a friend died in prison after being tortured. After leaving prison, he found it difficult to deal with his psychological challenges without continuing to use drugs. Finally, he was able to stay clean for one year, during which he completed a rehabilitation program and made a pilgrimage to Mecca. Then, one night, Ehan was 'drinking vodka. I was hung over. [My friends] said smoke some, you'll feel better. I said I know. I've done this before. [It] progressed [and I] went back to heroin'. Soon enough, he was caught with just over a gram of heroin, which incurs a 16-year sentence.

Another interviewee, Faisal, started selling heroin at age 15 to help support his family. Soon after, he started using, without understanding addiction: 'One day I was really depressed about a little problem going on in my family. One of the guys I sold drugs to said you look really depressed, listen, use some of this, you'll feel better. As long as you don't use it all the time, you'll be okay'. Faisal experienced painful withdrawal symptoms when he stopped using, recalling, 'I started getting really sick, fever. I had no idea what it was. I didn't know what it was. [The] supplier showed up and said yeah, you're sick, [and the] only way you will get over it is if you use it more. It turned out to be true'. Faisal's substance abuse was exacerbated by the confusion and unfairness that he perceived during the change in government in the Maldives:

> When I was first sentenced to jail, I quit. It was difficult but I got over it and then I was trying to be really good. Then, when the coup happened, when the military took over, when the Vice President took over and became the President, I got a pardon. I had married someone when I was in prison. I went to Male' and she had come to pick me up. There was a group who was being released one at a time. I asked why I haven't been released. There is my wife outside. They sent her away [and said] we're sorry but your pardon was a mistake. I [had] seen the letter. How can it be a mistake? They returned me to jail. I relapsed. I used as soon as I got back, and I had been clean for two years. I never quit again.

Just as the militant jihadists were able to exploit a lack of Islamic knowledge while at the same time offering religious education to those desperate to learn, they also promised drug users detoxification and rehabilitation programming. Indeed, ten (58.8 percent) of the men and one of the women were motivated to join militant jihadist groups by the idea that joining such groups would help them be rehabilitated from their substance abuse problems. This was apparently effective for some, a notable finding given that rehabilitation from heroin use is rarely successful without medication such as methadone (Mattick, Breen, Kimber, & Davoli, 2009). Studies have also found that higher levels of spirituality and religiosity are predictive of lower rates of relapse among heroin users in the United States (Schoenthaler et al., 2015). Said Najib, 'I was clean for six years. I was with people who followed the Sunnah for six years'. Recalled Bilal, 'After I stopped using, [I] started praying and learning about religion. I felt a lot of satisfaction that I could stop, and not use again [...] My hope is that my sins are forgiven. I get really good feelings when I pray and fast'. Recounted Hakim, who was still struggling with a heroin addiction, 'I realise the only way [to get clean] is leading a good religious life. I could only go 30 min [without using]; now I can go 48 h. I know I need to do this'.

Seeking redemption

A common thread attaching all three primary vulnerabilities exploited by the Maldivian militant jihadists were feelings of insignificance and hopelessness. Many of the interviewees were afraid that they had been condemned, both societally and divinely, for their past sins. Eight of the men and two of the women reported that they had been motivated to join the militant jihadists because they felt that doing so would lead to their redemption and forgiveness in the eyes of God. Badia, one of the women, had experienced a great deal of trauma in her life prior to her incarceration on drug charges. Her redemption came in the form of religious education, both formally and informally, in prison:

> I learned a lot from prison, how to pray, met a lot of people over the years, I've learned how to understand feelings and experiences from others, advise others, I have learned in the religious programs, I became a good mother in prison. I learned how to pray in prison, recitation in prison, I told my mother I'm not sad because I've learned so much here in prison.

Two of the men who were incarcerated for murder were profoundly concerned over whether they could be forgiven for this sin. Recall Abbas, quoted previously, who told of the militant jihadists telling him that he was serving an unjust sentence if his victim's family had forgiven him. This message came as a great relief to Abbas, who had been previously told by a mainstream Maldivian imam that he could not ever be forgiven for his crime, thereby condemning him to eternal hellfire, which Abbas took literally. Similarly, Ibrahim said that the militant jihadists in prison told him that 'what you have done [drug use] is bad and it's going to be alright. You should pray, it will be alright'. The same individuals also told him, however, that 'the laws here [in the Maldives] are against Islam and this government is not good'.

Discussion

Research which provides holistic and broadly generalisable understandings of the psychosocial processes leading to radicalisation to terrorism nevertheless emphasises the importance of context to an individual's trajectory into violence (e.g. Kruglanski et al., 2022; Speckhard, 2016). The present article aimed to illustrate the way that the psychosocial process of radicalisation is influenced by context among Maldivian youth and young adults. Using a small but relevant sample of incarcerated Maldivian men and women holding varying levels of militant jihadist beliefs, we identified three particularly salient and interconnected vulnerabilities that are exploited by militant jihadist recruiters in the Maldives. These vulnerabilities, lack of education and employment opportunities, lack of nuanced Islamic education, and substance abuse, converged to produce feelings of insignificance and worthlessness, if not outright fear of eternal damnation. In and out of prison, Maldivian militant jihadists seised on these feelings among these vulnerable young people and offered them increased self-worth, rehabilitation, and redemption. Notably, the first vulnerability, lack of education and employment opportunities, was also exploited by gang members, who recruited many of the participants as teenagers to work for them as drug dealers and thieves. But gang membership typically brought about the third vulnerability, substance abuse, and created susceptibility to in-prison arguments by militant jihadist self-proclaimed Islamic scholars that joining the militant jihadists would bring about both physical detoxification and spiritual forgiveness. Moreover, the militant jihadists did not negate the employment opportunities provided by gangs, telling their potential recruits that they could continue to earn money for themselves, their families, and their cause by committing crimes against non-Muslim tourists or Muslims whom the militant jihadists *takfir*-ed, that is, declared apostates, including the Maldivian government.

Importantly, although the contextual factors impacting radicalisation among young people in the Maldives are the focus of this article, the needs for rehabilitation and redemption as motivators of radicalisation are not unique. Both were reported by and observed among ISIS defectors, returnees and prisoners from Iraq, Syria, and abroad (Speckhard & Ellenberg, 2020; Stern, 2016), particularly those with criminal histories (Basra & Neumann, 2016). Indeed, De Graaf and Van den Bos (2021) highlight redemption through religious radicalism as a means of coping with social stressors, such as discrimination and humiliation, as well as the social alienation that can arise from lack of employment, substance abuse, and involvement in criminality, as described by the interviewees in the present study. Thus, the three vulnerabilities highlighted presently do not represent idiosyncratic sources of radicalisation in the Maldives, but rather specific manifestations of and triggers for universal needs (Kruglanski et al., 2022) that play a role in cases of radicalisation around the world.

Limitations and directions for future research

This study is not without limitations, however. First and foremost, the sample size is small, and the results are therefore preliminary and should not be generalised to the broader population of violent extremists or criminal offenders in the Maldives or elsewhere. Future research should aim to replicate this work using larger and more diverse samples of Maldivian violent extremists and criminal offenders, as well as populations in the broader Indo-Pacific region. Moreover, the participants who were interviewed for this study had been presented to the researchers by prison officials as prisoners potentially holding violent extremist beliefs or belonging to the militant jihadist cell within the prison but had not yet undergone the screening that was later put in place, after which radicalised prisoners were transferred to a separate facility for rehabilitation and deradicalization programming. Thus, they do not necessarily represent the typical violent extremist offender in the Maldives but are rather taken from the general offender population. Future research should explore the potential differences in the radicalisation processes of Maldivian prisoners who are incarcerated for violent extremism offenses and those who hold militant jihadist beliefs but are incarcerated for non-ideological crimes. Future research on violent extremist recidivism among offenders who radicalised in prison is similarly warranted. Finally, the participants spoke retrospectively about their experiences with militant jihadists in the Maldives as youth and young adults, but all participants were older than 18 at the time of their interview. Thus, future research exploring contemporaneous accounts of militant jihadist radicalisation and recruitment efforts focused on youth may provide more detail than was provided by the interviewees in the present study.

Recommendations for policy and practice

The results of this article suggest that changes to the Maldivian educational system throughout the islands could be highly impactful in preventing radicalisation to violent extremism by minimising the vulnerabilities that militant jihadists in the Maldives exploit in their recruitment of youth and young adults. For instance, making upper secondary education more accessible to those living outside of the capital would increase young people's employment opportunities and allow them to remain in their parents' homes throughout adolescence, both of which would lessen their risk of gang involvement (Eitle, Gunkel, & Van Gundy, 2004; Salaam, 2011; Seals, 2009). Further, improving Islamic education by adding nuance and directly addressing the false claims made by violent extremists will proactively create a population of young adults who are better able to resist the promises of significance, dignity, and redemption made by both gang members and militant jihadists (Speckhard, Ellenberg, & Ali, 2022). Prior literature has suggested that the *Wahhabi* ideology adhered to by many Saudi-educated Maldivian

Islamic scholars validates aspects of the extreme interpretation of Islam preached by militant jihadists that legitimizes overthrowing what is defined by the jihadists as an apostate government, making it more difficult for these scholars to dispute the militant jihadists' claims and condemn militant jihadist violence against the government (Ranjan, 2023). Finally, providing comprehensive drug education that explains the neurobiology of addiction and goes beyond a 'Just Say No' model, will better protect young people from the temptations of substance abuse (Pan & Bai, 2009). Although these changes are broad, they are feasible given the Maldives' small population, relatively high GDP in comparison to other countries in the region (U.S. Department of State, 2022), and stated motivation to curb terrorism in the country through preventative means in addition to more traditional kinetic strategies (Speckhard, Ellenberg, & Ali, 2022).

Conclusion

The present article aimed to elucidate factors involved in militant jihadist recruitment of youth and young adults in the Maldives. The research, based on interviews with 20 incarcerated Maldivian men and women, found three primary contextual factors which may be exploited in the process of militant jihadist recruitment in the Maldives. These factors – lack of education and employment opportunities, lack of nuanced Islamic education, and substance abuse – each contribute to feelings of significance loss and need for redemption, as well as an inability to refute ideological arguments that they will find drug and criminal rehabilitation, purpose and forgiveness through militant jihad. The confluence of these factors, as well as the presence of militant jihadist networks both inside and outside of prisons – and the absence of supportive, prosocial alternative networks – creates the perfect storm through which radicalisation to militant jihadist extremism can arise (Kruglanski et al., 2019; Speckhard, 2016). The findings from this study are therefore consistent with prior research on the process of radicalisation (e.g. Kruglanski et al., 2014). They are also consistent with prior findings on youth disenfranchisement in the Maldives (Templer, 2019) and the tactics through which gangs recruit in the Maldives (Naaz, 2012), which are remarkably similar to those used by militant jihadists. Thus, the present research delves into the psychological effects of these vulnerabilities as they relate to militant jihadist radicalisation and recruitment within the Maldivian context, but does not deny that these factors are also at play in gang recruitment in the Maldives as well as violent extremist radicalisation and recruitment elsewhere.

Notes

1. We use the term 'militant jihadist' in order to clarify the ideology adhered to by these individuals and groups (as opposed to the broader term 'terrorist') and to reflect what these actors call themselves (i.e., 'jihadists'), despite scholarly interpretations of Islam that do not condone terrorist violence. Likewise, we use the term *militant* to specify that these are not typical religious adherents but actually violent, non-state actors.
2. The IRB information for the authors' organization is available upon request.
3. One such text noted by the third author, a respected Islamic scholar, is *Kitab al Tawhid* by Muhammed bin Abdulwahab.

Disclosure statement

No potential conflict of interest was reported by the author(s).

Funding

This work was supported by Transparency Maldives.

References

Basra, R., & Neumann, P. R. (2016). Criminal pasts, terrorist futures: European jihadists and the new crime-terror nexus. *Perspectives on Terrorism, 10*(6), 25–40.

Bonofer, J. A. (2010). The challenges of democracy in Maldives. *International Journal of South Asian Studies, 3*(2), 433–449.

Bureau of Counterterrorism and Countering Violent Extremism. (2015). Maldives. *Country Reports on Terrorism 2015.*

Charmaz, K. (2014). *Constructing grounded theory*. London: SAGE.

De Graaf, B. A., & Van den Bos, K. (2021). Religious radicalization: social appraisals and finding radical redemption in extreme beliefs. *Current Opinion in Psychology, 40*, 56–60.

Dharmawardhane, I. (2015). Maldives. *Counter Terrorist Trends and Analyses, 8*(1), 63–69.

Di Biase, R., & Maniku, A.A. (2021). Transforming education in the Maldives: The challenges of a small island developing state. In P. M. Sarangapani & R. Pappu (Eds.), *Handbook of education systems in South Asia* (pp. 545–573). Singapore: Springer Singapore.

Doosje, B., Moghaddam, F. M., Kruglanski, A. W., De Wolf, A., Mann, L., & Feddes, A. R. (2016). Terrorism, radicalization and de-radicalization. *Current Opinion in Psychology, 11*, 79–84.

Eitle, D., Gunkel, S., & Van Gundy, K. (2004). Cumulative exposure to stressful life events and male gang membership. *Journal of Criminal Justice, 32*(2), 95–111.

Horgan, J. (2008). From profiles to pathways and roots to routes: Perspectives from psychology on radicalization into terrorism. *The ANNALS of the American Academy of Political and Social Science, 618*(1), 80–94.

Kruglanski, A. W., Bélanger, J. J., Gelfand, M., Gunaratna, R., Hettiarachchi, M., Reinares, F., … Sharvit, K. (2013). Terrorism—A (self) love story: Redirecting the significance quest can end violence. *American Psychologist, 68*(7), 559.

Kruglanski, A. W., Bélanger, J. J., & Gunaratna, R. (2019). *The three pillars of radicalization: Needs, narratives, and networks*. New York: Oxford University Press.

Kruglanski, A. W., Gelfand, M. J., Bélanger, J. J., Sheveland, A., Hetiarachchi, M., & Gunaratna, R. (2014). The psychology of radicalization and deradicalization: How significance quest impacts violent extremism. *Political Psychology, 35*, 69–93.

Kruglanski, A. W., Molinario, E., Jasko, K., Webber, D., Leander, N. P., & Pierro, A. (2022). Significance-quest theory. *Perspectives on Psychological Science, 17*(4), 1050–1071.

Makan, A. (2007). Bomb blast wounds 12 tourists in Maldives capital. *Reuters*. https://www.reuters.com/article/us-maldives-explosion/bomb-blast-wounds-12-tourists-inMaldives-capital-idUSCOL8415420070929

Maldives Bureau of Statistics. (2006). Youth population in the Maldives. *Census Analysis 2006.*

Maldives Democracy Network. (2016). Preliminary assessment of radicalization in the Maldives. http://mdn.mv/wp-content/uploads/2016/09/Preliminary-Assessment-of-Radicalisationin-the-Maldives-Final.pdf

Mashal, M. (2021). Former Maldives president is critically injured in bombing. *The New York Times*. https://www.nytimes.com/2021/05/07/world/asia/maldives-presidentbombing.html

Mattick, R.P., Breen, C., Kimber, J., & Davoli, M. (2009). Methadone maintenance therapy versus no opioid replacement therapy for opioid dependence. *Cochrane Database of Systematic Reviews*, 3.

McCauley, C., & Moskalenko, S. (2017). Understanding political radicalization: The two-pyramids model. *American Psychologist, 72*(3), 205.

Naaz, A. A. (2012). Rapid situation assessment of gangs in Male'. The Asia Foundation. http://saruna.mnu.edu.mv/jspui/bitstream/123456789/5532/1/Rapid%20Situation%20Assessment%20of%20Gangs%20in%20Mal%C3%A9.pdf

Niyaz, A. (2010). Terrorism and extremism: a threat to Maldives tourism industry. *Revista UNISCI, 24*, 221–231.

Pan, W., & Bai, H. (2009). A multivariate approach to a meta-analytic review of the effectiveness of the D.A.R.E. Program. *International Journal of Environmental Research and Public Health, 6*(1), 267–277.

Ramakrishna, K. (2021). The global threat landscape in 2020. *Counter Terrorist Trends and Analyses, 13*(1), 1–13.

Ranjan, A. (2023). Foreign policy choice or domestic compulsion? Maldives' deep ties with Saudi Arabia. *Journal of Asian and African Studies, 58*(4), 518–534.

Salaam, A.O. (2011). Motivations for gang membership in Lagos, Nigeria: Challenge and resilience. *Journal of Adolescent Research, 26*(6), 701–726.

Sayed, A., & Hamming, T.R. (2023). *The growing threat of the Islamic State in Afghanistan and South Asia*. Washington, DC: United States Institute of Peace.

Schoenthaler, S.J., Blum, K., Braverman, E.R., Giordano, J., Thompson, B., Oscar-Berman, M., ... Gold, M.S. (2015). NIDA-Drug Addiction Treatment Outcome Study (DATOS) relapse as a function of spirituality/religiosity. *Journal of Reward Deficiency Syndrome, 01*(1), 36.

Seals, A. (2009). Are gangs a substitute for legitimate employment? Investigating the impact of labor market effects on gang affiliation. *Kyklos, 62*(3), 407–425.

Shahid, H. (2014). *National security policy and security challenges of Maldives*. Fort Leavenworth: Army Command and General Staff College Fort Leavenworth KS.

Shama, A. (2018). Islamic radicalization in the Maldives: An analysis of the role of religious networks and proliferation of different religious narratives. *Journal of Advances in Humanities and Social Sciences, 4*(5), 206–213.

Shiuna, M., & Sodiq, A. (2013). *Improving education in the Maldives: Stakeholder perspectives on the Maldivian education*. Male: Maldives Research.

Speckhard, A. (2016). *The lethal cocktail of terrorism: the four necessary ingredients that go into making a terrorist & fifty individual vulnerabilities/motivations that may also play a role*. McLean: International Center for the Study of Violent Extremism: Brief Report.

Speckhard, A., Ellenberg, M., & Ali, S. (2022). *Prison radicalisation in the Maldives*. Male: Transparency Maldives & Ministry of Home Affairs.

Speckhard, A., & Ellenberg, M. D. (2020). Isis in their own words: Recruitment history, motivations for joining, travel, experiences in ISIS, and disillusionment over time – analysis of 220 In-depth interviews of ISIS returnees, defectors and prisoners. *Journal of Strategic Security, 13*(1), 82–127.

Stern, J. (2016). Radicalization to extremism and mobilization to violence: What have we learned and what can we do about it? *The Annals of the American Academy of Political and Social Science, 668*(1), 102–117.

Templer, R. J. (2019). *Youth vulnerability in the Maldives*. Male: United Nations Development Programme.

Thoha, N. (2020). *Assessing potential climate-related security risks in the Maldives: Exploring the future climate-induced migration*. New York: Issue Brief, United Nations Development Programme (UNDP).

UNICEF. (2015). *Assessment of the situation of students who migrate to Malé for education: Abridged report*. Male: UNICEF.

UNICEF. (2018). *The Maldives: Education*. Male: UNICEF.

U.S. Department of State. (2022). Integrated Country Strategy: Maldives.

Zahir, A. (2020). Islamic State terror in the Maldives as COVID-19 arrives. *The Diplomat*. https://thediplomat.com/2020/04/islamic-state-terror-in-the-maldives-as-covid-19arrives/

Evolving dynamics of China-Pakistan counter-terrorism cooperation

Khuram Iqbal, Muhammad Shoaib and Sardar Bakhsh

ABSTRACT
Counter-terrorism cooperation is a crucial aspect of China-Pakistan bilateral security relationship. Originating from a shared understanding of the threat of Uygur separatism facing China, it has encompassed the TTP and Baloch militants targeting CPEC projects and Chinese nationals in Pakistan. However, with Beijing's growing economic influence in Pakistan after the BRI and the US withdrawal from Afghanistan, the dynamics of counter-terrorism cooperation have transformed in two ways. Firstly, Pakistan's regional influence has diminished and Beijing no longer relies solely on Islamabad for safeguarding its interests vis-à-vis regional terrorism. Secondly, this relationship shows a dynamic of its own, largely independent of the India-factor.

Introduction

Security cooperation remains a crucial component of China–Pakistan relations. Apart from the 'Indian threat' that binds both countries in one strategic continuum, counterterrorism is perhaps the second most important area of cooperation in the security sector. Terrorism poses a formidable challenge to both countries. Over the past two decades, Pakistan has been ranked among one of the worst-hit countries by terrorism. According to the Global Terrorism Index (2011–2014), Pakistan ranked second, ahead of Afghanistan and just below Iraq, regarding the frequency of terrorist attacks. In 2015, Pakistan's rank improved slightly from second to fourth. 2021 marked a significant decline in terrorist incidents, and Pakistan's standing improved to nine. Although the intensity and frequency of violence and terrorism in China are much lower than in Pakistan, Beijing has placed the issue at the top of the three evils of terrorism, extremism, and separatism. The transnational nature of the terrorist threat has led China to cooperate closely with the countries in its neighbourhood.

China–Pakistan counter-terrorism cooperation spans more than three decades, and the patterns of cooperation continue to evolve along China's expanding regional footprint. Great power politics in sub-regions of Asia and the geopolitics surrounding China's Belt and Road Initiative (BRI) have strengthened the common threat perception and resolve to counter extremism and terrorism. Therefore, over time, counter-terrorism cooperation between China and Pakistan has expanded significantly, encompassing various measures to address shared security challenges. In this regard, the 2003 bilateral extradition treaty provides them with a legal framework to cooperate in bringing suspected terrorists to justice, while joint counter-terrorism exercises allow the exchange of expertise and experience. The informal intelligence-sharing arrangement strengthens their ability to anticipate and prevent terrorist attacks.

In addition to these measures, China and Pakistan have consistently presented a united front against terrorism at regional and global forums, such as the Shanghai Cooperation Organisation (SCO) and the UN. Their representatives agree on refraining from using terrorism as a diplomatic tool. At the UN, China has frequently vetoed, delayed, and held the efforts by India and other countries to categorise Pakistani-based organisations and individuals as terrorists under the rules of the UNSC's 1267 committee and measures to support action against Pakistan. (China's position in the UN indicates that its understanding of 'terrorists' differs from that of India and Western countries). Islamabad reciprocates Beijing's efforts by shielding it at the Organisation of Islamic Cooperation (OIC) on the Uyghur issue. It has consistently resisted international pressure to criticise China publicly on the issue and dealt with it in its own way. It has encouraged prominent leaders from religious parties to visit China to assure the Chinese of their cooperation and goodwill. China has used these visits to enhance its approach's legitimacy to address the situation in Xinjiang.

Both China and Pakistan favoured bilateral arrangements for counter-terrorism efforts in the region, as divergent positions of India and Pakistan on terrorism can impede any multilateral progress. India-Pakistan tensions underscore the complexity of counter-terrorism cooperation in the region and the challenges posed by conflicting perspectives and interests (Adil, 2023). They disagree on the causes and contours of terrorism. However, the challenges to counter-terrorism cooperation in the region are not limited to their enmity. There are instances of disagreements over the issue between China and Pakistan as well. Under such circumstances, China leverages its influence to promote its counter-terrorism goals in Pakistan. However, it avoids using diplomatic coercion involving explicit threats of harm to push Pakistan to change its tactics. China induces behavioural changes in Pakistan to align its policies in addressing mutual concerns, particularly regarding the ETIM and Uyghur separatism. Its demands generally do not entail actions Pakistan would otherwise refuse to undertake because it shares a common perception of ETIM and Uyghur separatists with the former.

An important reason for the alignment in perceptions of Pakistan and China is China's economic imprint and Pakistan's growing reliance on China in security and economic sectors. Pakistan's weak economy, domestic instability and divergence with the US have also pushed Pakistan to cooperate more closely with China. Therefore, Pakistan's political and military leadership heeds China's advice on terrorism. Infrastructural investments and military exports, especially after the 2013 announcement of the China–Pakistan Economic Corridor (CPEC), also increased China's influence on Pakistan's counter-terrorism policy. Although the Chinese leadership largely refrains from publicly criticising Pakistan's policies, they convey their concerns privately and, at times, shape Pakistan's response to violence and terrorist incidents.

The study of the origins of China–Pakistan counter-terrorism cooperation helps us understand the contours of their collaboration and China's influence on the counter-terrorism policy of Pakistan. This study explores the origins of bilateral cooperation to highlight the shifting nature of the threat and how these shifts have affected their cooperation. It specifically examines how China–Pakistan counter-terrorism cooperation has evolved in the backdrop of geopolitical shifts in the South Asia region.

To answer the research question, the study utilises a historical analysis framework, which involves a systematic examination and interpretation of past events to understand their significance, causes, and consequences within a political context. This methodology employs a chronological framework to trace the evolution of China–Pakistan counter-terrorism cooperation, dividing it into three distinct periods: the 1990s, when China sought Pakistan's cooperation in suppressing Uyghur separatism at home; the early 2000s, when both countries worked together to limit Uyghur presence in Pakistan; and 2013 onward when China prioritised the protection of its personnel and investments in Pakistan. Comparative analysis of these three temporal phases allowed us to identify patterns, similarities, and differences in China–Pakistan counter-terrorism cooperation during the last three decades.

Existing research on China–Pakistan relations primarily focuses on bilateral relations as the fundamental unit of analysis. Our study acknowledges the significance of bilateral relations but seeks to augment the existing literature by providing a more focused examination of the counter-terrorism cooperation aspect. In doing so, the study goes beyond the counter-India aspect of China–Pakistan relations and argues that the counter-terrorism relationship between the two countries should not be seen as driven wholly through the lens of a counter-India 'threshold alliance' (Lalwani, 2023). Geo-political shifts in Afghanistan, not India, play a pivotal role in shaping the dynamics of counter-terrorism cooperation between China and Pakistan.

The study is divided into four sections. The first section covers the 1990s when China faced a Uyghur separatist threat within its boundaries. The second section details the joint efforts of China and Pakistan to deal with the transnational presence of separatists. The third section discusses the measures taken by China and Pakistan to respond to the terrorist threat in Pakistan. This section includes details of attacks on Chinese nationals and investments in Pakistan and covers China's efforts to strengthen Pakistan to deal with the threat. The fourth section highlights the shifts in counter-terrorism cooperation between the two sides. The concluding section analyzes the dynamic nature of the threat of terrorism and how this dynamism has led Beijing to improvise its counter-terrorism approach with Islamabad.

The 1990s: dealing with the consequences of post-anti-Soviet Afghan Jihad

China–Pakistan counter-terrorism cooperation started immediately after the Soviet withdrawal from Afghanistan in 1989. Both sides sought to mitigate the fallout of an ambitious Jihadi project in their neighbourhood. As for China, it provided arms to Mujahideen during the war to supplement the US-led effort in Afghanistan. Training camps were established in Xinjiang to train Uyghur fighters. Approximately 300 Chinese instructors and advisors spent time in training camps in Pakistan (Haider, 2005). Since China and Pakistan had actively participated in the anti-Soviet Jihad, the threat of spillover effects was real. Many Uyghurs who fought alongside Mujahideen returned to Xinjiang and initiated anti-China local Jihad.

Within months, the frequency of violent incidents in Xinjiang rapidly increased. From 1990 to 2001, 162 people died, and 440 were injured due to 200 terrorist attacks (Chung, 2002). High-profile attacks, such as the Baren uprising in Kashghar in1992, prompted China to initiate its 'Strike Hard' campaign against the three evil forces (Wayne, 2007, p. 42). China closed the road linkage with Pakistan for a few months to prevent new enforcement of Uyghur fighters from Mujahedeen camps. Some Uyghurs still fled to Pakistan, where they founded ETIM and used a madrassa as their base (Wayne, 2007, p. 6).

Over time, the decision-making authorities in Beijing realised that closing the land route with Pakistan was not a permanent solution. In 2003, China and Pakistan signed the extradition treaty. Before the treaty, they relied on informal collaboration between their intelligence communities. For instance, after the Baren episode, Islamabad acted swiftly against Uyghurs taking shelter in different parts of Pakistan. When China launched an offensive in 1997 to eradicate subversive activities, the level of violence increased in China (Castets, 2003). Four bomb blasts in Urumqi killed nine people and injured 74 (Castets, 2003). The subsequent Chinese crackdown constrained many protestors to flee to neighbouring countries, including Pakistan and Afghanistan. In response, Pakistan identified and detained the supporters and sympathisers of the Uyghur uprisings. In 1997 it reportedly deported 14 Chinese Uyghur students for organising demonstrations supporting the Ghulja uprising.

China reciprocated with enhanced military support to Pakistan. From 1990 to 1999, Chinese arms exports to Pakistan amounted to $2.4 Billion (Boni, 2019, p. 111) This increase occurred against the backdrop of their June 1990 MoU for ten years of cooperation in research and development, technological transfer, co-production, and procurement. In December 1990, they also signed a military protocol agreement under which Beijing would provide credit facilities for Islamabad's procurement of defence equipment. In September 1990, Pakistan's President Ghulam Ishaq Khan visited China, overseeing the signing of a bilateral agreement on humanitarian assistance to Afghan refugees. In the following year, the Chinese Premier and President visited Pakistan. Premier Li Peng appreciated Islamabad's role in the Afghan peace process, especially in providing humanitarian assistance to the refugees (Boni, 2019, p. 122). President Fang Shang Kun followed his visit in October. During the visit, China and Pakistan signed two agreements which provided Pakistan with an interest-free loan of 50 million Yuan for an unspecified project and additional assistance for the refugees (Boni, 2019, p. 122).

China's economic support, transfer of military equipment, and occasional diplomatic pressure on Pakistan worked in its favour. However, the tough talks on the issue of terrorism occurred privately as both sides avoided the media limelight. Following a failed uprising in Baren, China reportedly communicated to Pakistan that it could freeze bilateral ties if Islamabad failed to take effective action against Islamist militants (Haider, 2005). Beijing's reluctance to implement an agreement in 1995 to improve a highway to enable transit trade between Pakistan, Kazakhstan, and Kyrgyzstan indicated its seriousness. Rashid argues that 'China was apprehensive that the mobility through the highway could heighten the fundamentalist threat to Xinjiang' (Haider, 2005).

China was also apprehensive of drugs and weapon smuggling from Pakistan (Haider, 2005). In February 1998, the Xinjiang Legal Daily reported, 'There is also evidence of trade in heroin and weapons over Xinjiang's borders with Pakistan, Afghanistan and three Central Asian Republics' (Haider, 2005). In January 1999, China protested with the interior ministry of Pakistan after the arrest of 16 Uyghurs in Xinjiang. The arrested individuals confessed to the Chinese authorities that they trained in camps at Jalalabad (Afghanistan) and Landi Kotal (Khyber Agency, Pakistan) (Fayaz, 2012). Pakistan denied that it harboured, trained, armed, or supported Uyghur militancy and extended all-out support to China in countering militancy in Xinjiang. To epitomise cooperation, after the fall of Kabul to the Taliban in 1994, Pakistan's intelligence agencies influenced the Islamic Emirate not to take up the cause of 'East Turkistan'. They became facilitators between China and militant groups to strike deals to keep militants from targeting China. China received guarantees from Taliban leader Mullah Omar that his force would not allow East Turkistan Islamic Movement (ETIM) any base in Afghanistan. Mullah Omar assured the Chinese ambassador that 'Afghanistan never had any interest or wished to interfere in China's domestic issues and affairs, nor would Afghanistan allow any group to use its territory to conduct any such operations or support one to that end' (Fayaz, 2012).

The Taliban kept their assurances. They allowed Uyghurs to participate in local battles but not to wage any struggle against China for a separate homeland. They were directed to move from the neighbouring region with China to fight against the Northern Alliance in the northern region of Afghanistan (Fayaz, 2012). As a group, ETIM did not operate independently but worked under the Islamic Movement of Uzbekistan (IMU). The understanding reached with Mullah Omer and cooperation with Pakistan significantly improved China's counter-terrorism capacity and efforts causing a noticeable decline in the number of attacks (Figure 1) (Small, 2015, p. 129). According to the Chinese government, it eliminated 195 cells in 1998 and 76 cells in 1999, along with two violent extremist organisations based in Kashgar and Hotan. Pakistani authorities closed two important settlements of the Uyghur community in Rawalpindi, known as Hotanabad and Kashgharabad, in 1999 and 2000. When asked about the reason for the closure, they told the Uyghur settlers that they were under pressure from China to do it (Haider, 2005).

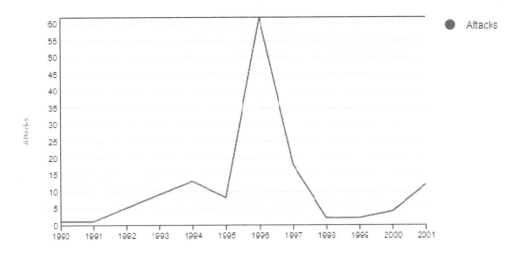

Source: (Global Terrorism Database, 2023)

Figure 1. Frequency of terrorist attacks in China (1990–2001).
Source: (Global Terrorism Database, 2024).

In June 2000, Qazi Hussain, the Chief of Jamaat-e-Islami – arguably, Pakistan's most prominent religious political party of the 1990s – visited China. Qazi conveyed to his hosts the eagerness of various religious parties in Pakistan to maintain favourable relations with China (Ali, 2017, p. 147). His gesture assured China of the goodwill and cooperation of Pakistani religious organisations. China used such visits and engagements strategically to bolster its approach's legitimacy to address the situation in Xinjiang. By highlighting the support of influential religious figures and parties in Pakistan, it sought the validation of its actions and policies in the region.

China–Pakistan counter-terrorism cooperation amid the Global War on Terror (2001–2010)

The US-led Global War on Terror (GWOT) created a global consensus on combating and eradicating anti-state militancy. China seized the opportunity presented by this consensus and extended counter-terrorism operations beyond its borders. It shifted the focus of its counter-terrorism approach from domestic issues to broader regional and international engagement. The shift allowed China to collaborate with other nations in sharing intelligence, conducting joint operations, and taking measures to defuse the threat of Uyghur separatism in the neighbouring countries and the West.

Pakistan played a crucial role in China's renewed efforts. In December 2001, President General Pervez Musharraf visited China only two months after joining the War on Terrorism. He had two primary objectives: first, to assure the Chinese leadership of his decision to align with the US in the war; second, to travel to areas with a significant Muslim population to express unwavering support for Beijing's efforts to counter-separatism and terrorism. During the visit, Musharraf held an important meeting with the Imam of the Grand Mosque of Xian and other Muslim leaders. He emphasised the importance of Chinese Muslims remaining patriotic and loyal to their government. He delivered the message to foster a sense of unity and cooperation among Chinese Muslims in the fight against separatism and terrorism. He stated, 'Islam is a religion of peace, and we do not believe in any violence; therefore, you, being a part of China, have to be very patriotic, and all Muslims in China should work for the good of China' (Ali, 2017, p. 147).

In addition to extending political support for China's counter-terrorism efforts, Pakistan also conducted operations against anti-China militants on its soil. Following the fall of the Taliban in 2001, the ETIM relocated to the tribal region of Pakistan. Some Uyghur fighters tried to return to China, while others stayed in Afghanistan to fight alongside the Taliban. As per the Chinese authorities, China arrested 100 Uyghur fighters upon their return, 300 were captured in Afghanistan, and the remaining 600 were either in Afghanistan or Pakistan. China also swayed Pakistan to act against Uyghur militants in the tribal areas. In May 2002, Pakistan detained Ismail Kadir and handed him over to the Chinese authorities (The separatist leader, 2002). Kadir was one of the top ten leaders who spearheaded the separatist movement in Xinjiang. After his arrest, Chinese intelligence agencies identified Hassan Mehsum as the new leader of ETIM and requested their Pakistani counterparts to neutralise him.

Musharraf again visited China in November 2003 and met with his counterpart President Hu Jintao. Both vowed to fight against the three evil forces (Dawn, 2003)). Pakistan and China signed eight agreements, including extradition and preferential trade agreements. When China released a list of designated terrorist organisations and individuals in December 2003 that included ETIM and Mahsum, Pakistani authorities immediately released their response. The Pakistani side announced that Mehsum was killed on 2 October 2003 in a military operation against al-Qaeda hideouts in South Waziristan (Haider, 2005). Mahsum's death boosted China's confidence in Pakistan's resolve to counter anti-China militant organisations. In October 2004, Pakistan and China conducted their first-ever joint anti-terrorism exercise, Friendship-2004, in Xinjiang's Taxkorgan Tajik Autonomous County, which borders Tajikistan, Afghanistan, and Pakistan. About 200 soldiers from both sides participated in the exercise (Jize & Yang, 2010).

China and Pakistan signed a 'Treaty of Friendship, Cooperation and Good Neighbourly Relations' in April 2005 (Mehmood, 2005). Under the treaty, which came into force in January 2006, they signed 20 agreements, including 'Combating Terrorism, Separatism and Extremism'. During the visit of President Hu Jintao to Islamabad in November 2006, they renewed their commitments 'to substantive cooperation under bilateral and multilateral frameworks to jointly combat the "three evils" and maintain regional peace, stability and security'. In December 2006, the People's Liberation Army (PLA) and Pakistan Army troops conducted joint-terror operations exercise in Abbottabad. In 2007, the Chinese embassy in Islamabad formed a task force to collaborate with several branches of administration in Pakistan (Ministry of Interior, Ministry of Foreign Affairs, Ministry of Defense, Military of Finance, and the government secretariat) on counter terrorism.

However, military operations and counter-terrorism collaboration with China also triggered a response from militants. In the 1990s, ETIM or other militant organisations avoided targeting Chinese interests in Pakistan. However, China–Pakistan cooperation in the mid-2000s, especially after July 2007, prompted militant groups to launch attacks against Chinese targets in Pakistan. In this regard, the Red Mosque incident in 2007 (involving the abduction of seven Chinese citizens in Islamabad and causing a near-diplomatic crisis between the two countries) was the breaking point (Small, 2015, p. 111). It was the first time the Chinese government publicly demanded action against militants in Pakistan (Small, 2015, p. xv) Beijing used the incident to securitise the Uyghur presence in Pakistan. It attributed this incident to Uyghurs in the mosque and complained that 'Islamabad was negligent in guaranteeing the security of Chinese citizens … and tolerated terrorist threats to China itself' (Small, 2015, p. xiv). Pakistani security forces immediately launched an operation against the extremists taking refuge in the Red Mosque and killed 103 people, including 12 Uyghurs, to clear the site (Small, 2015, p. xiv).

The Red Mosque operation was a catalyst for anti-state militants in Pakistan. They launched a full-scale operation against the state. The militancy spilt over from tribal areas to the mainland, and casualties increased exponentially (Figure 2). Some militant leaders also considered China the culprit that pushed the Pakistan Army to launch the operation. These allegations forced China to declare that, 'China did not push Pakistan for operations in the Red Mosque. It is a consistent policy of China not to meddle in the domestic affairs of other countries (Small, 2015, p. xv)'. Small (2015) considers China's declaration 'too late' because the militants were convinced about China's role in the Red Mosque operation. Local Jihadis were convinced that 'Operation Silence' would not have happened if the Chinese had not demanded action. In 2008 when a Chinese worker was kidnapped, the Taliban spokesperson cited 'Chinese pressure to

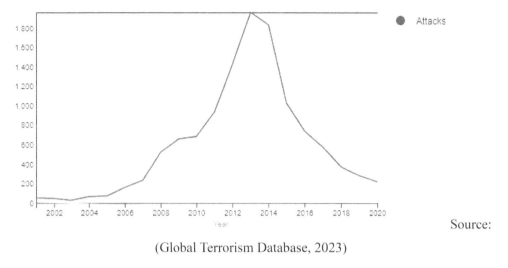

Figure 2. Frequency of terrorist attacks in Pakistan (2001–2020).
Source: (Global Terrorism Database, 2023).

launch Operation Silence' in Red Mosque as the rationale for the kidnapping. Chinese Ambassador to Pakistan Luo Zhaohui was also on the Taliban's hit list (Small, 2015, p. xv).

Militant organisations also used the operation for propaganda. After the operation, some radical elements in Pakistan and their international allies, including al-Qaeda, aligned with Uyghurs as they saw China suppressing their 'Muslim brethren' across the border and pushing Islamabad to be more assertive against Mujahideen. Nonetheless, China–Pakistan counter terrorism cooperation increased in the following months. To complement the Chinese efforts, Pakistan launched combing operations in the tribal areas, exchanged actionable intelligence on ETIM with the Chinese authorities, sealed the border with Xinjiang to prevent the cross-border movement of militants, and extended political support through high-profile visits to legitimize Chinese measures to ensure safe and secure Olympics in Beijing.

The shift in the threat landscape occurred concurrently with the emergence of ethno-nationalist groups operating from the Balochistan province of Pakistan. Baloch militant groups also adopted an anti-China agenda. These groups considered the growing economic presence of China, especially after the Saindak Copper–Gold project and Gwadar port, in Balochistan a threat to their resources and cultural identity. Between 2001 and 2010, nine terrorist incidents targeting Chinese nationals occurred in Pakistan (Table 1).

The expansion in the threat spectrum, with both Uyghur militants and local anti-state groups (mainly Taliban and Baloch separatists) targeting Chinese citizens and investments in Pakistan, posed a significant challenge to the security situation and threatened the prospects of any significant Chinese economic engagement in Pakistan (Duchâtel, 2011).

China–Pakistan counter-terrorism cooperation in the era of the BRI

Terrorism became an existential threat to Pakistan after the Red Mosque operation. On the one hand, Pakistan's Western allies questioned its role in the War on Terror and

Table 1. Attacks targeting Chinese interests/personnel in Pakistan (2001–2010).

Date	Location	Attack type	Causalities	Claim of responsibility
3 May 2004	Gwadar	Car bomb	Three dead and nine wounded	Balochistan Liberation Army (BLA)
22 September 2004	FATA	Engineer wounded	One wounded	Pakistani Taliban
9 October 2004	South Waziristan	Kidnapping	One dead and one wounded	al-Qaeda
15 February 2006	Hub, Balochistan	–	Two dead	BLA
24 June 2007	Red Mosque, Islamabad	Kidnapping	No casualties	Radical Islamist students from Jamia Hafsa
9 July 2007	Khazna, near Peshawar	Chinese workers assassinated	Three dead, and one wounded	Assassination related to the Red Mosque episode
19 July 2007	Hub, Balochistan	Chinese convoy blown up	No Chinese casualties	BLA
29 August 2008	Swat	Kidnapping	Two Chinese nationals were kidnapped and released	TTP
22 December 2008	Peshawar	Drive-by Shooting	One wounded	Unknown

Data Source: (Boni, 2019).

blamed its security apparatus for playing a double game. On the other hand, terrorist incidents claimed thousands of lives in the country (Moreau, 2010). Anti-state militants blamed the government and armed forces for their partnership with the US and for launching military operations on the local population. Some militant groups like TTP, based in the border areas of Pakistan and Afghanistan, embraced the Uyghur cause and equated China with the US as an adversary of Islam. In March 2012, the Pakistani Taliban, for the first time, attributed the killing of a Chinese national to 'revenge for the Chinese government killing our Muslim brothers in the Xinjiang province' (Small, 2015, p. 37).

Xinjiang region also witnessed a sharp increase in terrorist attacks. The region experienced 190 'violent terrorist' incidents in 2012 (Kaiman, 2013). Terror incidents also spread from border regions of China to the mainland when terrorists attacked Tiananmen Square on 28 October 2013. Turkistan Islamic Party (TIP) leader Abdullah Mansoor, who was featured in a video threatening the Beijing Olympics in 2008, claimed responsibility for the attack (Kaiman, 2013). In response, Beijing labelled terrorism the 'most direct and realistic security threat' (Rajagopalan, 2013). In March 2014, an unidentified group of knife-wielding men and women attacked people at the Kunming Railway Station. The attack left 31 civilians and four perpetrators dead, with more than 140 others injured. Xinjiang's capital Urumqi witnessed the first-ever suicide bomb just hours after President Xi Jinping had completed his visit to the area.

Following the attacks, Beijing paid more attention to Uyghur-aligned armed groups in Afghanistan and Pakistan. It requested Pakistan to designate ETIM and IMU as terrorist organisations, which Islamabad did in 2013 (Biberman, Schwartz, & Zahid, 2023). However, Islamabad failed to capture Abdullah Mansour in the following months. In March 2014, he gave a telephone interview to Reuters from his hideout in Pakistan in which he called the 'fight with the Chinese a holy act' and 'labelled China as the enemy of all Muslims' (Mehsud & Golovnina, 2014). In August 2014, a Chinese state media report stated that Memetuhut Memetrozi, a co-founder of ETIM serving a life sentence in China for his involvement in terrorist attacks, had been indoctrinated in a madrassa in Pakistan. The report was a rare proclamation by Chinese authorities of Pakistan's ties to Uyghur militancy (Xu, Fletcher, & Bajoria, 2014). On the diplomatic front, China reportedly delayed the official announcement of CPEC until Pakistan's crackdown on China-centric militant organisations, both local (Baloch insurgent groups and TTP) and foreign (ETIM, TIP, and IMU).

Pakistan's Prime Minister Muhammad Nawaz Sharif visited China the same year and met President Xi Jinping. Both agreed to a 'common vision for deepening China–Pakistan strategic cooperative partnership in the new era'. They signed an MOU on the 'Cooperation of Developing CPEC Long-term Plan and Action'. Pakistan awarded a Chinese company the contract for constructing and operating Gwadar Port (Boni, 2019)). As China had sought security guarantees from Pakistan's government and military leadership, the Chief of Army Staff General Raheel Sharif also paid a visit to China in June 2014 to assuage Chinese concerns (ISPR, 2014). His visit came at a time when the leadership in Pakistan was contemplating a military operation against the militants.

Pakistan got the impetus to launch a military operation in the tribal areas after the Karachi Airport attack on 8 June 2014. IMU, a group aligned with the ETIM and TIP, claimed responsibility for the attack (BBC, 2014). On 14 June 2014, Pakistani armed forces launched Operation Zarb-e-Azab in North Waziristan. Although Defense Minister Khawaja Asif called the airport attack the ultimate impetus of the campaign, consistent Chinese pressure to act against Islamist groups, which threatened China's security, also influenced the decision. Unsurprisingly, the military operation (that was scaled up after the TTP attack on Army Public School Peshawar on 16 December 2014) brought about positive results. Terrorist incidents decreased, and so did the civilian and military casualties. China also acknowledged.

Pakistan's counter-terrorism gains. In September 2015, Pakistani President Mamnoon Hussain visited China and conveyed to President Xi Jinping that the recent anti-terror operations had successfully eradicated the ETIM elements. President Xi assured him of 'China's unswerving support for Pakistan's efforts in safeguarding its national security' (Reuters, 2015). Pakistan's successes also boosted the confidence of Chinese leadership to initiate the CPEC formally (Ahmed, 2020). A secure Pakistan served Chinese interests in two ways: (a) security of Chinese nationals and investments in Pakistan and (b) improved security situation in Xinjiang. Since the end of Zarb-e-Azab in 2016, Xinjiang has not witnessed any major terror attacks. Peace in Xinjiang is an important reason for China's unwavering support for Pakistan's counter-terrorism efforts in the following years. It provided material and political support to Pakistan in dealing with anti-state militants in tribal areas and Balochistan. In Balochistan, it assumed significant security risks in building a trade-and-energy corridor (Duchâtel, 2011).

Baloch separatists released multiple videos threatening to target Chinese nationals and investments. They also organised multiple attacks on Chinese nationals, irrespective of their work status. However, China supported Pakistan's decision to launch military operations and enhanced military-to-military cooperation. Pakistan also took measures to assuage China's concerns. The government established two security divisions and a naval task force to protect Chinese nationals working on CPEC projects (Basit, 2019). It allowed non-CPEC companies and workers to hire private security firms.

However, all these measures have thus far failed to ensure fool-proof security of Chinese personnel and investments in Pakistan. Since the beginning of CPEC in 2015, China has faced some of the deadliest attacks against its personnel and investments in Pakistan. The following table (Table 2) reflects the spike in anti-China terrorism in Pakistan from 2010 onwards.

As the above table shows, TTP and Baloch separatists successfully launched terror attacks against Chinese interests in Pakistan. These attacks perturbed the Chinese leadership. After the June 2022 attack on Chinese nationals affiliated with the Confucius Institute, Beijing demanded stern actions against the perpetrators and foolproof security for its citizens. Some unconfirmed reports suggested that the Chinese leadership insisted on sending PLA troops to Pakistan for the security of its citizens.

Pakistan's failure to prevent attacks from its soil pushed Beijing to adopt a more assertive approach. For instance, after a deadly attack killed 10 Chinese nationals and seriously injured 26 others in July 2021, Chinese contractor China Gezhouba demanded compensation of USD 37 million (The Economic Times, 2022). Although in the past, Pakistan has paid heavy compensation after each attack targeting the Chinese, the demanded amount by Gezhouba was 500 per cent more than what China pays to its nationals if killed in a similar attack in their own country. The issue was only resolved when Islamabad agreed to pay over USD 11.4 million to the 36 Chinese nationals hit by the blast (The Economic Times, 2022). Through such measures, China perhaps expects Pakistan to demonstrate a more assertive approach to achieving shared policy objectives in counterterrorism.

The growing threat of terrorism in Pakistan has also tested Beijing's policy of non-interference. In 2018, the Financial Times reported that Beijing engaged directly with the BLA to secure its USD 60 billion projects (Bokhari & Stacey, 2018). Although Beijing denied these reports, counter-terrorism experts believe that Chinese firms, if not officials, established contacts with the Baloch insurgents. With Islamabad's knowledge, the negotiations appear to have been regularly held with local militant and economic interest groups. Indirectly, China has been the impetus for negotiation between the Pakistani government and Baloch militants. Evidence shows that the former also opened backchannels to Baloch leaders in 2021, potentially leading to some insurgents' demobilisation.

Evolving threat spectrum and the shift in China-Pakistan counter-terrorism cooperation

China and Pakistan have made significant progress in the collaboration in counter terrorism. Their bilateral understanding has shifted from the Uyghur separatist threat in Xinjiang to military operations in Pakistan, arms supplies, anti-terror exercises, and a similar stance on terrorism at global forums. In the past, both sides took advantage of the US military presence in Afghanistan to jointly work on quelling ETIM and other militant organisations. The pretext of the War on Terror allowed the Chinese to label the anti-state separatists as terrorists. The state targeted separatists with legal impunity. On the other hand, Pakistani military operations and the US drone strikes in the border region neutralised several militants – either from ETIM or their sympathisers and allies. For instance, in February 2010, a US drone strike killed an ETIM leader Abdul Haq Turkistani in North Waziristan. In June 2012, Abu Yahya al-Libi, a senior al-Qaeda ideologue who

Table 2. Attacks targeting Chinese interests/personnel in Pakistan (2010 onwards).

Date	Location	Attack type/Dynamics of attack	Causalities	Claim of responsibility
22 November 2011	Balochistan	Attack on a convoy with Chinese engineers	No casualties	BLA
28 February 2012	Peshawar	A Chinese woman was shot dead	One dead	TTP
22 June 2013	Gilgit Baltistan	Gunmen dressed as paramilitary killed nine tourists	Two dead, and one rescued in unknown conditions	TTP
19 May 2014	Durban area of Dera Ismail Khan	Chinese tourist kidnapped	No casualties: Tourist rescued on 24 August 2015	TTP
30 May 2016	Karachi	Roadside bomb explosion	Two wounded	Sindhudesh Revolutionary Army (SRA)
October 2016	Hub	Claymore blast	Two killed	BLA
8 June 2017	Quetta	Two Chinese teachers were kidnapped and then killed	Two dead	Islamic State
21 December 2017	Kahuta	Chinese national missing from Karot Hydropower Project	No news about the whereabouts of the man, and a kidnapping case registered	–
5 February 2018	Karachi	Chinese shipping executive shot in his car	One dead	–
11 August 2018	Dalbandin region	A small truck exploded along the route of a bus carrying Chinese engineers	Two Chinese engineers wounded	BLA
22 November 2018	Karachi	Attack on Chinese Consulate in Karachi	Two civilians and two police officers killed, no Chinese nationals killed	BLA
23 April 2020	Karachi	A Chinese National was kidnapped from DHA Karachi	No casualties	–
15 December 2020	Karachi	A bomb planted on the car of a Chinese restaurant owner in Clifton	No casualties	–
15 March 2021	Karachi	Two men on a motorcycle opened fire at a vehicle	One Chinese national and one civilian injured	–
15 July 2021	Dasu, Upper Kohistan	Suicide attack on Chinese convoy	One civilian, two FC troops, and 10 Chinese nationals killed	–
28, July 2021	Karachi	An unidentified assailant opened fire on a car transporting two Chinese nationals	One Chinese national injured	Baloch Liberation Front (BLF)
20 August 2021	Gawadar	A suicide attack targeting Chinese nationals' vehicle	One Chinese national injured and three civilians killed	–
26 April 2022	Karachi	A female suicide bomber blew herself up, targeting the van transporting Chinese nationals from Karachi University (KU) hostel to Confucius Institute	Two civilians and three Chinese nationals killed	BLA Majeed Brigade
16 May 2022	Kech	A female suicide bomber of BLA, identified as Noor Jehan, along with her accomplice, who wanted to target a Chinese convoy on the CPEC route arrested	One injured and one wounded	BLA Majeed Brigade
28 September 2022	Karachi	Unidentified gunmen killed a Chinese national, Ronald Raymond Chou, in a private dental clinic	One Chinese national killed and two injured	SRA

(Continued)

Table 2. Continued.

Date	Location	Attack type/Dynamics of attack	Causalities	Claim of responsibility
3 November 2022	Karachi	A terrorist arrested who allegedly intended to kill a Chinese doctor in Hyderabad	No casualties	SRA
3 March 2023	Kech	A military post established to protect the CPEC was attacked	No casualties	BLF
10 May 2023	Karachi	A suspected suicide bomber was shot dead by Sindh Police when he was planning to attack Chinese nationals	No casualties	–
13 August 2023	Gawadar	A convoy of Chinese workers was attacked by BLA's Majeed Brigade	No casualties	BLA

Data Source: Authors.

had called for Jihad against China, was hit by four missiles fired at a North Waziristan compound. The following month, a drone strike killed six Uzbeks from an IMU splinter organisation close to ETIM. In August 2012, two US Hellfire missiles struck Abdul Shakoor Turkistani, the head of ETIM and a member of al-Qaeda's executive council, in Shawal. According to Pakistani news sources, the armed forces neutralised dozens of anti-China militants during Operation Zarb-e-Azab.

As global power dynamics evolved and the US–China competition intensified, Pakistan also felt diplomatic pressure. In October 2020, the US delisted ETIM as a terrorist organisation and US rhetoric on China's policy in Xinjiang changed. This shift is reflected in the growing emphasis on addressing human rights violations, advocacy for Uyghur rights, and imposing economic sanctions on Chinese officials and entities allegedly involved in human rights abuses in the region. The delisting occurred concurrently with several other developments. For instance, in December 2019, the US House of Representatives passed a bill 'demanding a tougher response' from the Trump administration (Westcott & Byrd, 2019). The US Congress also passed several acts in 2020 and 2021 criticising China's policy in Xinjiang. The EU also approved the Magnitsky Act in December 2020 to place targeted sanctions on gross human rights abuses involved in Uyghur rights violations in Xinjiang (UHRP, 2023).

Notwithstanding the economic dependence and historical alignment with the West, Pakistan resisted the pressure from the Western nations to criticise China publicly. It emphasised the principle of non-interference in China's internal matters (Arab News, 2022). Former Prime Minister Imran Khan publicly debunked the reports of mass castrations and forced labour in Xinjiang (Al Jazeera, 2021). Other Pakistani leaders frequently praised the China model and emphasised bilateral cooperation. No mainstream media channel in the county reported on the 'Muslim persecution' issue in Xinjiang. A significant number of social media accounts criticised the US advocacy of Uyghurs in Xinjiang by comparing the foreign policies of China and the US. The responses from Pakistan reflected mutual trust between China and Pakistan and the strength of their bilateral relationship at both official and unofficial levels.

The declining influence of Pakistan over multiple local and regional terrorist organisations has had a significant impact on Beijing's approach, prompting a shift towards an increased reliance on direct contacts rather than heavy dependence on Pakistan, as seen in the past. Pakistan's Afghan strategy did not unfold as expected, as the Taliban's takeover of Kabul in August 2021 resulted in a major setback. This turn of events left Pakistan disheartened and disillusioned. The Afghan Taliban refused to act against anti-Pakistan groups, most notably the TTP, which had been their ally in the fight against international forces for nearly two decades.

Moreover, the Afghan Taliban expressed a desire for an independent foreign policy, including seeking improved relations with India (Baweja, 2022) further straining its ties with Pakistan. The Taliban also established contacts and discussions with countries such as the US, China, Russia, and Iran, indicating diversification of its diplomatic engagements beyond Pakistan. This diversification suggests that the Taliban is less reliant on Pakistan for its international support and legitimacy, reducing Pakistan's influence over the group's decision-making processes. The Afghan Taliban's independent stance helps it to distance itself from the perception of being solely a proxy of Pakistan. It also appeases a significant segment of Afghan society that holds Pakistan responsible for interference and aspirations of dominance.

Consequently, Pakistan increasingly depends on Chinese diplomatic initiatives to secure assurances from the Afghan Taliban. Following the devastating attack on Chinese engineers in Dasu, suspected of having been orchestrated by the TTP-ETIM nexus in collaboration with certain 'hostile agencies', the Chinese Foreign Minister, Wang Yi, hosted a high-level delegation of the Taliban. During the meeting, the Chinese Foreign Minister urged the Afghan government to take decisive action against the ETIM. In response, the Afghan Taliban provided assurances to China that they would not permit any individual or group to employ Afghan soil to launch attacks against China's interests. The Taliban have moved ETIM members out of the area immediately adjacent to the strategic Wakhan Corridor and shut down Baloch safe havens in southern Afghanistan. This diplomatic engagement showcases China's growing reliance on direct contact with the Taliban as Pakistan's leverage continues to wane. Through direct engagement with the Taliban, China also seeks to neutralise ISKP (Webber, 2022) which has emerged as a new challenge to Chinese interests in the region.

China's continuous engagement with the Taliban and participation in trilateral meetings implies a shared understanding of both sides on engaging the regime in Afghanistan. Both have also conveyed their concerns to the Taliban regime occasionally, (given China's diplomatic outreach to the Taliban, Pakistan has reportedly used Chinese officials occasionally to convey its concerns to the Taliban regime.) However, they agree on economically integrating Afghanistan, as an unstable and impoverished Afghanistan may attract violent non-state actors. Pakistan and China, Afghanistan's largest and third-largest trading partners, have welcomed the Taliban's desire to extend the CPEC into Afghanistan. In January 2023, China and Afghanistan signed a 25-year deal to drill oil from the Amu Darya basin (CGTN, 2023). The agreement also raised hopes for agreements on the extraction of minerals, including lithium and copper.

China-Afghanistan economic agreements are important for regional stability. Unlike the 1990s, it is not dependent on Pakistan to reach the Taliban regime. Taliban's economic dependence on China will likely limit the support for anti-China Pakistani militants hiding in Afghanistan. Any understanding reached between China and the Taliban regime may keep TTP from Baloch militants, who have orchestrated most anti-China, anti-CPEC terrorist attacks in recent years. Chinese efforts to limit cooperation between TTP and BLA, with the support of the Afghan Taliban, would also help Pakistan's counter-terrorism initiatives.

Conclusion

In tracing the trajectory of China–Pakistan counter-terrorism cooperation from the 1990s onward, two main conclusions emerge. Firstly, this relationship reveals a dynamic of its own, largely independent of the India factor. Contrary to certain scholarly emphasis, the India-centric perspective does not have the dominating influence that some suggest. Instead, a myriad of factors has significantly shaped bilateral counter-terrorism collaboration. These include the global context of the War on Terrorism, the implementation of the Belt and Road Initiative, the resurgence of the Taliban, and the emergence of the Islamic State Khorasan Province.

Secondly, a distinct shift in the dynamics is observed, particularly during the 1990s and the subsequent decade marked by the War on Terror. Beijing, during this period, relied on Pakistan to secure cooperation from the Afghan Taliban against anti-China militants. However, the dynamics have evolved, with the current scenario witnessing a reversal. Pakistan now looks to Beijing not only for support but also to leverage its influence with Kabul, aiming to prevent safe havens for groups antagonistic to Pakistan, including the TTP and Baloch rebels.

This shift raises questions about the viability of Chinese-funded developmental projects in Pakistan. The increasing number of attacks against Chinese targets inside Pakistan may increasingly expose the relations to some new challenges. As these developments unfold, the narrative of their counter-terrorism cooperation takes on a more complex and multifaceted dimension, reflecting the need for examining how the evolving geopolitical landscape and mega developmental projects such as BRI impact terrorist ideology and target selection in the region.

Disclosure statement

No potential conflict of interest was reported by the author(s).

References

Adil, H. (2023, May 8). At the SCO summit, India, and Pakistan squabble over Kashmir, 'terrorism'. *Aljazeera English*. Retrieved from https://www.aljazeera.com/news/2023/5/8/at-sco-summit-india-pakistan-squabble-over-kashmir-terrorism

Ahmed, Z. (2020, May). China-Pakistan: A journey of friendship (1950–2020). *Global Times*. Retrieved from https://www.globaltimes.cn/content/1189007.shtml

Ali, G. (2017). *China-Pakistan relations: A historical analysis*. Oxford University Press, Karachi.

Basit, S. H. (2019). Terrorizing the CPEC: Managing transnational militancy in China–Pakistan relations. *The Pacific Review*, 32(4), 694–724. doi:10.1080/09512748.2018.1516694

Baweja, H. (2022, August). Taliban government wants to have positive ties with India, says Suhail Shaheen. *Times of India*. Retrieved from https://timesofindia.indiatimes.com/india/taliban-government-wants-to-have-positive-ties-with-india-says-suhail-shaheen/articleshow/93548302.cms/

Biberman, Y., Schwartz, J., & Zahid, F. (2023). China's security strategy in Pakistan: Lessons for Washington. *Asian Security*, 19(1), 43–58. doi:10.1080/14799855.2023.2176224

Bokhari, F., & Stacey, K. (2018, February). China Woos Pakistan, Militants to secure belt and road projects. *Financial Times*. Retrieved from https://www.ft.com/content/063ce350-1099-11e8-8cb6-b9ccc4c4dbbb

Boni, F. (2019). *Sino-Pakistani relations: Politics, military and regional dynamics*. Routledge, Abingdon.

Castets, R. (2003). The Uyghurs in Xinjiang–The Malaise Grows. After September 11th 2001, the Chinese regime strove to include its repression of Uyghur opposition within the international dynamic of the struggle against Islamic terrorist networks. *China Perspectives*, *2003*(49). doi:10.4000/chinaperspectives.648

Chief of Army Staff Reheel Sharif's visit to China. (2014, June). *ISPR*. Retrieved from https://ispr.gov.pk/press-release-detail?id=2563

China, Afghanistan sign an oil extraction contract. (2023, January). *CGTN*. Retrieved from https://news.cgtn.com/news/2023-01-06/China-Afghanistan-sign-oil-extraction-deal-1gntb6PHJNm/index.html

Chung, C. P. (2002). China's "war on terror": September 11 and Uighur separatism. *Foreign Affairs*, *81*, 8–12. doi:10.2307/20033235 Retrieved from https://www.jstor.org/stable/pdf/20033235.pdf

Dawn. (2003, November 4). Pakistan China signed eight accords: Defence industrial cooperation, preferential trade included, November). *The Dawn*. Retrieved from https://www.dawn.com/news/123203/pakistan-china-sign-8-accords-defence-industrial-cooperation-preferential-trade-included.

Duchâtel, M. (2011). The terrorist risk and China's policy toward Pakistan: Strategic reassurance and the 'United Front'. *Journal of Contemporary China*, *20*(71), 543–561. doi:10.1080/10670564.2011.587158

Fayaz, S. (2012). China's Xinjiang Problem and Pakistan. *The Dialogue*, *7*(3), 235–254. Retrieved from https://www.qurtuba.edu.pk/thedialogue/The%20Dialogue/7_3/Dialogue_July_September2012_235-254.pdf

Global Terrorism Database. (2024, February 7). Retrieved from https://www.start.umd.edu/gtd/search/Results.aspx?start_yearonly=1990&end_yearonly=2000&start_year=&start_month=&tart_day=&end_year=&end_month=&end_day=&asmSelect0=&country=44&asmSelect1=&dtp2=all&success=yes&casualties_type=b&casualties_max= .

Haider, Z. (2005). Sino-Pakistan relations and Xinjiang's Uighurs: Politics, trade, and Islam along the Karakoram highway. *Asian Survey*, *45*(4), 522–545. doi:10.1525/as.2005.45.4.522

International Responses to the Uyghur Crisis. (2023, June). *UHRP*. Retrieved from https://uhrp.org/responses/

Jize, Q., & Yang, A. (2010, July). China, Pakistan holding joint military exercises. *China Daily*. Retrieved from https://www.chinadaily.com.cn/china/2010-07/03/content_10054204.htm

Kaiman, J. (2013). Islamist group claims responsibility for attack on China's Tiananmen Square. *The Guardian*. Retrieved from https://www.theguardian.com/world/2013/nov/25/islamist-china-tiananmen-beijing-attack

Karachi airport: Islamic Movement of Uzbekistan claims attack. (2014, June). *BBC*. Retrieved from https://www.bbc.com/news/world-asia-27790892

Lalwani, S. P.(2023). A Threshold Alliance: The China-Pakistan Military Relationship. USIP. Retrieved from: https://www.usip.org/publications/2023/03/threshold-alliance-china-pakistan-military-relationship.

Mehmood, S. (2005, April). Pakistan China sign accord. *The New York Times*. Retrieved from https://www.nytimes.com/2005/04/07/world/asia/pakistan-and-china-sign-accord.html

Mehsud, S., & Golovnina, M. (2014, March 14). From his Pakistan hideout, Uighur leader vows revenge on China. *Reuters*. https://www.reuters.com/article/us-pakistan-uighurs-idUSBREA2D0PF20140314

Moreau, R. (2010). Pakistan is the world's most dangerous country. *The Newsweek*. Retrieved from https://www.newsweek.com/pakistan-worlds-most-dangerous-country-72033

Pakistan mentions the principle of non-interference while responding to UN report on the Uyghur community. (2022, June). *Arab News*. Retrieved from https://arab.news/gyasf

Pakistan says "almost all" Uighur militants eliminated. (2015, September). *Reuters*. Retrieved from https://www.reuters.com/article/china-pakistan-idINKCN0R20DB20150902

Pakistan's Khan backs China on Uighurs, praises one-party system. (2021, July). *Aljazeera*. Retrieved from https://www.aljazeera.com/news/2021/7/2/pakistan-imran-khan-china-uighurs

Pakistan to pay USD 11.6 mn in compensation to 36 Chinese victims of hydropower project terror attack. (2022, June). *The Economic Times*. Retrieved from https://economictimes.indiatimes.com/news/international/world-news/pakistan-to-pay-usd 11-6-mn-in-compensation-to-36-chinese-victims-of-hydropower-project-terror attack/articleshow/93214131.cms?from=mdr

Rajagopalan, M. (2013). China security chief blames Uighur Islamists for Tiananmen attack. *Reuters*. Retrieved from https://www.reuters.com/article/uk-china-tiananmen-idUKBRE9A003J20131101

Small, A. (2015). *The China Pakistan axis: Asia's new geopolitics*. Random House, Gurugram.

The separatist leader handed over to China. (2002, May). *The Dawn*. Retrieved from https://www.dawn.com/news/37943/separatist-leader-handed-over-to-china

Wayne, M. I. (2007). *China's war on terrorism: Counter-insurgency, politics and internal security*. Routledge, New York.

Webber, L. (2022, June). Islamic State in Afghanistan promises attacks on Chinese and Iranian cities, threatens Uzbekistan and Tajikistan. *Militant Wire*. Retrieved from https://www.militantwire.com/p/islamic-state-in-afghanistan-promises

Westcott, B., & Byrd, H. (2019, December). US House passes Uyghur Act calling for tough sanctions on Beijing over Xinjiang camps. *CNN*. Retrieved from https://edition.cnn.com/2019/12/03/politics/us-xinjiang-bill-trump-intl-hnk/index.html

Xu, B., Fletcher, H., & Bajoria, J. (2014). The East Turkestan Islamic Movement (ETIM). *Council on Foreign Relations, 4*. Retrieved from https://www.cfr.org/backgrounder/east-turkestan-islamic-movement-etim

An Indonesian way of P/CVE and interpreting the whole-of-society approach: lessons from civil society organisations

Chaula Rininta Anindya

ABSTRACT
In 2016, The United Nations (UN) issued the Plan of Action to Prevent Violent Extremism that prescribes member states to adopt a National Action Plan (NAP) to combat violent extremism through whole-of-government and whole-of-society approaches. A key aspect of the whole-of-society approach is to involve civil society organisations (CSOs). The collapse of the New Order regime in Indonesia, coupled with shifting global focus to P/CVE agendas, granted them wide latitude to pursue their objectives and the right environment to flourish. However, the mushrooming of P/CVE CSOs in Indonesia exposes the country to challenges such as uncoordinated programmes and competition. This article argues that these experiences prompted Indonesia to interpret the concept of the whole-of-society approach and to formulate a common NAP for relevant stakeholders to refer to. The NAP provides an official categorisation to assess the implementation of P/CVE programmes and identify required interventions. It also encourages all relevant stakeholders in the field to develop a unified database and a formal working mechanism among them. The availability of such regulations and mechanisms is critical to enhancing the impact of P/CVE initiatives, including the contributions of CSOs.

Introduction

In 2021, President Joko 'Jokowi' Widodo issued Presidential Regulation (*Peraturan Presiden* or *Perpres*) No. 7/2021 on the National Action Plan (NAP) on Preventing and Countering Violent Extremism (P/CVE). This regulation aligns with the United Nations (UN)'s Plan of Action on Preventing Violent Extremism (2016) which urges member states to formulate their respective NAPs. A fundamental element of NAP as formulated by the UN is the involvement of both governmental and non-governmental entities in P/CVE, also known as the whole-of-government and whole-of-society approach.

To implement the whole-of-society approach, the role of civil society organisations (CSOs) is indispensable. In Indonesia, experienced CSOs on P/CVE issues have been conducting a wide range of programmes, including the creation of a peace education module, and assisting in the reintegration of former terrorist inmates into society (Anindya, 2019; Barton, Vergani, & Wahid, 2022; Sumpter, 2017). These organisations play a role in filling the gaps in the government's own P/CVE initiatives through their wide-ranging activities. Furthermore, Indonesian CSOs have gained regional recognition; a 2018 study on P/CVE CSOs in Southeast Asia highlighted that Indonesian CSOs are far more established and have a vast network of partners to support their programmes compared to their Southeast Asian counterparts (Goodhardt, Vergani, Barton, & Kruber, 2022).

Interest in studying P/CVE CSOs in Indonesia is growing with a primary focus on understanding their contributions to P/CVE efforts. Sumpter (2017), for instance, discusses the tailored approach of CSOs, addressing gaps in the government's policy and programmes. Despite the valuable initiatives undertaken by CSOs, the Indonesian government failed to actively engage them, opting for a top-down approach instead (Sumpter, 2017). The most recent study conducted by Barton et al. (2022) discusses a wide range of CSOs' programmes, providing insights into their success and limitations. There is also intriguing research on the 'colonial-isation' of CSOs by foreign funders. While CSOs recognise that their programmes would be mutually beneficial for both themselves and the funders, they only have limited knowledge of how their contributions are utilised by the funders (Ilyas, 2021). It demonstrates the intricate relationships between CSOs and their foreign partners, considering the CSOs' heavy reliance on foreign funding to maintain their organisations. Conversely, discussions on the enabling environment and factors that lead to the emergence of P/CVE CSOs in Indonesia remain relatively sparse. Understanding them is critical to gaining insight into current developments and initiatives.

There are various dynamics of localising or interpreting global narratives to fit the Indonesian context. Localisation refers to the process of adapting foreign ideas to fit into local practices or beliefs (Acharya, 2004). This article will delve into the process of interpreting the whole-of-society approach through experience. Therefore, this article will address the following questions: How did P/CVE CSOs emerge in Indonesia? What are the necessary conditions to augment the impact of the whole-of-society approach? The article will first examine the earlier dynamics of P/CVE initiatives in Indonesia and subsequently assess the latest efforts to enhance the initiatives.

Context: Indonesia's counterterrorism landscape

The 2002 Bali Bombings[1] changed the counterterrorism landscape in Indonesia in at least two ways. First, the attack carried out by Jemaah Islamiyah (JI) prompted the Indonesian government to swiftly adopt Law No. 15/2003 on Terrorism, as a legal basis to act against terrorism. This law empowers security forces to arrest the perpetrators of the Bali Bombing, as well as hunt down suspected individuals associated with radical extremist groups, among others. The primary focus, both nationally and internationally, was to capture the individuals behind the attack. Second, the 2002 Bali Bombings prompted Indonesia to develop counterterrorism capabilities. The Indonesian National Police (Kepolisian Negara Republik Indonesia or Polri), the forefront of Indonesia's counterterrorism initiatives, received substantial funding assistance and training from foreign partners, notably the United States through President Bush's Global War on Terrorism (GWOT) campaign and Australia.[2] The assistance was consequential in the establishment of Polri's special counterterrorism unit known as Detachment 88 (Densus 88) in 2003. With this external support, Detachment 88 excels in honing its counterterrorism skills and successfully arrests hundreds of terrorist suspects each year.

In 2010, President Susilo Bambang Yudhoyono (2004-2014) established the National Counterterrorism Agency (Badan Nasional Penanggulangan Terorisme or BNPT) which serves as the coordinating body of Indonesia's counterterrorism efforts. Before its establishment as an agency in 2010, BNPT operated as a counterterrorism desk under the Coordinating Ministry of Political, Legal, and Security Affairs (Kementerian Koordinator Bidang Politik, Hukum, dan Keamanan or Kemenkopolhukam). Its ascension as a separate agency was the result of the discovery of a terrorist plot to assassinate President Yudhoyono.[3] The government argued that such an agency was essential to coordinate Indonesia's counterterrorism efforts, which involve a myriad of law enforcement and security agencies – including the police, military, and state prosecutors offices, among others. BNPT, however, was established under a Presidential Regulation (Peraturan Presiden or Perpres), which provides a weaker legal foundation to serve as the basis of its primary function as a coordinator for other state agencies, including the ministries that were established under a more robust law (Undang-Undang or UU). The establishment of BNPT was also seen as a means to accommodate the military's involvement in counterterrorism policy. Notably, a person of active military background has always held the position of Deputy I Prevention, Protection, and Deradicalisation (Haripin, Anindya, & Priamarizki, 2020).

Terrorism challenges in Indonesia are continuously evolving, with the emergence of the Islamic State (IS) posing a new challenge. Indonesia must address a myriad of new issues, including the scattered terrorist networks, the ever-increasing trend of women and children as perpetrators of terrorist attacks, and the issues of returnees and deportees.[4] Following the 2016 Thamrin Attack perpetrated by IS-affiliated individuals, the Indonesian government saw fit to begin the process of amending the Law on Terrorism given its insufficiency in dealing with the contemporary challenges. The amendment process took roughly two years to complete due to disagreement on various clauses, such as the involvement of the Indonesian Armed Forces (Tentara Nasional Indonesia or TNI) and the definition of terrorism. An important milestone prompting lawmakers to expedite the process took place following the 2018 East Java Bombings, where Indonesia witnessed the involvement of entire family members, including women and children in terror attacks.[5] In response to the attack, Law No. 5/2018 was ratified to further enhance the security apparatus' power. This law grants Detachment 88 the authority to arrest individuals affiliated with the proscribed terrorist organisations[6] and those conspiring to carry out terror attacks. Furthermore, it also entrenches BNPT's status as the leading coordinating body for counterterrorism efforts in Indonesia.

The law may deter aspiring terrorists from initiating attacks, but it does not fully eradicate terrorism threats. As the influence of IS begins to wane, JI once again comes into the spotlight. JI gradually shifts its strategy to maintain its survival by infiltrating formal political organisations, engaging in legal business to finance its organisation, and exploiting charity organisations as a guise for its activities (Chew, 2023). Addressing these challenges over the long term requires immediate, comprehensive, and multistakeholder efforts.

Methodology

This research employs qualitative research, employing elite interview methodology and literature reviews. I conducted interviews with relevant stakeholders in Indonesia's P/

CVE; CSO activists, government officials, and scholars from the relevant field. The interview with the government officials mainly targeted the staff of BNPT. I also interviewed CSO activists who were involved in the formulation process of Indonesia's NAP and have conducted various P/CVE programmes, both at national and regional levels. Lastly, I also interviewed scholars who have been observing Indonesia's P/CVE programmes and are engaged in the formulation process of P/CVE policies.

The interviewees were informed in advance about the nature of the interview and the expected outcome of the research; to publish it as a journal article and thesis. They were asked for verbal consent to participate in the research. The interviews were partially transcribed which will be shown in this article through quotations. Due to the sensitive nature of the information given by the interviewees, most of their names will be identified with general identifications, such as staff, CSO activists, or researchers. The length of the interview ranged between 30 min to two hours. The interviewee could choose between in-person and online interviews due to the pandemic during the research period. However, this research has yet to interview relevant UN bodies and foreign aid agencies due to limited access. In the future, this research could be repolished by incorporating the donors' perspectives for a more balanced view.

The enabling environment

Understanding the socio-political conditions that enable the emergence of P/CVE CSOs is valuable to provide a better context of Indonesia. This section will discuss the complex interactions between the international community and the government. The transition to the *reformasi* (reform) era opened the floodgates of domestic factors that constructed a conducive environment for civil society to work on P/CVE issues. First, the collapse of Suharto's authoritarian New Order regime gave rise to the mushrooming of CSOs and provided ample opportunities for non-governmental entities to shape and take part in the policymaking process. The number of CSOs during the New Order and, more importantly, their role in policymaking was very limited due to the government's suppression of individuals and/or organisations who were deemed to be a 'threat'.

In the early stage of the *reformasi* era, a coalition of civil society named Propatria Working Group (Propatria WG) emerged as the leading coalition that pushed for Security Sector Reform (SSR) agenda. ProPatria WG consisted of leading experts in the field of defence and security in Indonesia. ProPatria WG had the privilege of being actively involved in the policy-making process thanks to their close relationship[7] with high-ranking government officials and military officers (Sukma, 2012). ProPatria demonstrates the importance of both expertise and networks with government officials to be successful, and as evidence that CSOs can take part in the policymaking process. This case also shows that the Indonesian government has acknowledged the role of CSOs in the policy-making process. It can be seen as an attempt to show its commitment to reform into a more democratic governance.

Second, the shifting donors' agenda and aid landscape. Before the 9/11 tragedy, the focus of foreign donors in Indonesia was to promote democratisation. Propatria WG benefitted from this focus, receiving a substantial amount of funds from the United States Agency for International Development (USAID) and other funders (Scarpello, 2014). Although Propatria received a large amount of funds from USAID, they argued that their agenda had never been driven by the interest of the funders (R. Sukma, member of ProPatria, personal communication, March 15, 2022). However, the 9/11 attacks and the 2002 Bali Bombings shifted the impetus away from democratisation to counterterrorism. Groups that previously benefitted from the initial focus on democratisation such as Propatria subsequently lost most of their funding and their influence in policymaking waned after 2004. As donors shifted the allocation of funds to counterterrorism-related projects, it paved the way for relevant CSOs in counterterrorism issues.

Third, the continuing cycle of terrorism and the policy gap. Indeed, although Detachment 88 has significantly enhanced its counterterrorism capabilities and arrested and/or eliminated numerous known/suspected terrorists, the law enforcement approach does not break the cycle of terrorism. The perpetrators of the 2009 J.W. Marriott and Ritz-Carlton Hotel Bombings and more than two dozen individuals behind the Aceh training camps (2010) were former inmates; the majority were former terrorist inmates and some were ordinary inmates who were radicalised or recruited in the prison (IPAC, 2013). These cases show that law enforcement alone is ineffective in preventing future terror attacks. The police were cognisant of this and thus came up with an ad-hoc deradicalisation programme. They gave humane treatment to selected inmates and provided necessary assistance for their families. Due to the ad-hoc nature of the programme and other constraints, the implementation was premature and limited only to certain inmates. It is not uncommon for detained and/or convicted terrorist suspects to experience torture during the investigation process. The police suggested that they did not have enough budget and human resources to carry out sustainable deradicalisation programmes (Chernov-Hwang, 2018). This underlines the need for other relevant stakeholders to jump in and provide support for rehabilitation and reintegration programme.

Lastly, the shifting global discourses towards comprehensive counterterrorism policy and a whole-of-society approach. In the aftermath of 9/11, the global discourse of counterterrorism was highly associated with the use of a hard approach that emphasised kinetic actions and law enforcement. However, the discourse was gradually replaced by Preventing and Countering Violent Extremism or P/CVE.[8] Started with the UN Global Counterterrorism in 2006 which called for the involvement of CSOs, the idea of a whole-of-government and whole-of-society approach was formally introduced through the UN Plan of Action in 2016. The Plan of Action outlines that the P/CVE strategy requires a multidisciplinary approach and should engage both the national and local stakeholders. This approach is also known as the whole-of-government and whole-of-society approach. The whole-of-society approach involves a wide range of actors, including CSOs, think tanks, universities, media, private sectors, and community leaders. This global narrative of whole-of-government and whole-of-society approach also became the trigger of the Indonesian government to engage CSOs in P/CVE initiatives.

These discussions show the inextricable link between international trends and Indonesia's domestic conditions. The conducive national socio-political environment, the rising international interests in counterterrorism and P/CVE post 9/11, and the continuing terrorism threats are some of the factors enabling P/CVE CSOs' ever-increasing relevance in Indonesia. The process leading to the emergence of P/CVE CSOs can also be analysed from the lens of localisation. A regime may frame the localisation process of global narratives to enhance their legitimacy and justification (Acharya, 2004). From the Global War on Terrorism (GWOT) to the UN's Plan of Action, there was a strong international demand for each country to work together and formulate their policy in combating terrorism. Indonesia was also pursuing democratisation and trying to convince the public it was no longer an authoritarian regime. Providing more opportunities for CSOs to voice their concerns and carry out their initiatives, allows the government to prove to the public its commitment to pursue a democratic regime. At the same time, the civil society activists could earn support from the donors and contribute to the implementation of P/CVE initiatives.

The early stage of P/CVE CSOs initiatives

This section will show a wide range of P/CVE CSOs in Indonesia and their primary focus. Many national-based P/CVE CSOs were established from 2004 to 2009, a couple of years after the 2002 Bali Bombings. The discussion in the previous section highlights that the momentum for P/CVE CSOs to gain more relevance in Indonesia's counterterrorism did not come instantaneously. Furthermore, developing P/CVE programmes requires time, an extensive learning process, and support from external funders to mature. Indeed, various CSOs operating in Indonesia drew upon P/CVE experiences in other parts of the globe to figure out suitable programmes, but they ultimately need to tailor them to fit into the Indonesian context (T. Andrie, a civil society activist, personal communication, December 23, 2021). In the early stage, the global discourses on counterterrorism emphasise a comprehensive approach but there were limited examples of how to carry out the programme. Indonesia went through its own learning process to develop P/CVE programmes for local initiatives.

In the earlier wave of 'P/CVE-sation' in Indonesia, two prominent CSOs were working on rehabilitation programmes and prison management programmes. One of the notable CSOs is an international CSO, Search for Common Ground (SFCG). SFCG established its presence in Indonesia in 2002 and has been working on tolerance and peace advocacy programmes in the country. The other was spearheaded by Noor Huda Ismail[9], a former journalist, who established the Institute for International Peace Building (Yayasan Prasasti Perdamaian or YPP) in 2008, which focuses on the implementation of a soft approach to eradicate terrorism. In 2009, the two organisations and the Directorate General of Corrections (Direktorat Jenderal Pemasyarakatan or DitjenPAS) worked on conflict management training for the inmates and prison officers. The programme aimed to encourage the participants to pursue peaceful and constructive conflict resolution through emotional management and confidence building (SFCG & DitjenPAS, 2010).

On top of rehabilitation and prison management programmes, another line of focus of CSO is on counter-radicalisation or prevention. The leading organisation in this area is the Wahid Institute (currently known as Wahid Foundation), led by Yenny Wahid, the daughter of former President Abdurrahman Wahid. Wahid Foundation (WF) was established in 2004 to address the problem of communal conflicts. WF frequently conducts surveys on radicalisation, peace, and tolerance. It also carries out programmes to promote peace and tolerance among youth, as well as countering extremist propaganda (Osman, 2014).

Unlike the majority of P/CVE CSOs in Indonesia that focus on individual terrorists and the general community, a handful of CSOs focus on the survivors of terror attacks. While many CSOs' programmes focus on the offenders, limited attention is given to the survivors of terror attacks. The survivors and their families came up with their own initiatives and established their own CSOs to advocate their rights. In 2009, the survivors and the families of survivors established the Associations of Indonesian Bombing Victims (ASKOBI). The association aims to assist the survivors and their families to receive appropriate medical treatment and compensation by lobbying the government and other relevant institutions. ASKOBI also actively campaigns in the fight against terrorism and engages youth in their campaigns (a survivor of terrorist act, personal communication, November 9, 2022).

Besides civil society, universities and scholars have also started their own research centre on P/CVE. Research centres carry out both research and rehabilitation or reintegration programmes for the inmates and their families. For instance, a university-based research centre, Universitas Indonesia's Research Center for Police Studies (PRIK) was established in 2009. This centre created initiatives involving reformed radicals in the rehabilitation programme (Wildan, 2021).

Following the early wave of P/CVE-sation, the number of P/CVE CSOs increased. Some of them were not necessarily new CSOs or research institutions, but long-established ones that expanded their agenda on P/CVE programmes, such as the International NGO Forum on Indonesia Development (INFID).[10] There are also think tanks that expanded their research scope to this issue, including The Habibie Center and CSIS Indonesia. Various wing organisations of Islamic organisations in Indonesia also take part in the P/CVE initiatives, such as the women's wing organisation of the two largest Islamic organisations in Indonesia, Fatayat of Nahdlatul Ulama and Aisyiyah of Muhammadiyah. There are also groups or individuals who established their own organisation or research centre after building a good rapport in their past organisation, such as the Division for Applied Social Psychology Research (DASPR). As for the victims, they established other organisations called The Survivors Foundation (Yayasan Penyintas Indonesia or YPI) and The Survivors Family Foundation (Yayasan Keluarga Penyintas or YKP). The list of CSOs still goes on as they are more diverse and active at both national and regional levels.

The merit and challenges

The increasing number of CSOs has both merit and challenges. Their presence fills the policy gaps by crafting initiatives on overlooked issues, such as gender mainstreaming and the rights of terror attack survivors. They also expand the outreach of P/CVE programmes. In the past few years, Indonesia has witnessed women's active role in terrorism, such as the 2018 East Java Bombings. A collaboration platform of CSOs and governmental agencies called the Working Group on Women and P/CVE (WGWC), campaigns for the issue of gender mainstreaming and active involvement of women in P/CVE initiatives. WGWC's programmes involve wives or mothers who belong to the Family Welfare and Empowerment (Pemberdayaan dan Kesejahteraan Keluarga or PKK)[11] to understand the phenomenon of radicalisation hence they could be the first identifier and responder in their family (R. Kholifah, steering committee WGWC, personal communication, July 31, 2022). This initiative can be seen as CSO's way to localise the P/CVE initiatives. They utilise the role of existing groups within the community. They seek assistance from a movement that has been a part of society for decades to reduce resistance from society. Meanwhile, for a specific group, DASPR has developed the Resilience Program for Families (the Resilience Program for Families of Terrorism-Related Convicts). This programme provides psychological and economic empowerment programmes for women who are family members of terrorist inmates. The programme managed to encourage them to start a small business and to change their views on other groups into a more positive perspective (DASPR, 2021).

Civil society activists also introduce a breakthrough programme to pursue peaceful dialogues between survivors and perpetrators. The Alliance for Peaceful Indonesia (Aliansi Indonesia Damai or AIDA) has been working closely with YPI. This dialogue aims to create a peaceful reconciliation between the two. It was not easy for the survivors to bring themselves to meet the perpetrators, but it shed a new perspective on peaceful resolutions once they joined the programme. In an interview, a survivor claimed:

> When I met him [the perpetrator], I was very angry and could not control my emotions. I thought I could just ignore him, but we had an intensive one-week programme. I was very angry when he bragged about his involvement in the attack. He expressed his remorse after listening to all my anger. It took me one year to realise that my anger would not change anything. I asked AIDA to facilitate another meeting with him. I told him that I was sorry for being so emotional toward him. I felt relieved after talking to him. (A terrorist attack survivor, November 9, 2022)

The presence of CSOs also helped the government to reach out to individuals who have yet to be exposed to the government's programmes. Due to limited human resources and the vast geography of Indonesia, CSOs offer an extra pair of hands to handle those individuals. Local-based CSOs can provide intensive programme for targeted recipients. A leading example is the Peace Circle Foundation (Yayasan Lingkar Perdamaian or YLP) founded by Ali Fauzi Manzi, the youngest brother of the Bali Bombing perpetrators. His foundation is in Lamongan, East Java where there are many former terrorist inmates and their families. This strategic location is an advantage for his foundation to provide an intensive reintegration programme for the former inmates and their families.

Nonetheless, there were various obstacles to managing all CSOs' initiatives. First, the absence of a clear coordination mechanism among relevant stakeholders. BNPT who was supposed to be the coordinating body could not perform its role well. The lack of a communication platform among stakeholders led to duplication of programmes, undermining their effectiveness (Amali & Nurhasanah, 2022). A case in point is the repetitive profiling process by various stakeholders, including CSOs and research institutions. This repetitive process allowed the inmates to study each question and answer what they deemed appropriate for the interviewers (DASPR, 2018). Lack of coordination among the donor countries also undermines the effectiveness of the programmes. Personal communication was the only means to avoid duplication of programmes. CSO activists shared their experience and views on the problems of coordination:

> I was the advisor for two organisations who wanted to assist the regional governments. When the first organisation came to me, they told me that they wanted to do their project in East Java and West Java. The second organisation also came to me and told me that they would cover Central Java and West Java. Then, I told the second organisation to switch the area from West Java to other regions. They received funding from two different countries, Australia and the US. There was no coordination among these two organisations and the donors. (A civil society activist, October 17, 2022)

> Ideally, the donor should have had meetings together. However, the 'sectoral ego' among donors hinders them from doing so. A simple example would be the administrative

procedure for minutes of handover [Berita Acara Serah Terima or BAST]. When USAID and the Australian Department of Foreign Affairs Trade (DFAT) worked together on a project, they questioned who should be written on the BAST or to whom the BAST belongs. (A civil society activist, October 26, 2022)

Second, the competing interest among CSOs. The foreign donor is the main source of funding for P/CVE CSOs. The CSOs need to build their reputation and earn credit for their work. Many CSOs tend to work in a region they are more familiar with, thus they can produce a better result (a civil society activist, October 17, 2022). The absence of coordination and proper work distribution led to competition among CSOs. Some of them express their frustration over unhealthy competition and domination by certain CSOs:

When I returned from an international conference, I got a phone call from BNPT who requested a meeting with me. It seems that the head of BNPT was angry to receive a report from this lady [another CSO who attended the conference]. She reported that, in my speech, I did not thank our country for their support. (A terror attack survivor, November 9, 2022).

I do not like the way the collaboration platform [a platform run by CSOs] operates. The activities are in the name of the platform but the one who benefits the most is the organisations that is run by one of the steering committees of the platform. Those organisations will receive both the money and the credit for the work done. (A civil society activist, October 21, 2022).

Without a firm coordinating body, such competition is inevitable. CSOs are pivotal in assisting the country to conduct P/CVE initiatives but these problems show that the government should take action to augment the impact of P/CVE CSOs. There is an urgent need for a coordinating body that could map out the initiatives and the expertise of CSOs, so that the government could link them up with the donors.

This article does not aim to downplay the work of CSOs nor suggest that the number of CSOs should be decreased. Indonesia faces a complex challenge of terrorism threats in the country. There is a wide range of issues that should be handled and a large number of individuals and communities that should be taken care of. The increasing number of CSOs will be more beneficial to the country if there is proper coordination that could distribute the resources of CSOs across the country.

The Indonesian way: RAN-PE and I-KHUB

The international call for NAP on P/CVE and the past coordination problem encouraged Indonesia to formulate its own NAP that fits into the Indonesian context. The UN facilitated a workshop for Indonesia and other countries to prepare the NAP where each country shared their experiences in developing NAP (UNODC, 2017). The process of formulation started back in 2017 and BNPT worked closely with WF in engaging other CSOs. The involvement of CSOs in the drafting process marked a significant development of CSOs' role in P/CVE. The Indonesian government formally acknowledges their role.[12] The final product of NAP was issued in 2021 through Perpres No. 7/2021 on Rancangan Aksi Nasional Pencegahan dan Penanggulangan Ekstremisme Berbasis Kekerasan yang Mengarah pada Terorisme or known as RAN PE. RAN PE consists of three pillars: (1) Pillar 1: prevention (preparedness, counter radicalisation, and deradicalisation); (2) Pillar 2: law enforcement, witness and victims' protections, and enforcement of national regulations; (3) Pillar 3: International partnership (Table 1).

Table 1. The Pillar and Focus of Programme of RAN-PE.

Pillar	Aspects	Focus of Programmes
Pillar 1	Preparedness	• Supporting data • Stakeholders' awareness and capabilities • Child and youth resilience • Enhancing the effectiveness of securing critical infrastructure
	Counter-radicalisation	• Effectiveness of campaign • Resilience of vulnerable communities
	Deradicalisation	• In-prison deradicalisation • Out-of-prison deradicalisation
Pillar 2	Law Enforcement	• Coordination of law enforcement agencies • Capacity of law enforcement agencies
	Protection of Witnesses and Victims	• Protection of witnesses and victims
	Empowerment of the National Legislation Framework	• Synchronisation of national and international legal frameworks • Harmonisation of relevant national legislation and/or regulations
Pillar 3	Partnership	• Supporting partnerships among stakeholders
	International Collaboration	• Enhancing international cooperation

Source: K-HUB & Laboratorium Psikologi Politik UI (2023)

This framework enables the country to identify relevant stakeholders and map out the distribution of programmes. Two leading studies by CSOs mapped the initiatives based on RAN-PE's categorisation; INFID and Knowledge Hub (K-HUB). INFID (2020) refers to the earlier draft of NAP as a framework for assessing 144 CSOs' programmes from 2014 to 2019. Within the draft, the protection of witnesses and victims had not been incorporated which resulted in the lack of assessment of the programme for victims and survivors. INFID's research indicates a high percentage of programmes on Pillar I (74,3%), followed by Pillar 2 (16%), and Pillar 3 (9,7%). This report is useful for identifying the challenges to carrying out P/CVE programmes. Although Pillar 1 is the highest among all, deradicalisation programmes only made up 9,35% of the whole programmes in Pillar 1. It was due to the resistance of highly radicalised inmates and the sensitivity of the issue, limiting CSOs' engagement. Due to security concerns, CSOs have very limited access to the inmates unless there is support from relevant authorities (INFID, 2020).

A more recent and comprehensive study was conducted by K-HUB Team (a database platform for P/CVE CSO initiatives, developed by Peace Generation (PeaceGen)) and the Political Psychology Laboratory of Universitas Indonesia. This research was based on programmes of 81 CSOs. The study refers to the final version of RAN-PE. It finds a similar trend of high concentration on Pillar 1 (84,6%), followed by Pillar 2 (11,6%) and Pillar 3 (3,79%). Deradicalisation programmes are also the lowest among Pillar 1 (6,3%). The report suggests there is no programme to develop an appropriate method for handling juvenile terrorism offenders. Access to juvenile inmates, who are also terrorism offenders, is delicate. CSOs cannot work on this matter alone and should be supported by relevant governmental agencies, such as Ministry of Law and Human Rights (Kementerian Hukum dan HAM or Kemenkumham) and Ministry of Women Empowerment and Child Protection (Kementerian Pemberdayaan Perempuan dan Perlindungan Anak or KemenPPPA) (K-HUB & Laboratorium Psikologi Politik UI, 2023). Another important finding from this research is the limited programme on the protection of victims and witnesses. The research only found five programmes under this category and only five CSOs working on this issue (K-HUB & Laboratorium Psikologi Politik UI, 2023). This finding echoes the concern of survivors that P/CVE programmes in Indonesia tend to be offender-oriented instead of survivor-oriented (a terrorist attack survivor, November 9, 2022). This mapping helps relevant stakeholders to identify what is lacking and with whom partnerships should be established.

Besides the types of programmes, the mapping is also useful for identifying the area distribution. K-HUB finds a high concentration of programmes in Java. 252 out of 330 (76%) programmes are carried out in Java, particularly West Java (K-HUB, 2023). One of the reasons why CSO programmes are highly concentrated in Java Island is due to the focus of funders. The funders tend to focus on provinces in Java Island (a civil society activist, October 26, 2022). This mapping will be useful as a backgrounder for donors and CSOs to consider expanding their projects to other regions. Terrorist activities are not only in Java and for the past three years the hotspot has shifted from Java to Sumatera. Yet, there is very limited CSOs engagement in Sumatera (Pokja Tematis RAN PE, 2023).

To support the implementation of RAN-PE, the Indonesian government is developing the Indonesia Knowledge Hub or I-KHUB. One of the points of RAN-PE emphasises the creation of an integrated database of P/CVE initiatives. BNPT aspires to create a digital platform called Indonesia Knowledge Hub or I-KHUB which was formally launched in October 2020 (BNPT, 2020). The catalyst of I-KHUB is to create an accessible and comprehensive database to address the problems of coordination and competition. BNPT realises that not all CSOs have access to funders. Also, discrepancies exist between the donors' initiatives and the government's agenda. I-KHUB attempts to provide information for the funders on the required assistance to fulfil the Indonesian government's agenda and relevant CSOs that they can contact to work with based on the CSOs' expertise (BNPT staff, personal communication, March 2, 2022). This effort also seeks to minimise monopoly by certain CSOs and aspires to provide more opportunities for regional-based CSOs.

I-KHUB is a government-led database initiative, meanwhile, there are also other databases created by CSOs, which are K-HUB by PeaceGen and K-HUB WGWC. Although there are various database platforms in Indonesia, these platforms do not seek to outdo each other. Instead, they aspire to support each other in creating a comprehensive database for P/CVE initiatives in Indonesia. I-KHUB focuses on the government-led P/CVE initiatives, while PeaceGen's K-HUB focuses on CSOs-led initiatives. K-HUB WGWC creates a database on P/CVE programmes focusing on gender mainstreaming issues. In addition, there are also other databases created by research institutions, such as the Center for Detention Studies (CDS)' database on terrorists and the incidents based on trial documents.

I-KHUB will serve as a collaborative platform for governmental and non-governmental agencies. Compiling comprehensive information is taxing and cannot be done by one agency. The other knowledge hub and database systems will complement I-KHUB database. PeaceGen has been assisting BNPT to develop I-KHUB through its experience in developing K-HUB on P/CVE initiatives by CSOs. A prototype of a collaborative database was a partnership between I-KHUB and CDS in 2021. CDS created geospatial data on terrorist activities based on court documents (I-KHUB Team, personal communication, February 2, 2023). This partnership is reciprocal for both; CDS could gain access from the Supreme Court (Mahkamah Agung) with the assistance of BNPT, while BNPT could earn data and analysis from CDS (Aranoval, 2022).

By the time of writing this article, I-KHUB's website is far from perfect. The data is incomplete, and the website is hard to navigate. The I-KHUB Team suggests that collecting information from relevant stakeholders remains an obstacle due to the lack of awareness of the importance of digital databases. BNPT seeks to enforce the submission of the database from the stakeholders by requiring each agency to create an account to report the implementation of NAP P/CVE (I-KHUB Team, personal communication, February 2, 2023). For the past few years, I-KHUB also published policy analysis documents on NAP P/CVE and I-KHUB to provide information for the stakeholders about the merit of an integrated database. Polishing I-KHUB to become an ideal integrated database platform is still a long way to go. It requires a step-by-step approach to convince relevant stakeholders to fully take part in this initiative. Despite the existing flaws, I-KHUB would be useful in the future to map out P/CVE initiatives in Indonesia.

Closing and policy lessons

Starting from an unfamiliar idea of a whole-of-society approach, P/CVE CSOs in Indonesia initiated their work individually or through small collaborations. The supporting socio-political conditions of Indonesia at the beginning of the *reformasi era* enabled CSOs to show their significance. The government gave the freedom for CSOs to carry out their activities, but no formal working mechanism between them. When the number of players increases, the conditions on the ground become more complicated. At the same time, there is a wide range of issues that should be addressed. It took years of trial-and-error to realise what should be done to formulate suitable programmes for the country and to augment the impact.

The obstacles to implementing programmes, the socio-political dynamics, and the evolving threat shape the 'Indonesian way' of interpreting the call for a whole-of-society approach and engagement of CSOs. Those conditions pushed Indonesia to formulate its NAP. Indonesia's NAP is relatively new, and it is too early to judge its effectiveness. But it is a remarkable progress from a messy beginning. Each country has its own way of interpreting the whole-of-society approach, yet the lessons from Indonesia's experience may be useful as a reference for other countries to develop their NAP (Figure 1).

Based on this article's discussions, there are three important takeaways on the importance of NAP in supporting CSOs' initiatives. First, NAP provides opportunities to nurture coordination between agencies. NAP is relatively new; it may be folly to assume that it has fully eliminated the clash of interests. However, the creation of RAN-PE has led to other initiatives, such as the Thematic Working Group. It provides a formal coordination and meeting platform between the CSOs and governmental agencies to regularly assess the implementation of RAN-PE. This platform allows relevant stakeholders to learn about other programmes and report their programmes for future assessment.

Second, identifying necessary interventions based on an official categorisation. The classification will ease the mapping process. Through the mapping process, relevant stakeholders can discover which areas are still lacking and need more support. The number

Figure 1. P/CVE Efforts with and Without NAP.
Source: Author.

of CSOs is increasing but most of their expertise is on Pillar 1 which also requires a vast engagement in a vast country like Indonesia. The mapping can be utilised as a basis to develop training programmes for other CSOs, including the region-based CSOs. They are the closest stakeholders to the targeted recipients which will ensure the sustainability of the programme and ease the monitoring systems.

Third, the importance of collaborative initiatives between CSOs and governmental agencies. There are targets of programmes that have not been fulfilled or that lack engagement. Lack of authority hinders CSOs to further their engagement in those areas. For instance, law enforcement is the area where CSOs cannot further intervene without access from the government (K-HUB & Laboratorium Psikologi Politik UI, 2023). The government may be hesitant to grant full access to CSOs due to security concerns. Nonetheless, the government can make use of CSOs' research capabilities to prepare necessary documents for the programmes or to assess the programmes. The government may have too many things on its hands thus experienced CSOs will be valuable partners in reducing the burden.

Notes

1. In 2002, Jemaah Islamiyah (JI) launched a terror attack against a club and a bar in Bali, Indonesia. A total of 202 people died, including 88 Australians. JI is also responsible for various terror attacks in Indonesia in the early 2000s.
2. Prior to 1998, the Indonesian Armed Forces (Tentara Nasional Indonesia or TNI) was at the forefront of Indonesia's counterterrorism effort. However, the collapse of the authoritarian regime and the transition to the *reformasi* (reform) era forced the military to give up its internal security role. During the authoritarian regime, the military was notorious for its repressive measures through its internal security role. Subsequently, the internal security role was passed to the police and the military only served as an Auxiliary Force (Bantuan Kendali Operasi or BKO) to the police (see Honna, 2013; Haripin et al., 2020).
3. The idea to establish a new counterterrorism agency initially began during the formulation process of the bill on terrorism in early 2000s. The proposal was dropped due to criticism from the civil society activists who suggested that such agencies may become an oppressive tool of the government. At that time, Indonesia had just transitioned from an authoritarian regime to the *reformasi* (reform) era, hence the fear of oppression. However, the government proceeded with the proposal after the 2002 Bali Bombing. Instead of a new body or agency,

President Megawati established a counterterrorism desk under the Coordinating Ministry of Political, Legal, and Security Affairs led by Susilo Bambang Yudhoyono. A high-ranking police officer, Ansyaad Mbai, was appointed as the head of the desk.
4. The Syrian Civil War and the Islamic State (IS) propaganda lured many aspiring jihadis to emigrate to Syria. The individuals who have spent their time in Syria and returned to Indonesia are identified as returnees. Meanwhile, the individuals who were unable to enter Syria and were deported back to Indonesia before doing so are identified as deportees. Deportees also include individuals who were exposed to radical ideologies while they were overseas and deported to Indonesia (see Anindya, 2019; Sumper, 2018).
5. In May 2018, two families detonated bombs in East Java. The first attack targeted three churches, while the second attack targeted a police headquarters. The perpetrators of the church bombings, Dita Oepriarto and his family, were initially under police surveillance. However, the family blended well into society to deceive the security apparatus (see IPAC, 2018).
6. The Indonesian government officially banned Jemaah Islamiyah (JI) in 2008 and Jemaah Ansharut Daulah (JAD), the umbrella organisation of IS-symphatisers in Indonesia, in 2018.
7. ProPatria members have established track records in the country's defence and security field since before the beginning of the *reformasi* era in 1998. They were engaged in the education programme of the Military Command and Staff College (Sesko). The members also established vast networks in the defence and security fields, including prominent military officers and other defence and security related institutions. Some of them are also relatives of high ranking military officers which helped them to build trust with the military (see Sukma, 2012; E. Prasetyono, member of ProPatria, personal communication, February 25, 2022).
8. P/CVE programmes originated as early as 2003 in Europe. The United Kingdom started its own strategy, CONTEST which outlines the four 'Ps': pursue, prevent, protect, prepare. The CONTEST strategy was developed over time and the incident of the 2005 London Bombing further shaped the focus of the strategy. The strategy emphasises a community-based approach that engages local stakeholders to prevent an individual from joining and supporting terrorist organisations. Other Western countries followed suit by acknowledging the importance of a comprehensive approach in eliminating terrorist threats but had yet to conceptualise the programme of P/CVE as early as the UK did. From 2005 to 2006, for instance, American and Australian policymakers underlined the link between poverty and terrorism, hence focus shifted to aid allocation. The scope of recipients expanded to other relevant agencies which worked on developmental issues (see Howell & Lind, 2009; Harris-Hogan, Barelle, & Zammit, 2016; Mastroe, 2016; Ucko, 2018).
9. Noor Huda Ismail is a Pesantren (Islamic boarding school) Ngruki graduate whose former roommate was involved in the 2002 Bali Bombing.
10. During the New Order Regime, INFID was very vocal in criticising Suharto's developmental policy but in recent years the trend has shifted whereby they began working on P/CVE projects.
11. PKK was established under the New Order regime. This movement is mainly located in rural areas. It focuses on the role of women in the family. The movement was infamous as a tool of the Suharto government to control and dictate the role of women. However, the collapse of the New Order regime and the transition to the *reformasi* era gradually changed the role of PKK. It has incorporated the perspectives of gender mainstreaming in its activities. Their roles in campaigning for alternatives or improvement of policy is pivotal in enhancing the quality of the policy (see Dewi, 2023).
12. In 2022, the Indonesian government established a Thematic Working Group or Kelompok Kerja (Pokja) Tematis as a formal platform of coordination between governmental and non-governmental agencies. This working group allows the stakeholders to sit together and discuss the gaps in RAN PE's implementation (see Pokja Tematis, 2023).

Acknowledgments

The author thanks Prof. Jun Honna and Keoni Marzuki for their valuable feedback.

Disclosure statement

No potential conflict of interest was reported by the author(s).

Funding

This research was supported by the Japanese Monbukagakusho Scholarship and Ritsumeikan University.

ORCID

Chaula Rininta Anindya http://orcid.org/0000-0001-7898-7245

References

Acharya, A. (2004). How ideas spread: Whose norms matter? Norm localization and institutional change in Asian regionalism. *International Organization, 58*(2), 239–275. doi:10.1017/S0020818304582024

Amali, I., & Nurhasanah, U. (2022). *Kolaborasi dan Aksi Kolektif Masyarakat Sipil Bersama Pemerintah Dalam Upaya PE*. Retrieved from I-KHUB Commentary: https://ikhub.id/produk/kebijakandaerah/97181538.

Anindya, C. R. (2019). The deradicalisation programme for Indonesian deportees: A vacuum in coordination. *Journal for Deradicalization, 18*, 217–243.

Aranoval, M. A. (2022). *Strategi Collaborative Governance Dalam Memperkuat Penyediaan Data Kejahatan Terorisme: Praktik Baik Kerjasama CDS-BNPT*. Retrieved from I-KHUB: https://ikhub.id/produk/kebijakandaerah/51689864.

Barton, G., Vergani, M., & Wahid, Y. (2022). *Countering Violent and Hateful Extremism in Indonesia: Islam, Gender, and Civil Society*. Singapore: Palgrave Macmillan.

BNPT. (2020, October 19). *BNPT Luncurkan I-KHUB on CT/CVE, Era Baru Kolaborasi Penanggulangan Terorisme Manfaatkan Teknologi Informasi*. Retrieved from BNPT: https://www.bnpt.go.id/bnpt-luncurkan-i-khub-on-ctve-era-baru-kolaborasi-penanggulangan-terorisme-manfaatkan-teknologi-informasi.

Chernov-Hwang, J. (2018). *Why terrorists quit: The disengagement of Indonesian Jihadists*. Ithaca, New York: Cornell University Press.

Chew, A. (2023, June). JI's infiltration of state institutions in change of tactics. *Counter Terrorist Trends and Analysis, 15*(3), 10–14.

DASPR. (2018). *Kegiatan Asesmen Program-Program Deradikalisasi dalam Lembaga Pemasyarakatan*. Retrieved from DASPR: https://daspr.org/publikasi/policy-brief-kegiatan-asesmen-program-program-deradikalisasi-dalam-lembaga-pemasyarakatan/.

DASPR. (2021, February 25). *Policy Brief Program Resiliensi Keluarga Narapidana Kasus Terorisme*. Retrieved from Buletin KPIN: http://buletin.k-pin.org/index.php/daftar-artikel/791-policy-brief-program-resiliensi-keluarga-narapidana-kasus-terorisme.

Dewi, K. H. (2023). The city, PKK leaders. *Women's Empowerment. Asian Journal of Women's Studies, 29*(1), 121–135. doi:10.1080/12259276.2023.2170047

Goodhardt, D., Vergani, M., Barton, G., & Kruber, S. (2022). Capacity gap analysis of civil society organisations working against violent extremism in Indonesia and Southeast Asia. In G. Barton, M. Vergani, & Y. Wahid (Eds.), *Countering Violent and Hateful Extremism in Indonesia: Islam, Gender, and Civil Society* (pp. 279–295). Singapore: Palgrave Macmillan.

Haripin, M., Anindya, C. R., & Priamarizki, A. (2020). The politics of counter-terrorism in post-authoritarian states: Indonesia's experience, 1998–2018. *Defense & Security Analysis, 36*(3), 275–299. doi:10.1080/14751798.2020.1790807

Harris-Hogan, S., Barelle, K., & Zammit, A. (2016). What is countering violent extremism? Exploring CVE Policy and Practice in Australia. *Behavioral Sciences of Terrorism and Political Aggression, 8*(1), 6–24. doi:10.1080/19434472.2015.1104710

Honna. (2013). Security challenges and military reform in post-authoritarian Indonesia: The impact of separatism, terrorism, and communal violence. In J. Rüland, G. Manea, & H. Born (Eds.), *The Politics of Military Reform: Experiences from Indonesia and Nigeria* (pp. 185-200). Berlin, Heidelberg: Springer.

Howell, J., & Lind, J. (2009). *Counter-Terrorism, Aid, and Civil Society: Before and After the War on Terror*. London: Palgrave Macmillan.

Ilyas, M. (2021). Decolonising the terrorism industry: Indonesia. *Social Sciences, 10*(2), 1–16. doi:10.3390/socsci10020053

INFID. (2020). *Laporan Pemetaan Program Pencegahan Ekstremisme Kekerasa: Oleh Pemerintah dan Lembaga Non-Pemerintah di Indonesia (2014-2019)*. Jakarta: INFID.

Institute for Policy Analysis of Conflict [IPAC]. (2013). *Prison Problems: Planned and Unplanned Releases of Convicted Extremists in Indonesia*. Jakarta: Institute for Policy Analysis of Conflict.

Institute for Policy Analysis of Conflict [IPAC]. (2018). *The Surabaya Bombings and The Future of ISIS in Indonesia*. Jakarta: Institute for Policy Analysis of Conflict.

Kelompok Kerja Tematis RAN-PE [Pokja Tematis RAN-PE]. (2023). *Laporan Kelompok Kerja Tematis RAN PE Tahun 2022*. Jakarta: Kelompok Kerja Tematis.

K-HUB. (2023). *K-HUB P/CVE Outlook #1 Melacak Dampak Organisasi Masyarakat Sipil (OMS) PCVE di Indonesia*. Retrieved from K-HUB: https://khub.id/outlook/melacakdampak.

K-HUB, & Laboratorium Psikologi Politik UI. (2023). *K-HUB P/CVE Outlook #1, Melacak Dampak Organisasi Masyarakat Sipil (OMS) PCVE di Indonesia*. Jakarta: K-HUB.

Mastroe, C. (2016). Evaluating CVE: Understanding the recent changes to the United Kingdom's implementation of prevent. *Perspectives on Terrorism, 10*(2), 50–60. Retrieved from: https://www.universiteitleiden.nl/binaries/content/assets/customsites/perspectives-on-terrorism/2016/206-evaluating-cve-understanding-the-recent-changes-to-the-united-kingdom-s-implementation-of-prevent-by-caitlin-mastroe.pdf.

Osman, S. (2014). Radicalisation, recidivism, and rehabilitation: Convicted terrorist and Indonesian prisons. In A. Silke (Ed.), *Prisons, Terrorism, and Extremism: Critical Issue in Management, Radicalisation, and Reform* (pp. 214–229). New York: Routledge.

Scarpello, F. (2014). Stifled development: The SSR – Civil society organizations community in post-authoritarian Indonesia. In F. Heiduk (Ed.), *Security Sector Reform in Southeast Asia: From Policy to Practice* (pp. 131–158). London: Palgrave Macmillan.

SFCG & DitjenPAS. (2010, August). *Pelatihan Manajemen Konflik: Rangkuman Kegiatan*. Retrieved from Search for Common Ground: https://www.sfcg.org/articles/SFCG%20CMT%20CLIPPINGS%20FINAL%208-10.pdf.

Sukma, R. (2012). The Role of Civil Society in Indonesia's Military Reform. In J. Rüland, M.-G. Manea, & H. Born (Eds.), *The Politics of Military Reform: Experiences from Indonesia and Nigeria* (pp. 147–160). Berlin, Heidelberg: Springer.

Sumper, C. (2018). *Returning Indonesian Extremists: Unclear Intentions and Unprepared Responses*. ICCT Policy Brief. 1-14. https://www.icct.nl/publication/returning-indonesian-extremists-unclear-intentions-and-unprepared-responses.

Sumpter, C. (2017). Countering violent extremism in Indonesia: Priorities, practice and the role of civil society. *Journal for Deradicalization, 11*, 112–147.

Ucko, D. H. (2018). Preventing violent extremism through the united nations: The rise and fall of a good idea. *International Affairs, 94*(2), 251–270. doi:10.1093/ia/iix235

UNODC. (2017, November 29). Cross Regional Workshop Assists ASEAN Region with the Development of National Action Plan to Prevent Violent Extremism. UNODC. https://www.unodc.org/roseap/en/2017/11/asean-prevent-violent-extremism/story.html

Wildan, M. (2021). Countering violent extremism in Indonesia: The role of former terrorists and civil society organizations. In G. Barton, M. Vergani, & Y. Wahid (Eds.), *Countering Violent and Hateful Extremism in Indonesia: Islam, Gender, and Society* (pp. 195–214). Singapore: Palgrave MacMillan.

The false dawns over Marawi: examining the post-Marawi counterterrorism strategy in the Philippines

Tom Smith and Ann Bajo

ABSTRACT
Following the 2017 siege of Marawi, the Philippines' counter-terrorism approach has grappled with an increasingly fragmented and unpredictable landscape. Despite claims of victory, the aftermath of Marawi underscores the need to reassess and critique the country's counter-terrorism strategy. This paper provides a comprehensive analysis of the post-Marawi terrorist environment and evaluates the efficacy of strategies adopted by Philippine security forces. While detailing changes in strategy, policy and capacity-building efforts, the paper argues that the focus on the Abu Sayyaf Group (ASG) in Sulu has overshadowed broader security concerns, including the resurgence and the proliferation of other rebels. The paper concludes that 7 years after Marawi, while steps have been taken in the right direction, the opportunity to fundamentally reset counterterrorism has been squandered. A more nuanced and comprehensive approach requiring further investment and infrastructure is needed. This represents the first assessment of both the new military and non-military interventions by the Philippine state. The analysis reveals how US security assistance to the Philippines has become more politicized on anti-corruption and human rights issues and how progressive policy changes will be undone if Marawi itself is not rescued from bad governance and the neglect of the community that lost the most.

Introduction

The 2017 siege of Marawi serves as a pivotal event in assessing the trajectory of counter-terrorism efforts in the Philippines. While initial military engagements may have been deemed successful, the prolonged aftermath reveals significant challenges in rebuilding, assisting displaced populations, and addressing alleged breaches of international humanitarian law (Amnesty International, 2017). This introduction sets the stage for a critical examination of the Philippines' post-Marawi counter-terrorism strategy, emphasizing the need for a comprehensive post-mortem analysis of the siege's implications.

The objectives of this paper are twofold: to analyse both military and non-military interventions since Marawi and to evaluate the effectiveness of these interventions in addressing the evolving terrorist threat landscape. By adopting a holistic approach, this study aims to shed light on the persistent challenges faced by Philippine security forces, including the complexities of understanding adversaries and garnering public support. These two riddles continue to limit the success of counter-terrorism measures in the Philippines, and it is important to recognise that recent exposure to the military – be that in Marawi or elsewhere, linger long in the memory of the public who the military desperately need in order to be successful. Old, as well as recent experiences of a politicised and heavy-handed military have undone decades of steadily built-up good will with the public, especially in Muslim majority communities in Mindanao where the Islamist and communist insurgencies and the states' response penetrate deep into the community's lives.

Drawing on existing literature, this paper situates itself within ongoing debates surrounding counter-terrorism strategies in the Philippines. While acknowledging past successes and failures, this study seeks to identify overlooked aspects and missed opportunities in post-Marawi interventions. In the subsequent sections, this paper will delve into the intricacies of the post-Marawi landscape, examining the resurgence of the Abu Sayyaf Group (ASG) and the recalibration of military strategies. Furthermore, it will assess the National Action Plan for Preventing and Countering Violent Extremists, highlighting both its strengths and limitations. By interrogating these developments, this paper aims to provide a nuanced understanding of the evolving security dynamics in the Philippines and offer insights for future policy considerations.

Background

The Maute clan's foray into jihadism with its alliance with the ASG during the siege of Marawi, initially led to speculation that some of the Philippines' most dangerous terrorists had been neutralized. However, a closer examination reveals that the security landscape post-Marawi is as, if not more, intricate than before, with the approaches taken since the Marawi crisis potentially contributing to this heightened complexity (Smith & Franco, 2020). During the siege, the Maute clan collaborated with the ASG, utilizing Marawi, once their stronghold, as a base for an assault on their own territory. However, their aspirations of becoming jihadists were short lived and ultimately led to their downfall. This does not discount the possibility that other influential warlords and pseudo-political factions in the Philippines may forge similar alliances with insurgent and terrorist entities when expedient.

Although the Marawi crisis was expected to contain and dismantle the ASG, subsequent developments indicate that the group has regrouped under new leadership, revitalizing its brand and operations from previous strongholds, albeit without immediate expansionist ambitions akin to those that culminated in the devastation of Marawi. However, their continued capability to carry out attacks and abductions beyond Sulu persists. In 2017, prior to the siege of Marawi, arrests were made in Negros in May (Espina, 2017) and attacks took place in April (Fonbuena & Cupin, 2017) in Bohol. The ASG has never just been a Sulu issue. Despite this evolving threat landscape, governmental responses, policy decisions, resource allocations, and attention remain disproportionately focused on jihadist groups, potentially overshadowing threats posed by other insurgent factions.

In response to the evolving terrorist threat, the Armed Forces of the Philippines (AFP) embarked on a heightened military campaign, notably concentrating efforts in Sulu through a substantial enhancement of Joint Task Force-Sulu's operational capacity. This expansion was underpinned by three pivotal strategic manoeuvres: augmenting JTF-Sulu's force structure, enhancing intelligence, surveillance, and reconnaissance (ISR) capabilities, and implementing proactive civil–military operations (CMO). By October 2023 JTF-Sulu would be expanded to JTF-Orion, incorporating JTSF-Basilan (Falcatan, 2023a). While these initiatives signify a proactive shift towards combating terrorism, their efficacy is contingent upon several factors which are examined. The aftermath of the Marawi siege has spurred adjustments in the Philippines' counterterrorism strategy. The full impact and context of these adaptations is examined below suggesting a new framework on security assistance to the Philippines has emerged. One that that will be limited for as long as open wounds like Marawi remain untreated.

Marawi an open wound

Over the past six years, displaced former residents of Marawi have consistently voiced their grievances regarding the lack of rehabilitation efforts and consultation processes, which also deny the autonomy promised by the Bangsamoro Organic Law (BOL). These concerns, ranging from cultural insensitivity to corruption within government channels and the fear of further displacement due to the establishment of permanent military encampments, underscore the deep-rooted challenges faced by the displaced population (Yee, 2018; Curato, 2019). Despite these ongoing issues, it was not until April 2022 that President Duterte signed the Marawi Siege Compensation Act, leading to the establishment of a Marawi Compensation Board tasked with distributing a modest $17.9 million to former residents in May 2023. This placed significant pressure on President Marcos to address the needs of the estimated 360,000 individuals displaced by the siege (Flores, 2023).

Furthermore, concerns regarding the long-term repercussions of inadequate reconstruction efforts have been raised. A year after the siege Franco warned that a botched reconstruction would drive more 'toward jihadism' (Franco, 2018). Indeed, the resurgence of jihadist groups in the region has only compounded these fears, as Marawi's plight risks becoming both another recruitment cause and a hub once again. In June 2023 the new supposed 'emir of the Islamic State or IS in Southeast Asia' – Abu Zacariah of the Dawlah Islamiyah (now considered the evolution of the Maute group) was killed by security forces from 'a safe house in Brgy. Bangon, not far from a military brigade camp' (Fonbuena, 2023) in what remains of the city of Marawi.

This sequence of events underscores the complex interplay between socio-economic grievances, security concerns, and the threat of radicalization in post-conflict settings like Marawi. The failure to adequately address the needs of displaced populations not only perpetuates their suffering but also creates fertile ground for extremist ideologies to take root. As such, efforts to rebuild Marawi must go beyond mere infrastructure reconstruction and prioritize community engagement, cultural sensitivity, and inclusive governance to address the underlying grievances fuelling extremism. Cornelio and Calamba have interviewed Marawi's displaced youth and given the authorities clear evidence of the demand and the value in giving young people a stake in the social and economic rehabilitation of Marawi (Cornelio & Calamba, 2023). Joined with this analysis we now have convincing social, economic and security arguments for how a more informed and collaborative reconstruction of Marawi needs to be a top priority for government across areas of policy.

The abu sayyaf group under new leadership

Following the death of ASG leader Isnilon Hapilon in November 2017 during the Marawi Siege, the ASG quickly regrouped. Under new leadership they persisted in violent activities in the island of Sulu little over a year later. Hatib Hajan Sawadjaan emerged as the group's new leader and orchestrated the Jolo Cathedral bombing in Jolo, Sulu, on 27 January 2019. However, his tenure was short-lived as he was killed by the Army in Basilan on 2 December 2023 (Falcatan, 2023b). The ASG's resilience, despite its defeat in Marawi, underscores the entrenched nature of terrorist networks within their communities, challenging the efficacy of a recurrent 'decapitation' strategy.

Since its inception in 1991, the ASG has capitalized on deep-rooted historic, economic, political, and social grievances between Muslim communities and the Philippine government (Banlaoi, 2006). Grievances stemming from oppressive regimes, under-representation, and lack of development have fuelled violent expressions, often intertwined with criminal activities aimed at financial gain (Reyes & Smith, 2015). Despite attempts to align themselves with jihadist ideologies and waving ISIS flags (as they previously did with the Al Qaeda brand (James & Cooley, 2006)), the ASG's primary identity remains that of kidnappers-for-ransom and bandits.

Notable post-Marawi acts of violence attributed to the ASG and its affiliates include:

- The bombing of Our Lady of Mount Carmel Cathedral in Jolo, Sulu, on 27 January 2019, resulting in the deaths of 20 individuals.
- The first recorded Filipino suicide bombing targeting the 1st Brigade Combat Team in Indanan, Sulu, on 28 June 2019, resulting in 8 fatalities and 22 injuries.
- A female suicide bomber detonated herself near the Philippine Army's 35th Infantry Battalion in Indanan, Sulu, on 8 September 2019.
- The kidnapping of a British man and his wife in Zamboanga on 4 October 2019, with their subsequent rescue in Sulu in November.
- An encounter with the Philippine Army in Indanan, Sulu, resulting in the deaths of three suicide bombers, including two Egyptians and a Filipino.
- The death of 14 individuals following two explosions carried out by a female suicide bomber on 24 August 2020, in Jolo, Sulu.
- The arrest of a female suicide bomber in Patikul, Sulu, on 10 October 2020.

These attacks underscore the ASG's enduring resilience and the continued exploitation of remaining deep-seated socio-political grievances in the region. Factors such as ethno-national identity and 'misgoverned spaces' (Mendoza, Ong, Romano, & Torno, 2021) contribute to the ASG's ability to recruit and perpetrate violence. A purely kinetic approach, focused on military interventions, fails to address the root causes of violence, such as mistreatment by the military and economic disenfranchisement, perpetuating a cycle of conflict. The failure to address these grievances, coupled with the reliance on military responses, highlights the missed opportunity to reset and rebuild Marawi, exacerbating public distrust and resentment towards the government's counter-terrorism efforts. As Smith and Franco noted in 2020 in a section of their chapter dedicated to the siege on Marawi, 'groups like the ASG and Maute function more as organized criminal organizations, whose financial motivations are no different from say extortion and kidnapping groups in Luzon and the Visayas'. They went on to warn, 'given the more material drivers of conflict, a fixation on de-radicalization and ideology-based counter-radicalization would be unproductive and unmerited policy which, crucially, is not evidence based'(Smith & Franco, 2020, p. 49). Before we examine the policy and military response since Marawi and whether this warning was heeded, we must also take account of the violence in the five years since Marawi from other rebel groups that garner less attention than the ASG.

The broader islamist rebel landscape post Marawi

The Bangsamoro peace process has garnered significant attention and political investment from Manila, with hopes pinned on it as a crucial component of the Philippines' counter-terrorism strategy (International Crisis Group, 2012). However, progress in this arena has been slow and marred by frequent violent disruptions, such as the bomb attack in Lamitan, Basilan, perpetrated by the ASG shortly after the passage of the Bangsamoro Organic Law (BOL) by the Philippine Congress. While the peace process aims to address the underlying grievances of communities across Mindanao, its impact is expected to materialize over an extended period. Notably, the Moro National Liberation Front (MNLF) and Moro Islamic Liberation Front (MILF) remain significant players in the Islamist insurgency, serving as the primary sources from which smaller splinter groups emerge, perpetuating internal conflict and resistance against the Armed Forces of the Philippines (AFP).

In Sulu, the stronghold of the ASG, the entrenched influence of local politics poses a formidable obstacle to eradication efforts (Teehankee, 2002). The pervasive lack of access to basic services for the local populace, often cited as a root cause of terrorism, is attributed to the governance failures and corruption among political elites (Mendoza et al., 2021). Moreover, there are allegations of collusion between political elites and militant groups, with the latter serving as private militias for the former (International Crisis Group, 2012). The inclusion of Sulu in the Bangsamoro Autonomous Region of Muslim Mindanao (BARMM) following the 2019 plebiscite has further complicated the dynamics, threatening the entrenched positions of political elites and introducing bureaucratic complexities to the Bangsamoro region (Bayot, 2018). Despite the aspirations for stability post-Marawi, the peace process has been elusive, exacerbated by ongoing violence between the MNLF and MILF, as well as MILF infighting, such as an incident in August 2022 in which fights between MILF factions in Cotabato City killed five people and displaced 100 families (Garcia, 2022; Fernandez & Magbanua, 2022). It is also worth noting that the communist insurgent group the New People's Army (NPA) continues to be active in violence against the military in Mindanao (Unson, 2023). On June 16 2023 the military response was severe and involved air strikes using attack helicopters newly acquired from Turkey (Gallardo, 2023). The protracted and multifaceted nature of the threat posed by rebel groups presents a formidable challenge to national security efforts.

If Sulu serves as the experimental ground for Philippine counterterrorism strategy, then current indications suggest that the experiment has yielded mixed results and, arguably, spiralled out of control (Yabes, 2021). Lieutenant Colonel Antonio Mangroban's proposition in 2012 for temporary military rule in Sulu to impose effective governance underscores the severity of the security situation in the region. The proposal entails military commanders assuming the roles of local chief executives under civil laws, aiming to establish a unified order of governance. This approach highlights the perceived inadequacy of civilian institutions to address the security challenges in Sulu, leading to a reliance on the military's resources and capabilities, including mobility assets for transportation due to limited civilian infrastructure (Aspinall & Hicken, 2020).

However, the suggestion of further militarization raises complex questions, particularly in light of the anti-military sentiment prevalent after the Marawi siege. The deep-seated grievances stemming from military presence and operations in conflict-affected areas pose a significant challenge to any strategy advocating for increased military involvement (Yabes, 2021). Deploying the military in this context risks exacerbating existing tensions and perpetuating cycles of violence, potentially entrenching communities in a state of perpetual conflict (De Castro, 2012).

Moreover, the reliance on military infrastructure and resources, even in ostensibly civilian-led initiatives, underscores the intricate entanglement of the military in the region's governance framework. The delicate balance between security imperatives and civilian governance becomes increasingly tenuous, necessitating sustained investment in public infrastructure and civil society initiatives to gradually reduce dependence on martial structures (Thompson, 2016). However, achieving this transition poses formidable challenges, requiring long-term commitment and strategic planning to navigate the complex interplay between security, governance, and community dynamics in Sulu.

The proposition of military rule as a solution in Sulu reflects the government's dilemma in addressing security concerns while grappling with public sentiment against militarization. The military's predominant role in counterterrorism efforts, coupled with its infrastructure advantage in remote regions like Sulu, presents a paradoxical challenge of dependency on military presence amid civilian resistance. In consolidating post-Marawi counterterrorism interventions, the Philippines has adopted a mixed approach encompassing both 'hard' military interventions and 'soft' policies aimed at addressing grievances. While military operations target groups like the ASG, soft approaches focus on preventing radicalization and terrorist recruitment through national action plans and community-based programs.

However, the complexity of the militant landscape extends beyond traditional Islamist rebel groups, with emerging factions like the Bangsamoro Islamic Freedom Fighters (BIFF) and Dawlah Islamiyah challenging the established hierarchy. The historic concentration of counterterrorism efforts on symptoms of the insurgency with a focus on high-profile groups like the ASG is now overlooking the broader spectrum of insurgency threats across Mindanao and beyond.

In essence, the post-Marawi landscape underlines the imperative of adopting a comprehensive and nuanced approach to address the underlying socio-political grievances fuelling the insurgency. By prioritizing inclusive peace processes, investing in community development, and diversifying counterterrorism strategies beyond military interventions, the Philippines can still navigate the challenges posed by Islamist rebel factions and clan violence to pave the way for lasting peace and stability in the region, but this navigation is becoming increasingly difficult (International Crisis Group, 2023). With every compromise in the peace process, the prospects for long term stability falter (Malan & Solomon, 2012).

Intensified focused military operations (FMOs)

In the immediate aftermath of the siege, Marawi emerged as a pivotal event catalysing heightened militarized responses to terrorism across Southeast Asia (Tan, 2018). Notably, the Philippines escalated its military campaigns in Sulu province, driven partly by President Duterte's stringent deadlines to quash the ASG (Smith, 2016). This surge entailed the expansion of military operations on the island, including the activation of the Philippine Army 11th Infantry Division and the enlargement of Joint Task Force-Sulu, all aimed at decisively neutralizing the ASG (Talabong, 2018). The deployment of the 1st BCT further exemplified this militarized approach, constituting a robust combined-arms force tailored for territorial defence. However, despite these efforts, hostilities and bombings continued demonstrating the persistent challenges faced in the region. This escalation culminated in a significant military presence, with an extensive deployment of army and marine battalions, notably disproportionate to the island's population size (Yabes, 2021). This disproportionate response demonstrates a strategic fixation on the ASG threat, which, despite intensive military operations, has remained resilient.

The protracted existence of the ASG since 1991 raises fundamental questions regarding the efficacy of solely kinetic approaches in counterterrorism strategies. This highlights the need for enhanced intelligence, surveillance, and reconnaissance (ISR) capabilities to gain deeper insights into the enemy's operations. However, the risk inherent in this strategic approach lies in the over-reliance on military force, as witnessed in the Marawi conflict. The adage 'if you only have a hammer for a tool, everything begins to look like a nail' has not been considered in the excessively militarized response to these complex security challenges.

Enhanced intelligence, surveillance, and reconnaissance

During the Marawi siege, the AFP faced a critical realization regarding the limitations of relying solely on human intelligence in navigating complex security environments (Franco, 2017). The strategic response to this challenge involved seeking support from established security partners, notably the United States and Australia, who provided crucial assistance by deploying Orion spy planes to augment the Philippines' surveillance capabilities during the crisis (Parameswaran, 2017). This collaboration emphasised the significance of international partnerships in enhancing the Philippines' counterterrorism efforts, particularly in the realm of ISR. Beyond the immediate crisis, Manila seized the opportunity to deepen its counter-terrorism cooperation with Washington, a move that was further solidified by its participation in the global coalition to defeat ISIS post-Marawi (Bureau of Counterterrorism, 2019). This alignment with the United States not only bolstered the Philippines' capabilities in addressing terrorism but also served broader strategic interests, particularly amid escalating tensions with China over disputed maritime territories. The subsequent acquisition of ScanEagle Unmanned Aerial Systems (UAS) from the US exemplified the tangible outcomes of this collaboration, providing the Philippines with advanced ISR capabilities valued at $4 million to support ongoing counterterrorism operations (U. S. Embassy Manila, 2021). Furthermore, the convergence of counterterrorism and geopolitical imperatives has intertwined the Philippines' security agenda with broader US-Philippines strategic interests, as evidenced by joint exercises, trainings, and advisory support provided by US Special Operations Advisors post-Marawi.

This multifaceted cooperation, which includes 'Humanitarian Civic Assistance (HCA) projects to improve infrastructure, enhance medical response, and strengthen ties between local communities and Philippine and American military forces' (U. S. Embassy Manila, 2023) emphasises the evolving nature of security partnerships in addressing complex security challenges, transcending traditional military-to-military engagements to encompass broader strategic dimensions. This is a move in the right direction. What remains unclear is which party is driving the more holistic cooperation and how long lasting it will be when implementation will have to be localised and embedded. The continued violence suggests the positive impact has yet to materialise.

In addition to its collaboration with the United States, the Philippines has actively pursued enhanced security cooperation with neighbouring countries within the ASEAN region, recognizing the transnational nature of contemporary security threats. The Marawi siege served as a wake-up call for ASEAN member states, prompting collective recognition of terrorism as a significant regional threat. While the siege had local origins, its broader implications, particularly the Maute-ASG group's aspiration to establish an ISIS caliphate in Southeast Asia, underscored the need for concerted regional responses to mitigate potential spillover effects on regional stability and security (Tan, 2018). In response, ASEAN member states have intensified military cooperation through joint patrols and intelligence sharing initiatives, as exemplified by the Trilateral Cooperation Agreement involving the Philippines, Malaysia and Indonesia, aimed at addressing maritime security challenges posed by the ASG in the Sulu Sea (Cook, 2017). Despite implementation challenges, such as territorial boundaries and limitations in law enforcement capacities, these initiatives signify a proactive effort to enhance regional security cooperation and border management. Furthermore, initiatives like the 'Our Eye' intelligence-sharing arrangement within ASEAN underline the growing recognition and imperative for collaborative approaches to counterterrorism at the regional level (Tan, 2018). This heightened regional engagement reflects a shared understanding among ASEAN member states of the interconnected nature of security threats and the necessity for collective action to address them effectively.

A new Dawn for international assistance?

The United States and Australia, have played a pivotal role in supporting ASEAN states' counterterrorism efforts, accentuating the global significance of regional security dynamics in Southeast Asia. However, while such partnerships had largely focused on tactical and diplomatic engagements, the enduring challenge lies in addressing underlying socio-economic and political grievances that fuel conflicts, rather than solely adopting a 'hard' counterterrorism approach focused on the ASG in Sulu. Thus far foreign assistance with addressing those underlying grievances has been muted and focused on the traditional routes of developmental aid and humanitarian assistance at times of crises – both of which continue to be impeded by corruption since Marawi (Trinidad, 2019; Mendoza et al., 2021; Arugay & Baquisal, 2023; Holden, 2023). That corruption has played a role in the lack of reconstruction of the city as examined below.

Since the Marawi crisis, issues concerning human rights abuses and corruption related to development aid and security assistance have become increasingly politicized. Corruption, once relegated to the periphery, now occupies a central position in discussions surrounding foreign aid, security assistance measures, and even private foreign investment in the Philippines (Robles, 2022). This heightened awareness has propelled corruption to the forefront of the political agenda, necessitating a collective response from all political stakeholders. While corruption remains a persistent challenge at the core of the Philippines' security issues, one potential positive outcome stemming from the Marawi crisis is the increased demand from donors and investors for transparency and accountability mechanisms from the outset. The devastation witnessed in Marawi and the subsequent failures to address it have raised the standards and discourse surrounding the aid-security-assistance nexus in the Philippines, prompting a more rigorous examination of internal shortcomings and the need for effective remedies.

In May 2020 the 'corrupt elites' were in the cross-hairs of the supposedly crusading Duterte (Thompson, 2022) when his government was resigned to offering a $600 reward to individuals who would report instances of aid distribution abuse during the COVID-19 pandemic. A 'reward' from one apparently pious branch of government concerning bribes from another. Subsequently, by September of the same year, the Philippine Human Rights Act was introduced in the U.S. House of Representatives, reflecting apprehensions that security assistance provided by the United States was potentially being misappropriated by the Duterte regime to perpetuate repressive measures (Smith, 2017). The proposed legislation aimed to compel the Philippines to institute significant human rights reforms within its military and police apparatuses, with the implicit threat of losing substantial security funding from the United States in the absence of tangible progress. This development represents a pivotal juncture in the historical trajectory of U.S.-Philippine relations, marking one of the most explicit instances wherein conditions on security assistance from the United States were openly articulated, coupled with discussions concerning internal corruption within the Philippine government (Aspinwall, 2020). Contrary to expectations that the aftermath of the Marawi crisis would catalyse increased military support from the United States, the prevailing trend has been one of heightened scrutiny and a shift towards more conditional engagement. Notably, in July 2022, the U.S. House of Representatives passed an amendment (PHRA, 2022) prohibiting assistance to the Philippine National Police, underscoring the continued influence of advocacy groups in shaping U.S. security policies toward the Philippines.

While the Marawi crisis served as a pivotal juncture for recalibrating U.S.-Philippine security cooperation, the concurrent human rights abuses under the Duterte administration were impossible to politically countenance. This shift in dynamics has become increasingly evident, particularly under President Marcos's administration. By 2024, the Philippines openly sought U.S. aid, 'to combat corruption and enhance revenue generation' (Leyco, 2024), from donors that had stopped support for seven years due to human rights concerns under Duterte. As noted earlier, the influence of the United

States on counterterrorism cooperation and policy in the Philippines intersects with another critical security challenge – China – a relationship that has also undergone re-evaluation since Marawi. Despite Duterte's failed attempts at appeasing China (De Castro, 2022) and his adversarial stance towards the U. S., the U.S. has persisted in conducting freedom of navigation operations in the South China Sea to counter China's expansive territorial claims. However, under the Marcos administration, the focal point of security cooperation has shifted from terrorism to the foundational issue of managing tensions with China, signifying a significant paradigmatic transformation in the bilateral relationship (Smith & Bajo, 2023).

Proactive civil-military operations

Civil Military Operations (CMO) now stand as a publicly declared and integral component of the framework of military operations aimed at countering terrorism and insurgency in the Philippines. Conceptually, CMO entail military collaboration with local stakeholders, embodying the principles of a whole-of-nation approach to engendering community support. Under the Duterte administration, the AFP, in conjunction with various stakeholders, formulated the Development Support and Security Plan (DSSP), also known as Kapayapaan, as the overarching campaign plan for internal security operations. This strategic blueprint delineates the expanded role of the military in bolstering government initiatives aimed at fostering good governance, sustainable development, and human security. Central to this endeavour is the execution of CMO, encompassing an array of social civic activities, including medical missions, school rehabilitation efforts, and the reintegration of former insurgents. However, comprehensive efficiency studies assessing the impact and efficacy of these initiatives are conspicuously lacking, thus underscoring the urgent need for empirical evaluation.

Civil Military Operations (CMO) serve as a crucial component of the broader military campaign, primarily facilitating community profiling and intelligence gathering. Simultaneously, when the military engages with local populations, it not only accentuates governmental presence but also aids in the provision of essential services, such as medical missions. However, the military finds itself inundated with the multifaceted responsibilities of CMO, particularly while concurrently conducting focused kinetic military operations. The effective execution of CMO requires specialized training and expertise within the military ranks, a process that, despite increased international cooperation and engagement, is anticipated to require several years to achieve professional proficiency. Presently, commanders are afforded considerable autonomy in implementing CMO strategies, albeit within the confines of limited resources and institutional frameworks (Yabes, 2021).

Regrettably, despite the military's endeavours in social civic engagement, it remains unpopular among local communities. The protracted conflict between the military and terrorist groups has resulted in the displacement of civilians and widespread disruption to livelihoods and developmental activities. For many locals, the military symbolizes destruction rather than protection, eroding trust in government forces (Yabes, 2021). Addressing this entrenched perception requires sustained commitment and nuanced CMO strategies aimed at rebuilding trust and fostering positive relationships with affected communities. However, the current risk is that rather than garnering support, government operations against terrorists may inadvertently alienate the very populations they seek to protect.

Realizing the potential of CMO to win hearts and minds necessitates unwavering commitment and comprehensive military reforms. Although promising initial steps have been taken in this direction, this commitment must transcend political administrations in Manila. These developments represent a positive shift in counterterrorism strategy following the Marawi crisis. Nevertheless, the journey toward effective CMO implementation and its attendant benefits for society demands a robust institutional dedication to bridge the gap between military operations and community perceptions.

Despite numerous military interventions and a concerted focus on Sulu and the ASG, the group remains entrenched on the island, illustrating the persistence of the security challenge (Engelbrecht, 2020). The establishment of mechanisms such as the Anti-Terrorism Council under the Human Security Act of 2007 has yielded limited results and lacks a solid legal foundation for proactive counterterrorism measures. However, the Marawi siege served as a catalyst for the Philippine government to reassess its counterterrorism strategy, with a new emphasis on preventing terrorist recruitment and promoting de-radicalization initiatives. Furthermore, incentivizing cooperation and implementing a robust law enforcement framework promises strategic advantage. A well-equipped and empowered local police force can bolster public trust in the justice system and undermine the alternative justice mechanisms offered by insurgent groups, which often exacerbate distrust in state institutions. Achieving this goal requires capacity building efforts in Sulu, including training for police officers and providing necessary resources for crime adjudication and prosecution, all aimed at fostering public confidence.

The post-Marawi period has triggered a shift in mindset towards this comprehensive approach, with civil society groups initiating capacity-building programs in Sulu and beyond. However, the success of these initiatives hinges on sustained support, both financial and in terms of security, to ensure independent implementation. These are long-term commitments requiring strategic patience, particularly in the face of persistent violent attacks from certain elements within the community and international pressures that can prioritize the eradication of terrorist strongholds over addressing domestic social unrest. This presents a test of strategic and political discipline, urging a redirection of resources towards capacity building efforts amidst prevailing pressures for more immediate and kinetic actions.

National action plan for preventing and countering violent extremism

The unexpected emergence of the Maute-ASG alliance in the western region of Mindanao, influenced significantly by ISIS propaganda, stressed the potency of social factors in recruitment efforts. Consequently, the 'push and pull' paradigm has informed the formulation of the National Action Plan for Preventing and Countering Violent Extremism (NAP-P/CVE), representing something of a positive outcome stemming from the Marawi siege. The NAP-P/CVE endeavors to mitigate radicalization leading to violent extremism through a comprehensive, whole-of-nation approach, involving governmental agencies, civil society organizations, religious institutions, and other key stakeholders, (Parameswaran, 2019). Addressing extremist narratives infiltrating Filipino communities, the plan adopts a synergistic blend of kinetic and soft approaches, wherein counterterrorism measures address terrorism directly, while efforts in preventing and countering violent extremism (PCVE) target underlying drivers. Endorsed by international bodies such as the United Nations and the Australian government, the NAP-P/CVE represents a significant step towards a nuanced and multifaceted response to terrorism. The policy is spearheaded by the National Security Council and endorsed by the Anti-Terrorism Council. Notably the Department of the Interior and Local Government (DILG) assumes responsibility for implementation and not the AFP. However, bureaucratic hurdles have impeded ground-level execution, hindering the realization of the plan's objectives. Nevertheless, these institutional reforms signify a nascent positive legacy from Marawi, albeit in its early stages.

Despite these initiatives, challenges persist in translating policy into action. Local government units, tasked with implementing the NAP-P/CVE, exhibit a lack of awareness or capacity to execute the plan effectively. Meanwhile, disparate efforts by the military, DILG, and civil society organizations, while well-intentioned, often diverge from the NAP-P/CVE's overarching objectives. Although military-led initiatives have shown efficacy in Sulu, their presence may inadvertently exacerbate tensions in conflict-affected areas. A one-size-fits-all approach, such as applying strategies from Sulu to the Bangsamoro Autonomous Region in Muslim Mindanao (BARMM), is untenable given the diverse contexts and challenges across regions. The path towards a stable and secure autonomous Muslim Mindanao remains fraught with obstacles. Therefore, bespoke counterterrorism strategies need to be tailored to local dynamics. The flexibility of the NAP-P/CVE and the bodies involved will be tested to the limit across Mindanao. The persistent prevalence of clan and rebel violence complicates these efforts, underscoring the need for sustained commitment and adaptive strategies to navigate the complex landscape of counterterrorism in the Philippines.

Task force ending local armed conflict

During the Duterte administration, the Task Force Balik Loob program underwent significant restructuring to aid former communist rebels in their transition to civilian life. This overhaul resulted in the establishment of the Task Force-Ending Local Communist Armed Conflict (TF-ELCAC), aimed at providing various government benefits, including cash grants, livelihood assistance, housing, health benefits, and education support (Unga, 2023). While these programs offer a semblance of hope for a model to address the Islamist and communist insurgencies, there remains a dearth of public accountability regarding their efficacy.

Since 2016, thousands of Islamist militants have surrendered to government authorities, with the demise of ASG commander Isnilon Hapilon serving as a key catalyst for surrenders among ASG members in 2018. Responding to this trend, the BARMM established its own iteration of TF-ELCAC, known as the Bangsamoro Task Force-Ending Local Armed Conflict (BTF-ELAC). This coordinating body oversees efforts to integrate former Moro rebels and terrorist members, including those from MILF, MNLF, BIFF, Maute group, and ASG (Bangsamoro Information Office, 2021). However, disparities between programs for former communist rebels and the Moro communities have created inequities in benefits and resources allocation. The implementation of BTF-ELAC remains hampered by delays, with an implementation plan for former rebels only completed in March 2021. This demarcation exacerbates existing tensions and divisions within the Muslim insurgency, particularly between MNLF-dominated Sulu and MILF-governed BARMM. The concentration of resources and attention on Maguindanao and Lanao provinces further marginalizes ASG members based in Sulu, perpetuating grievances and potentially fuelling further radicalization (International Crisis Group, 2012). The absence of synchronized efforts in counterterrorism between national and BARMM institutions underscores the need for coherent and equitable policy frameworks.

Parochial politics and intra-rebel rivalries persist in Sulu, hindering progress in improving living conditions for local populations. Without fair and equitable treatment for all rebel groups and a concerted effort to extend the positive initiatives of BARMM to Sulu, the risk of exacerbating violent rivalries remains. Present strategies largely prioritize addressing the ASG in Sulu, overlooking the broader complexities of the insurgency landscape. The nascent capacity of BARMM to implement a 'soft' approach further highlights the need for enhanced resource allocation and capacity-building efforts.

Anti-Terrorism law 2020

The enactment of the Anti-Terrorism Act of 2020 represents a significant evolution in the Philippines' legal approach to counterterrorism, particularly in the aftermath of the Marawi siege. This legislation, a revision of the Human Security Act of 2007, aims to address perceived shortcomings in the previous legal framework, which was perceived to favour suspects over law enforcement agencies. The earlier law's provisions, such as compensation for alleged suspects and stringent requirements for case-building, were rooted in historical contexts of abusive state power and past instances of human rights violations (Thongyoojaroen, 2023). However, the 2020 version of the law introduces contentious provisions allowing for the warrantless arrest of suspected terrorists and absolving law enforcement agencies of liabilities for false charges (Mendoza et al., 2021). In light of the Duterte administration's policies, including extrajudicial killings and the proliferation of 'red-tagging' these provisions raise concerns about potential human rights abuses and the erosion of due process safeguards.

The Anti-Terrorism Act of 2020 risks shifting too much power into the hands of an inadequately prepared security apparatus, potentially undermining 'soft' counterterrorism approaches and exacerbating existing human rights concerns. Furthermore, the Philippines' sluggish judicial process will struggle to cope with an influx of poorly evidenced terrorism cases, potentially delaying justice for victims of state abuses. As communities await accountability for past military abuses and extrajudicial killings, fast-tracking terrorism cases at the expense of security forces risks inflaming tensions and further eroding trust in state institutions.

Moreover, the singular focus on groups like the ASG in Sulu overlooks the persistent threat posed by longstanding insurgent groups such as the MNLF, MILF, and the NPA. By neglecting these 'old guard' factions and their splinter groups, the current counterterrorism strategy fails to address the broader landscape of extremist violence in the Philippines. A more holistic approach is necessary, one that has begun to be acknowledged in the counterterror policies examined here. The complex interplay of historical grievances, socio-economic factors, and regional dynamics shaping the country's security landscape demands further revision to the legal mechanism to keep pace.

Conclusion

In conclusion, the aftermath of Marawi has brought about a fundamental shift in mindset. The realization has dawned upon the military that a solely kinetic approach is insufficient in addressing the underlying causes of violence. Merely targeting the symptoms of extremism through force risks exacerbating grievances and further alienating communities, highlighting the critical need for clear messaging, trust-building, and institutional reforms, particularly in regions like Sulu. However, despite the deployment of new counterterrorism strategies, evidence of their positive impact remains elusive. The resilience of groups like the Abu Sayyaf and the enduring influence of longstanding insurgent factions such as the MNLF and MILF demonstrate the deep-seated nature of the challenges faced.

Philippine security forces must be receptive to developing softer skills and collaborating with civil society and international partners to gauge their impact on communities and strike a balance in their approach. This necessitates a commitment to ongoing training and reforms, particularly in community engagement and welfare operations. Moreover, addressing generational grievances requires sustained effort and a long-term perspective, with a focus on cultivating trust and respect within communities being paramount.

The success of these initiatives will be gradual and difficult to gauge for the actors on the ground, but continued scrutiny and support are imperative for their strategic effectiveness. While changes in strategy, resource allocation, and legal frameworks have been initiated, their tangible outcomes on the ground remain to be seen in terms of a reduction in terrorist violence across the country's complex landscape. As such, the journey towards effective counterterrorism in the Philippines post-Marawi is one that demands an as yet unseen perseverance and adaptability, and a steadfast commitment to rebuilding the city and lives destroyed in the previous epoch.

Disclosure statement

No potential conflict of interest was reported by the author(s).

ORCID

Tom Smith http://orcid.org/0000-0001-5882-1934
Ann Bajo http://orcid.org/0009-0001-4198-884X

References

Amnesty International. (2017). *The "battle of Marawi": Death and destruction in the Philippines.* Amnesty International. https://www.amnesty.org/en/documents/document/?indexNumber=asa35%2f7427%2f2017&language=en.

Arugay, A. A., & Baquisal, J. K. A. (2023). Bowed, bent, & broken: Duterte's assaults on civil society in the Philippines. *Journal of Current Southeast Asian Affairs, 42*(3), 328–349. doi:10.1177/18681034231209504

Aspinall, E., & Hicken, A. (2020). Guns for hire and enduring machines: Clientelism beyond parties in Indonesia and the Philippines. *Democratization, 27*(1), 137–156. doi:10.1080/13510347.2019.1590816

Aspinwall, N. (2020). Us bill aims to end aid to Philippines military and police. *The Diplomat*, 25 September 2020. https://thediplomat.com/2020/09/us-bill-aims-to-end-aid-to-philippines-military-and-police/.

Bangsamoro Information Office. (2021). Barmm gov't crafts work plan in ending insurgency in the Region. Bangsamoro Government Center. 26 March 2021. https://bangsamoro.gov.ph/news/latest-news/barmm-govt-crafts-work-plan-in-ending-insurgency-in-the-region/.

Banlaoi, R. C. (2006). The Abu sayyaf group: From mere banditry to genuine terrorism. *Southeast Asian Affairs*, *2006*(1), 247–262.

Bayot, A. B. E. (2018). *Elite bargains and political deals project: Philippines case Study*. UK Stabilisation Unit. https://assets.publishing.service.gov.uk/media/5c1912e1ed915d0c1bc0d614/Philippines_case_study.pdf.

Bureau of Counterterrorism. (2019). *Country reports on terrorism 2018*. United States Department of State Publication. https://www.state.gov/wp-content/uploads/2019/11/Country-Reports-on-Terrorism-2018-FINAL.pdf.

Cook, M. (2017). Opinion | unexpected benefits from a battle against ISIS. *The New York Times*, 5 November 2017, sec. Opinion. https://www.nytimes.com/2017/11/05/opinion/marawi-philippines-maute-duterte.html.

Cornelio, J., & Calamba, S. (2023). Going home: Youth and aspirations in postconflict marawi, Philippines. *Journal of Youth Studies*, *26*(5), 668–685. doi:10.1080/13676261.2022.2038781

Curato, N. (2019). Toxic democracy? The Philippines in 2018. *Southeast Asian Affairs*, 261–274.

De Castro, R. C. (2012). The cycle of militarization, demilitarization and remilitarization in the Philippines. S. Rajaratnam School of International Studies. https://www.jstor.org/stable/pdf/resrep05893.9.pdf.

De Castro, R. C. (2022). Caught between appeasement and limited hard balancing: The Philippines' changing relations with the eagle and the dragon. *Journal of Current Southeast Asian Affairs*, *41*(2), 258–278. doi:10.1177/18681034221081143

Engelbrecht, G. (2020). Violence in southern Philippines highlights resilience of militant networks. Australian strategic policy institute. *The Strategist* (blog). 16 September 2020. https://www.aspistrategist.org.au/violence-in-southern-philippines-highlights-resilience-of-militant-networks/.

Espina, M. P. (2017). Abu Sayyaf "relative" Nabbed in Negros Occidental. *RAPPLER*, 18 May 2017. https://www.rappler.com/nation/170193-abu-sayyaf-relative-negros-occidental-arrested/.

Falcatan, R. (2023a). Basilan and sulu army task forces give way to bigger, unified task force Orion. *RAPPLER*, 4 October 2023. https://www.rappler.com/nation/mindanao/basilan-sulu-army-task-forces-give-way-unified-task-force-orion/.

Falcatan, R. (2023b). Abu sayyaf leader killed in basilan Clash. *Rappler*, 3 December 2023. https://www.rappler.com/nation/mindanao/abu-sayyaf-leader-mudzrimar-sawadjaan-killed-basilan-clash-december-2023/.

Fernandez, E., & Magbanua, W. (2022). Clashes Erupt among Moro Factions in Cotabato. *INQUIRER.Net*, 13 August 2022. https://newsinfo.inquirer.net/1645757/clashes-erupt-among-moro-factions-in-cotabato.

Flores, H. (2023). Marcos orders measures to speed up marawi Recovery. *Philstar.Com*, 31 December 2023. https://www.philstar.com/headlines/2023/12/31/2322465/marcos-orders-measures-speed-marawi-recovery.

Fonbuena, C. (2023). Death of islamic state emir in marawi underscores failure to quash remnants of 2017 Siege. *Philippine Center for Inverstigative Journalism*, 17 June 2023. https://pcij.org/article/10260/death-isis-emir-marawi-underscores-failure-quash-remnants-2017-siege.

Fonbuena, C., & Cupin, B. (2017). 10 killed as gov't forces foil Abu Sayyaf attack in Bohol. *RAPPLER*, 11 April 2017. https://www.rappler.com/nation/166654-terrorism-bohol-abu-sayyaf/.

Franco, J. (2017). Freedom comes to Marawi after the defeat of the Islamic State. Australian Institute of International Affairs. *Australian Outlook* (blog). 23 October 2017. https://www.internationalaffairs.org.au/australianoutlook/freedom-marawi-defeat-islamic-state/.

Franco, J. (2018). Addressing Islamist militancy after the battle for Marawi. *International Crisis Group. Asia Commentary* (blog). 17 July 2018. https://www.crisisgroup.org/asia/south-east-asia/philippines/philippines-addressing-islamist-militancy-after-battle-marawi.

Gallardo, F. (2023). Soldiers kill 3 in surprise attack but face strong NPA defense in Butuan. *Rappler*, 17 June 2023. https://www.rappler.com/nation/army-attack-face-strong-npa-defense-butuan-june-16-2023/.

Garcia, T. (2022). Mnlf, MILF forces clash in Basilan. *Philippine News Agency*, 30 August 2022. https://www.pna.gov.ph/articles/1182487.

Holden, W. (2023). Climate change, neoauthoritarianism, necropolitics, and state failure: The duterte regime in the Philippines. *Asian Geographer*, 40(2), 145–167. doi:10.1080/10225706.2022.2029506

International Crisis Group. (2012). The Philippines: Local politics in the sulu archipelago and the peace process. Crisis Group Asia Report N°225,. http://www.crisisgroup.org/en/regions/asia/south-east-asia/philippines/225-the-philippines-local-politics-in-the-sulu-archipelago-and-the-peace-process.aspx.

International Crisis Group. (2023). *Making peace stick in the Bangsamoro. Asia Report No. 331*. Brussels: International Crisis Group. https://www.crisisgroup.org/asia/south-east-asia/philippines/331-southern-philippines-making-peace-stick-bangsamoro.

James, M. S., & Cooley, J. K. (2006). The Abu Sayyaf-Al Qaeda connection. *ABC News*, 6 January 2006. http://abcnews.go.com/International/story?id=79205&page=1.

Leyco, C. S. (2024). Gov't seeks US funding to combat corruption, improve revenue generation. *Manila Bulletin*, 3 February 2024. https://mb.com.ph/2024/2/2/gov-t-seeks-us-funding-to-combat-corruption-improve-revenue-generation-1.

Malan, C., & Solomon, H. (2012). Between conflict and compromise in the Philippines. *Indian Journal of Asian Affairs*, 25(1/2), 59–82.

Mendoza, R. U., Ong, R. J. G., Romano, D. L. L., & Torno, B. C. P. (2021). Counterterrorism in the Philippines: Review of key issues. *Perspectives on Terrorism*, 15(1), 49–64.

Parameswaran, P. (2017). What will Australia's new military terror aid to the Philippines look like? *The Diplomat*, 12 September 2017. https://thediplomat.com/2017/09/what-will-australias-new-military-terror-aid-to-the-philippines-look-like/.

Parameswaran, P. (2019). What's behind the Philippines' new strategy for countering violent extremism? *The Diplomat*, 23 July 2019. https://thediplomat.com/2019/07/whats-behind-the-philippines-new-strategy-for-countering-violent-extremism/.

PHRA. (2022). House passage of amendment to stop US aid to philippine national police. *Philippine Human Rights Act* (blog). 14 July 2022. https://humanrightsph.org/statements/coalition-for-philippine-human-rights-act-applauds-house-passage-of-amendment-to-stop-us-aid-to-philippine-national-police.

Reyes, Joseph Anthony L., & Smith, T. (2015). Analysing labels, associations, and sentiments in twitter on the Abu Sayyaf kidnapping of Viktor Okonek. *Terrorism and Political Violence*, 29(0), 1026–1044. doi:10.1080/09546553.2015.1105798

Robles, R. (2022). Can the Philippines draw investors amid inflation, debt and corruption woes? *South China Morning Post*, 30 July 2022, sec. This Week in Asia. https://www.scmp.com/week-asia/economics/article/3187110/can-philippines-overcome-crisis-investor-confidence-amid.

Smith, T. (2016). Panic about IS in the Philippines masks a very real war in the country. *The Conversation*, 3 October 2016. http://theconversation.com/panic-about-is-in-the-philippines-masks-a-very-real-war-in-the-country-65196.

Smith, T. (2017). Rodrigo Duterte's first year: A human rights disaster the world prefers to Ignore. *The Conversation*, 10 July 2017. http://theconversation.com/rodrigo-dutertes-first-year-a-human-rights-disaster-the-world-prefers-to-ignore-80442.

Smith, T., & Bajo, A. (2023). Philippines sides with US amid rising regional tensions between Beijing and Washington. *The Conversation*, 17 February 2023. http://theconversation.com/philippines-sides-with-us-amid-rising-regional-tensions-between-beijing-and-washington-199369.

Smith, T., & Franco, J. (2020). Mujahideen in Marawi: How local jihadism in the Philippines tried to Go global. In *Exporting global jihad: Critical perspectives from Asia and North America* (pp. 37–54). London: Bloomsbury Press (I.B. Tauris).

Talabong, R. (2018). Military's 2022 plan: New army division vs Abu Sayyaf in Sulu. *RAPPLER* (blog). 5 December 2018. https://www.rappler.com/nation/218280-military-create-infantry-divison-hunt-down-abu-sayyaf/.

Tan, S. S. (2018). Sending in the cavalry: The growing militarization of counterterrorism in Southeast Asia. *PRISM*, 7(4), 138–147.

Teehankee, J. (2002). Electoral politics in the Philippines. In A. Croissant (Ed.), *Electoral Politics in Southeast and East Asia* (pp. 149–202). Friedrich Ebert Stiftung Singapore. https://www.quezon.ph/wp-content/uploads/2006/09/Electoral%20Politics%20in%20the%20Philippines.pdf.

Thompson, M. R. (2016). Bloodied democracy: Duterte and the death of liberal reformism in the Philippines. *Journal of Current Southeast Asian Affairs*, 35(3), 39–68. doi:10.1177/186810341603500303

Thompson, M. R. (2022). Duterte's violent populism: Mass murder, political legitimacy and the "death of development" in the Philippines. *Journal of Contemporary Asia*, 52(3), 403–428. doi:10.1080/00472336.2021.1910859

Thongyoojaroen. (2023). Red-Tagging in the Philippines: A license to kill. *Human Rights Foundation* (blog). 10 April 2023. https://hrf.org/red-tagging-in-the-philippines-a-license-to-kill/.

Trinidad, D. (2019). Strategic foreign aid competition: Japanese and Chinese assistance in the philippine infrastructure sector. *Asian Affairs: An American Review*, 46(4), 89–122. doi:10.1080/00927678.2020.1723295

Unga, N. I. (2023). The surrender of islamist militants in mindanao: Why they left the Abu Sayyaf, BIFF, and Dawlah Islamiyah. Executive Policy Brief. National Defense College of the Philippines. https://ndcp.edu.ph/wp-content/uploads/2023/03/The-Surrender-of-Islamist-Militants-in-Mindanao-Why-they-left-the-Abu-Sayyaf-BIFF-and-Dawlah-Islamiyah.pdf?fbclid=IwAR08_ZOEpkGrZEDExG3gyh3jR6KxsMFZUkxNq-syWqS71IYyqVMeAqym9hw.

Unson, J. (2023). Npas in central Mindanao dwindling – local execs. *Philstar.Com*, 29 July 2023. https://www.philstar.com/nation/2023/07/29/2284757/npas-central-mindanao-dwindling-local-execs.

U. S. Embassy Manila. (2021). U.S. military delivers advanced unmanned aerial system to Philippine air force. *U.S. Embassy in the Philippines* (blog). 13 October 2021. https://ph.usembassy.gov/u-s-military-delivers-advanced-unmanned-aerial-system-to-philippine-air-force/.

U. S. Embassy Manila. (2023). Philippine, U.S. troops to hold largest ever balikatan exercise from April 11 to 28. *U.S. Embassy in the Philippines* (blog). 4 April 2023. https://ph.usembassy.gov/philippine-u-s-troops-to-hold-largest-ever-balikatan-exercise-from-april-11-to-28/.

Yabes, C. (2021). Creating sulu: In search of policy coalitions in the conflict-ridden island. *Southeast Asian Studies*, 10(2), 295–312.

Yee, D. K. P. (2018). First tragedy, then farce: Unlearned lessons of reconstructing ravaged cities. *New Mandala* (blog). 23 May 2018. https://www.newmandala.org/first-tragedy-farce-unlearned-lessons-reconstructing-ravaged-cities/.

Index

Note: **Bold** page numbers refer to tables; *italic* page numbers refer to figures and page numbers followed by "n" denote endnotes.

Abu Sayyaf Group (ASG) 111, 113–117, 120–122
Afghanistan/Afghan 3–5, 38, 77, 79–83, 85, 87, 90; Taliban 90–91
Amnesty International 6, 110
anti-China militants 82, 89, 91
anti-state militants 83, 85–86
anti-terror campaigns **15**
Anti-Terrorism Act 122
Anti-Terrorism Council 120–121
apostate government 69, 74
ASEAN member states 117
Auxiliary Force (Bantuan Kendali Operasi or BKO) 106n2

Badan Nasional Penanggulangan Terorisme or the National Counter Terrorism Agency (BNPT) 12, 43–44, 48–49, 96–97, 101–102, 104–105
Balochistan Liberation Army (BLA) 87, 91
Baloch militants 87, 90
Bangsamoro Autonomous Region of Muslim Mindanao (BARMM) 114
Bangsamoro Organic Law (BOL) 112, 114
Barton, G. 95
Beijing 77, 79–80, 83–85, 87, 91
Belt and Road Initiative (BRI) 77
Benjamin, Daniel 1
Briggs, Harold 31
British 32–35, 113
Bureau of Counterterrorism and Countering Violent Extremism 64, 69
Byman, Daniel 2

caregiving responsibilities 51–52
China/Chinese 6, 13, 26–34, 36–38, 77–87, 89–91, 116, 119; attacks on nationals 79, 87; authorities 81–82, 84, 86; education 28, 35–36; ethnic 27–28, 32, 36–37; government 81, 83; leadership 78, 82, 86–87; and Malays 28, 37;-medium schools 30, 33; nationals 79, 86–87; officials 89–90; and Pakistan 77–80, 83, 87, 89; policy 34; policy in Xinjiang 89; schools 30, 33; stateless 32, 37; terrorist attacks *81*
China-Pakistan counter-terrorism cooperation 77, 79; evolving dynamics of 79–91
China–Pakistan Economic Corridor (CPEC) 78
Chinese Communist Party (CCP) 26–27
civil-military operations (CMO) 112, 119
civil society 97, 100, 123; activists 99, 101, 104; groups 9, 120
civil society organisations (CSOs) 11, 15, 94–95, 97–106, 120–121; and governmental agencies 105–106
Cold War 25–27, 33–34
conflict 13, 20, 24–25, 36, 41–42, 47–48, 50, 62, 114
Connell, R. W. 46
contemporary counter-terrorism 34
contemporary radical Islamist terrorism 38
contemporary terrorism challenges 3, 5
cooperation 36, 77–83, 90
coordination 101–102, 104
counter-terrorism (CT) 4, 6, 9–20, 34, 42–43, 77, 83, 87, 98, 116–117, 122; approaches 79, 82, 117, 122; capabilities 95, 98; cooperation 77–79, 91, 116; efforts 11–12, 78, 96, 110, 115, 117; governance 11; missions 9, 13, 20; operations 11–14, 18; policy 78; purposes 48–49; strategies 43, 47, 48, 50, 116, 120, 122
countries 3–6, 10, 12, 36–37, 74, 77–79, 83, 85, 87, 90, 99, 102–103, 105
Crane, C. 26
cycle of terrorism 98

day-care facilities 54–55
Department of the Interior and Local Government (DILG) 121
deradicalisation: activities 49–50; programmes 49–50, 103

INDEX

Development Support and Security Plan (DSSP) 119
domestic counter terror operations 9–10
Drug Rehabilitation Center 65

East Indonesia Mujahideen 9, 13, **17**
East Java 43, 101
education, lack of 67, 72, 74; and employment opportunities 67, 72, 74
Embassy Manila 117
employment opportunities 67–68, 72, 74
extremist groups 42–43, 53

Federally Administered Tribal Areas (FATA) 3
female: agents 48–51, 53–55; bodies 44, 46, 53; suicide bomber 113
Feminist Security Studies (FSS) approach 44–45
foreign policies 4, 34, 89
foreign terrorist fighters (FTF) 61
front organisations 29–30, 49–50

gender/gendered 44–45, 51, 54, 64, 66; analysis 44, 47–48; discrimination 47, 56; equality 43–44, 47; habitus 45–46, 52; mainstreaming 43, 46–48, 55–56, 100; norms 45–46, 49, 54–55; organisations 45–46; performativity 45; relations 45–46, 49, 53; roles 51, 55
global security 2, 4
global terrorism 24, 35; threat 25, 38
Global War on Terrorism (GWOT) 82, 95, 98
government/governmental 4–5, 11, 14–15, 17, 20, 28–37, 66, 69, 71–72, 74, 85–86, 95–97, 99–102, 105–106, 118; agencies 100, 105–106, 120; response 4, 42
Greene, Hugh Carleton 31
groups 10–11, 14, 16, 25–26, 42–43, 46–47, 49, 62–63, 66–67, 70–71, 81, 90, 100–101, 113–114, 122–123
Gurney, Henry 30

hegemonic masculinity 44–46, 50
Hoffman, Bruce 1
Humanitarian Civic Assistance (HCA) 117
Human Security Act 120, 122
Hussain, Mamnoon 86
Hussain, Qazi 82
Hwang, J. C. 42

incarcerated people 65–67
India 3–5, 78–79, 90
individual vulnerabilities 62
Indonesia/Indonesian 5–6, 9–11, 13, 19–20, 36, 41–56, 61, 94–102, 104–106, 117; armed forces 48, 96; counterterrorism 99; CSOs 95; government 10, 13, 20, 37, 43, 47, 95–98, 102, 104; intelligence agencies 44, 55; intelligence community 43, 46, 55; intelligence services 44; military 11, 13, 15, 17–19; NAP 97, 105; National Armed Forces 9, 11; National Police 10, 12, 44, 48, 95; society 10, 41, 45; way of P/CVE 94–105; women 42, 48
Indonesia Knowledge Hub (I-KHUB) 102, 104–105
Indo-Pacific region 3, 61
information war 25, 31, 34, 38
The Institute for Policy Analysis of Conflict (IPAC) 41–42, 48, 50; report 56n2
institutional gender biases 47, 56
institutional gendered habitus 46, 52, 56
insurgent groups 120, 122
intelligence 10, 12, 16, 30, 41–51, 53–55, 117, 119; agencies 11, 43–45, 47, 49, 51, 53–56; agents 44; analysis 49–50, 54; sectors 44–45, 48, 52, 54–55
intelligence community (IC) 43, 44, 48, 51, 54–56, 80
intelligence operations 52–53; conducting 48–49
internal security 11, 19; operations 19, 119
international: community 41, 97; crisis group 114, 116, 122; development 31, 97; partnership 102, 116
International Labour Organisation 33
interviewees 64–71, 73, 97
interviews 44, 49–52, 64–67, 69, 73–74, 96–97, 101
ISIS's Khorasan Province (ISKP) 63
Islamabad 79–80, 83, 85, 87
Islamic education 68; nuanced 67–68, 70, 72, 74
Islamic Movement of Uzbekistan (IMU) 81
Islamic State (IS) 2–5, 13, 96, 112; ideology 25, 38; Khorasan Province 4, 91; propaganda 107n4
Islamic State of Iraq and Syria (ISIS) 10, 42, 62–63, 66, 70
Islam/Islamic/Islamist 3, 68–70, 72, 74, 82, 85; affairs 64, 69; insurgencies 114; militants 80, 121; scholars 65–66, 68, 74

Jaish-e-Mohammad (JeM) 5
Jamaah Ansharut Tauhid (JAT) 13
Jemaah Islamiyah (JI) 20n1, 42, 95, 106n1
jihadist: activism 42; groups 42, 112
Joint Information and Propaganda Committee (JIPC) 31
joint operations 9, 11, 14, 18, 20, 82
Joint Task Force-Sulu 112, 116
'Just Say No' model 74
J.W. Marriott hotel bombings 98

Kepolisian Negara Republik Indonesia 10, 95
Khan, Imran 89
Knowledge Hub (K-HUB) 103–104; Laboratorium Psikologi Politik UI 104, 106

INDEX

lactation rooms 54–55
law enforcement 16, 48, 96, 98, 102, 106; agencies 10, 122; approach 19–20, 98
law on terrorism 96
local Chinese 28, 32
local communities 15, 18, 117, 119
local government 33, 121
local Muslim communities 35–36, 38

Maafushi Prison 64–65, 70
Madago Raya Task Force 15–18
Malayan Communist Party (MCP) 25–31, 33, 35, 38
Malayan Peoples' Anti-Japanese Army (MPAJA) 27
Malaysia/Malayan/Malays 5, 28, 31–37, 117; Emergency 24–27, 29–30, 33–36; Emergency (1948–1960) 25
Maldives/Maldivian 61–68, 70–74; government 64, 66, 69–70, 72; militant jihadists 63; youth and young adults 63, 72
Mangroban, Antonio 115
Marawi 110–123; crisis 111, 118, 120; siege 110–113, 115–117, 120, 122
member states 6, 47, 94
Messerschmidt, J. W. 46
militant jihadism/jihadists 61–64, 66–74, 74n1; attacks 62; beliefs 69, 72–73; cells 67–68, 70, 73; exploitation of young adult vulnerabilities 63–73; groups 62–63, 69–71; radicalisation 61, 73, 74; recruiters 69, 72; terrorism 61
militants 4, 6, 49, 81, 83–84, 86–87; groups 4, 81, 85, 114; networks 3; organisations 83–84, 87
military/militaristic 3, 9–12, 14–20, 26, 43, 45, 48, 111, 114–115, 118–119, 121, 123; deployment 11, 20; deployment in counter terrorism 11, 20; force 9–10, 20, 30, 116; institutions 43, 45; interventions 113, 115–116, 120; involvement 10, 19; officers 14, 26, 97; operations 12, 18, 83, 86–87, 112, 116, 119–120; personnel 4, 10, 14–15, 18, 20; rule 12, 115
ministry, coordinating 43, 47–48, 96
Ministry of Islamic Affairs 64, 69
Ministry of Women Empowerment and Child Protection 54, 104
Moro Islamic Liberation Front (MILF) 114
Moro National Liberation Front (MNLF) 114
Musharraf, General Pervez 82
Muslim communities 36–38, 113

national: education system 36; identity 37; intelligence body 44, 48; police 11, 18; security 10, 43, 46–47, 86
National Action Plan (NAP) 4, 43, 47, 94, 102–103, 105, 111, 115, 120; P/CVE 105, 120–121

National Counterterrorism Agency (Badan Nasional Penanggulangan Terorisme or BNPT) 12, 44, 96
National Counter Terrorism Center 63–64
Nawaz Sharif, Muhammad 86
new terrorism 3, 5
non-governmental agencies 104
nuanced Islamic education, lack of 67–68, 72, 74

O'Brien, Kevin 2
operations 4, 9, 13–15, 17–20, 26, 29–30, 33, 35, 81–84, 111, 115; Camar Maleo 9, 13–14; Enduring Freedom 24; Madago Raya 9, 15–18, **16**, *16*; Tinombala 9, 14–15
organisations 11, 13, 27, 42, 45–46, 49, 52–54, 56, 63, 65, 94–97, 99–100

Pakistan/Pakistani 3–5, 36, 61, 63, 77–87, 89–91; authorities 81, 83; counter-terrorism cooperation 77–79, 82, 84, 91; relations 77, 79; Taliban 85; targeting Chinese interests/personnel **85, 88–89**; terrorist attacks *84*
participant 44, 48–53, 55, 65–69, 73, 99
Perkasa, Andika 17
personal communication 36, 63, 98–101, 104–105
Philippines 6, 110–112, 114–119, 121–122; army 113, 116; government 113, 118, 120; security forces 5, 111, 123
Pillar and Focus of Programme 102–103, **103**, 106
police: force 10–11, 19; officers 32, 120
policy analysis 41–42, 48, 50
policymaking process 97
politics/political 45–46; elites 9, 114; parties 30; violence 42, 45
Polri 9, 12–14, 18, 20, 95
Poso 9–15, 17–20
post-authoritarian Indonesia 11
preventing and countering violent extremism (P/CVE) 94–105, 121; efforts *106*; initiatives 95, 98–100, 104; programmes 97, 100, 103–104
preventing and countering violent extremism (P/CVE) CSOs 95, 97–100, 102; emergence of 97–98; in Indonesia 95, 99, 105; initiatives 99, 103
preventing violence extremism (PVE) 43, 47, 94
prison 35, 63–74, 98; interviews 64–65; management programmes 99
private Chinese schools 30, 32–33
programmes 17, 94–95, 98–101, 103–106
ProPatria 107n7
psychological operations 25–26, 28, 31
psychological war/warfare 25–27, 31, 32, 34–36, 38
psychosocial factors 61–62
psychosocial processes 62, 72
psywar operations 27, 29, 32–33, 35–38

INDEX

Qaeda 2–4, 6, 24, 61–62, 66, 70; -linked Jemaah Islamiah 6

radicalisation 5, 18, 45, 47, 62–65, 67, 72–74, 99–100
radical Islamism/Islamist 3, 6n1, 24–25, 35–36; ideology 2, 6, 35, 37; terrorism 5, 25
radical terrorist ideology, countering 25–37
rebel groups 114–115, 122
Red Mosque operation 83–84
religious education 6, 71
Republic of Indonesia 11, 47–48
Ritz-Carlton hotel bombings 98

Schulze, K. E. 42
security: affairs 43, 48, 96; agencies 32, 96; assistance 112, 118; cooperation 77, 119; forces 63, 95, 112; measures 35, 38; operations 13, 19; sectors 43–45, 47, 51–52, 55, 77; services 32, 35, 47; threats 10, 47, 85, 117
Security Sector Reform (SSR) 43, 52, 97
sexual violence 44–45
Shanghai Cooperation Organisation (SCO) 78
Simon, Steve 1
Simpson, Christopher 26
Singapore 29, 33–35, 37
social campaigns 15
societal expectations 52, 55
societal gender norms 45, 52, 56
South Asia 3, 5–6, 79
Southeast Asia 3, 5–6, 11, 34, 95, 112, 116–117
special counter terrorism unit 11, 13
special forces 16–17
Speckhard, A. 62
stakeholders 96, 98, 101, 103–105; organisations 64–65
state-sanctioned Islam 64, 69
'Strike Hard' campaign 80
substance abuse 63, 67, 70, 72–74
suicide terrorism 66
sulu 111–115, 117, 120–123
Sumpter, C. 95
Syrian civil war 21n3, 107n4

Taliban 3–4, 81–84, 90–91; regime 90
task force 15, 18, 83, 121
Task Force-Ending Local Communist Armed Conflict (TF-ELCAC) 121
Taylor, P. M. 25, 38
Tehrik-e-Taliban Pakistan (TTP) 3–4, 85–86, 90–91
Templer, Gerald 30
Tentara Nasional Indonesia (TNI) 9, 12–14, 18–20, 21n4, 96; involvement 11, 18–20
territorial operation 15, 18

terror/terrorism/terrorist 2, 4–5, 10, 14, 18–20, 35, 37–38, 45, 47–49, 54, 72, 74, 77–79, 82, 84, 85, 87, 95–96, 98–100, 104, 112, 116–117, 120; activities 6, 19, 104–105; attacks 3, 5–6, 10, 12–13, 19, 24, 77–78, 80, 85–87, 96, 98–99; attack survivors 99–100; challenges 2, 4–6, 10–122; countering 11, 41–55, 119; group 10–11, 16, 20; groups 2, 10, 18, 25, 42, 50, 119; incidents 6, 77–78, 84–86; networks 25, 113; organisations 10, 20, 85, 89; threats 4, 6, 10, 77, 79, 96, 98, 102, 112
Thematic Working Group 105
Thompson, Robert 30
Too, Henry C. C. 31–32
trade unions 29, 33
tribal areas 82–84, 86
Turkistan Islamic Party (TIP) 85

united front 26–27, 29–30, 33, 35, 78; organisations 33, 35
United Front Work Department (UFWD) 26
United Nations 94, 121; Development Programme 63–64; Security Council 3; Security Council Resolution 47
United States (US) 2, 24–25, 71, 95, 116–118; and Australia 116–117; military 87
United States Agency for International Development (USAID) 97
Uyghurs 13, 79–81, 83–84, 89; militancy 86

Vanguard Weekly 29
violent extremism/extremists 47–49, 61–62, 69, 73, 120; countering 64, 69, 94, 98, 120–121; extremists 73
VoA Indonesia 13–15, 18
Voice of the Malayan Revolution (VMR) 29
vulnerabilities **67**

war on terrorism 10, 48, 82, 91
Western governments 36–37
West Java 42, 104
whole-of-government 11, 94, 98
whole-of-society approach 11, 94–95, 98, 105
Widodo, Joko 'Jokowi' 94
women 41–55, 66–68, 71–72, 74, 85, 96, 100–101; bodies 45, 56; empowerment 47, 54, 104; involvement 43, 48; jobs 50–51, 56; recruitment of 46, 54; restroom 54; roles 42, 44–45, 47–48, 50–51, 55; roles in intelligence 56n3
Women, Peace and Security (WPS) 43, 47

Xinjiang 78–82, 84, 86–87, 89

Yew, Lee Kuan 33
young adults 63–64, 67, 70, 72–74
Yudhoyono, Susilo Bambang 96